ISLAND OF THE
DRAGON'S BLOOD

KU-360-855

ISLAND OF THE
DRAGON'S BLOOD

by

DOUGLAS BOTTING

Maps by A. Spark

Sketches by Janet Chandler

London
HODDER AND STOUGHTON

Copyright © 1958 by Douglas Botting

MADE AND PRINTED IN GREAT BRITAIN FOR
HODDER AND STOUGHTON LIMITED, LONDON
BY C. TINLING AND CO. LTD., LIVERPOOL, LONDON
AND PRESCOT

TO

MY MOTHER AND FATHER

O when shall we, all spent,

Row in to some far strand,

And find, to our content,

The original land

From which our boat once went,

Though not the one we planned.

W. R. Rodgers
Life's Circumnavigators

FOREWORD

It seems remarkable, in this present age, that one can still write a travel book which does not merely add to the heap of previous books already written about a particular country or tribe or journey. The fact is that no other general account of Socotra or its people has ever been published: there exist a number of scientific monographs and papers about specialist aspects of the island; one or two nineteenth-century accounts which form parts of larger volumes about Arabia in general; and brief mentions in historical works dating back to the days of the Roman Republic; otherwise, nothing. For this reason I felt an obligation to include a certain amount of purely factual information, particularly in historical and anthropological matters, that was new or else not generally known or readily available: but this book is not a work of reference—it remains a mainly personal narrative of places seen, people encountered, sensations felt and thoughts thought on this curious, little-visited and medieval island in the Arabian Sea.

The expedition which resulted in this book owes many debts of gratitude which cannot all be properly acknowledged here· I would, however, like to thank, briefly but especially, those officers of the Royal Air Force and the Government of Aden who did so much to make possible our unusual months 'on the island'. I would also like to thank the Oxford University Exploration Club, under whose auspices the expedition was organised, for every possible assistance, and the Principal and Fellows of St. Edmund Hall, Oxford, who most generously granted me a sabbatical year in which to fulfil my Socotran committments.

To the members of the expedition go my thanks for freely giving their diaries, notes, photographs and advice during the writing of this book, and for their companionship and invaluable co-operation during the period of the expedition; to my father, Leslie W. Botting, my sincere thanks for his unstinting help and advice at all stages of the book's production.

I would also like to thank Colonel I. E. Snell, O.B.E.,

for permission to include his account of witch-trials on Socotra; Mr. Harold Ingrams, C.M.G., O.B.E., and the Letchworth Publishing Agency Ltd., for permission to quote from the article 'Socotra—the Isle of the Blest' in the *Port of Aden Annual* 1955/6; Mrs. Yeats and Messrs. Macmillan and Co. for kind permission to quote on page 134 from 'The Old Men Admiring Themselves in the Water' in *Collected Poems of W. B. Yeats*; and Mr. W. R. Rodgers and Messrs. Secker and Warburg for kind permission to quote from "Life's Circumnavigator's" in *Awake! and Other Poems* by W. R. Rodgers. The two lines quoted on page 165 are from Mr. C. Day Lewis's translation of the *Aeneid of Virgil*, published by the Hogarth Press; the lines quoted on page 32 are from the poem 'For to Admire' in *Barrack-Room Ballads* by Rudyard Kipling, published by Macmillan and Co. I am grateful to the Royal Geographical Society for permission to base the maps in this book on their own; and to the Peninsular and Oriental Steam Navigation Co. for permission to make use of their files on the wreck of the *Aden*.

Finally, I wish to thank the Socotrans themselves, who were our unpredictable but always stimulating neighbours for two remarkable months. I have done my best to present them as fairly and as truthfully as I can; I have sometimes been critical but not, I hope, offensive; I only know that if they were to write about the eccentric visitors who appeared suddenly in their midst during the summer monsoon of 1956, they would be equally torn between sympathy and incredulity in their attempt at a fair description. I hope one day I may be allowed to visit them again—and one cannot say more than that.

CONTENTS

LIST OF ILLUSTRATIONS

The key figures shown in the above list identify
the names of the photographers as follows:

[1]Dr. Michael Gwynne   [4]Peter Shinnie
[2]Dr. Richard Lister   [5]John Weakley
[3]Douglas Botting   [6]Dr. Neil Orr

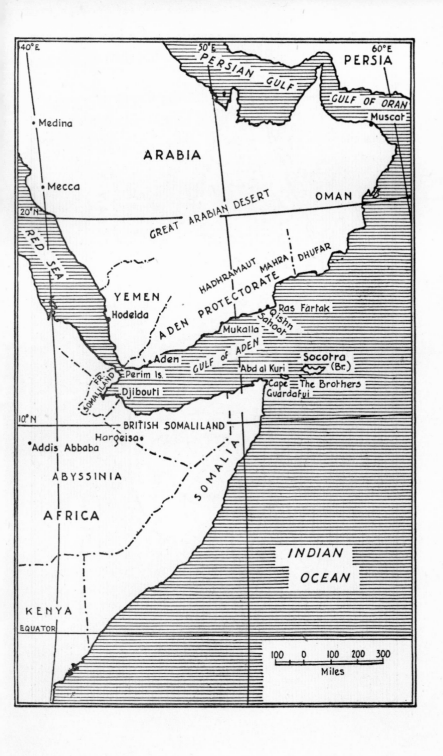

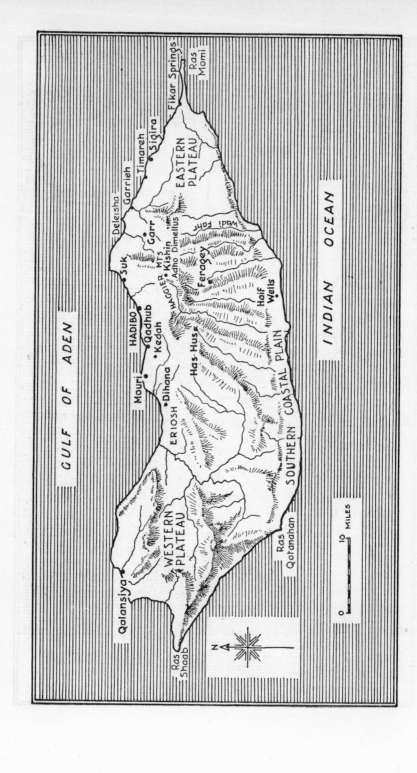

INTRODUCTION

AT THE PLACE OF THE CAVES

I MAY as well begin at Shimoni.

Shimoni is a small fishing village, about fifty miles south of Mombasa, on the shore of the Indian Ocean. Although it is the largest place between Mombasa and Tanga, there are only three Europeans and a few score African fisher families living there.

I stayed a few weeks at Shimoni, near the Colonel's house, in a tiny bungalow right on the seashore. Ernest Hemingway had stayed there a few weeks previously, recovering from concussion incurred in an air accident: the Colonel's small book-case was full of his novels with his signature on the fly-leaves. From my window I could look out over the narrow straits to the low little island of Wazin, covered with date palms, and with a white beach where the fishing people hauled up their canoes. When the tide came in I could lean out of the window and spit on the sea and if I lay awake at night I could hear the waves creeping on to the shore. I would listen for a long time to the sound the sea made, the whispering and the rattle of pebbles, and in the morning I need take only a few steps from the door to be in the water. I liked these morning swims, because then the day was still cool and lay all before me to go sailing, or fish or swim or take the truck down the coast over the coral roads between the coconut plantations. And the sea was always warm and clear so that you could spend hours in it and go down and chase surprised little fishes and look at the colours of the coral.

After breakfast the Colonel might take us out in the motor yacht. The Colonel ran a small fisheries business. Neither he nor the African fishermen took the business very seriously, but it gave them all something to do and a bit of money. The other Europeans living at Shimoni were a very old retired white hunter, who lived alone like a hermit in a star-shaped white house on a headland overlooking the sea, and a tea-planter, who had come down to the coast for his health and spent all the hours of daylight far out at sea fishing from a catamaran fitted with an outboard motor. I only saw each of them once. I saw the white hunter, who was very wrinkled and had a long white beard, stooping over the open bonnet of the Colonel's truck. He stared at the engine for a long time and then looked up at the Colonel and said, "Isn't it remarkable, how clever men are, making things like this?" I remember his face had the expression of wonder of a child who has learnt for the first time that tadpoles turn into frogs. A few days later I met the retired tea-planter. He wore nothing but a piece of coloured cloth round his waist and was burnt brown like an Indian. He seemed supremely happy.

We often spent the whole day in our boat, cruising along green shores overhung with creepers and thick shrubs and mangroves, and anchoring off tiny islands which were no more than lumps of mushroom-shaped coral rock and spits of sand that were covered at high tide. We would swim out a few yards in the clear warm water until we reached a sudden sea-cliff where the ocean reached deep down and everything was lost in blueness. On the sides of these cliffs were corals and waving sea-plants of colours we do not know this side of the water, and many fish of many sorts and many colours swam over and into the abyss. There were solitary fish and gregarious fish, of scarlet and gold and black and yellow, spotted and striped or all of one colour, or a shoal all of one colour, a twisting blur of red or brown, like smoke from a firework caught in an uncertain wind. There were fish shaped like pancakes and publicans and isosceles triangles, swimming in wide arcs and parabolas and circles, coming in and out of vision, their paths crossing and recrossing and merging and disappearing in a complex motif, till one's vision became a delirium and there seemed no other world but this silent world of shrieking colours, this antic and ritual dance. And when one came to the surface again, there was the spit of white sand, and the little boat bobbing at anchor, and Jamesi the boat-boy sitting at the stern, and the deep blue sky and the deep blue sea.

This was the period between the monsoons, and sometimes dhows would call at Shimoni on their way to Kilindini, cruising northwards from Pemba and Zanzibar, to take on spices and grain and lay up before the south-easter. The wind would come and take them up to Mogadishu and Aden, and veering eastwards perhaps to Mukalla, Muscat and Bombay. The dhows would come in towards dusk. You would hear the conch horn first and then see the dhow, low in the water and its sail slack, creeping down the strait between the far island and the near reef, and every so often someone would blow on the conch, producing a deep blaring sort of noise. I think dhows from a distance, under sail, are the most beautiful things on the sea, but close at hand you discover that they are dirty and smelly and look unseaworthy. Then some of the crew would row the Naqhoda ashore with heart-shaped paddles in a boat that might have been sinking, it was so low in the water, and then it seemed that time had stopped and it was Abdul Malik that had stepped ashore or da Cunha or Albuquerque. The Naqhoda would be fed, water put aboard and the poop-lamp lit, and in the morning the party would row back to their vessel, the crew would haul on the pulley ropes and raise the sail, and soon the dirty little ship would glide from its anchorage and sail like a swan through the morning-green sea.

It was on this Indian Ocean coast that I first saw Arabs and Arab dhows, and Arab houses with big carved wooden doors, and Arab coffee vendors with little cups on chains, and first heard of the ways of the monsoon winds, which did not penetrate the interior of Africa. The people of Shimoni were African but with some Arab intermixture. They were Muslims but seemed no different from other Africans except that they were more modest. The menfolk fished mostly in the early morning, and during the rest of the day they sat around in groups mending their tackle and making lobster pots out of palm fronds, and arguing and sleeping. The women were retiring, and dressed usually in the Muslim way, in black. Some of them were veiled, though they were not strict about this. One often saw them collecting shell-fish at low tide among the rocks and pools, and every day they would take food to the entrance of a deep subterranean cave and place it in a metal bowl for a certain snake to eat. The snake was said to be large and to share the cave with two lizard-like dragons, and it had to be placated with food offerings because it had supernatural powers. But it had been off its food for over a week when I arrived and I saw nothing in the caves except bats, whose droppings covered the floor ankle deep.

Shimoni is a Swahili word for "in the caves" or "at the place of the caves" and the caves there are large and extend farther than I ever explored.

We found an old mechanical gramophone in the Colonel's house and a record of *Mad Dogs and Englishmen*. We also had a record of a Bach Organ Prelude and Fugue in A minor (played on the piano) which I had bought in Nairobi when the train stopped there for a few hours on the way down from Uganda. We used to play these records most evenings, sitting on the veranda of the big old house. I suppose we had a whisky or two in front of us, and all around it seemed the world was burning and the glow of this almighty conflagration was reflected in the heavens; and then when the fire died out a large yellow star came and hung low over Wazin. I still have the Bach record and whenever I play it I remember very vividly Shimoni and all these things I have spoken about: the dhows gliding in at evening, and the canoes beached on the sand, and the Southern Cross, and the big fish and strange vegetables for dinner, and the old white house of wood and coral which once belonged to the East India Company, very many years ago; and the women collecting shell-fish at low tide on the rocks, and the magnolia blossoms and the sharp, upturned roots of mangrove trees that hurt your feet, and the Colonel telling us how he went around on camels in the Northern Province: the people in the village singing, and at night the crickets, and all the other insects, singing, and the dusk sky singing, and myself, inwardly, singing.

I remember especially standing on the shore looking over the sea to where the clouds rose and fell like great mountains, and resolving to myself that I would come back. I made this resolution for many varied and complex reasons, but principally, I think, because Africa had become a necessity for me, in the way that home for most people is an emotional, as well as a physical necessity

I found in Africa an excitement neither vicarious nor synthetic, which stemmed partly from the sheer novelty of my environment, and partly from that more than life-size force which seemed to work through people, places and events in Africa. When I first arrived I was told: "Don't be surprised by the way people behave here. Actually they're all mad. You may not believe me at first, but after a time you'll see that I'm right. And before you leave you'll be mad, too."

Certain images come to mind: returning from a bombing run over the Aberdares, flying at fifty feet in a Lincoln bomber up and down the ridges of the Kikuyu reserve, watching the tops of trees appear above the level of the wing tips, the chickens running in circles, the women flattening themselves to the ground, the pilot unperturbed that two bombs had jammed in the bomb rack and the undercarriage wouldn't come down; the women in the Lines wailing with a self-induced, ritualistic grief at the death of a child from fever or an askari who hung himself in the company office one breakfast time; a truck load of dead terrorists brought in from the forest and one of them raising himself slowly on one elbow and rubbing his eyes; *Bwana Ndevu*, the bearded Australian sergeant-major, firing his two Colt .45's at playing-cards pinned on the Mess wall. There was violence by Europeans and Africans, to each other, to themselves. I was in Africa at the wrong time, when the Mau Mau had split Kenya in half and worried all East Africa. But it seemed to me then only to emphasise the extremes, the conflicts and dissensions, the unbalance that was, I thought, indigenous to the country. And at that time it excited me, whatever the reasons.

I remember other things, small things, with greater affection. The young Acholi reading the Psalms in Latin to me, not understanding much but engrossed with the sounds of the words; the African who walked down a road with me and asked, "If my children go to England for a year, will they turn white like you?"; the hippopotami that rose from the lake at nightfall and paced across the golf-course and down Main Street, past the post office, till they came at length to the garden of my Company Commander—he would find them, when he opened his kitchen door, eating the chrysanthemums; marching alongside a squad of recruits in the raw early morning in time to the hypnotic chant of their tribal songs, the thorn trees looming out of the mist, dripping with moisture; Shimoni. . . .

I could go on and on. The point is that when the time came for me to leave I had already determined to come back at the first opportunity. The irony is that I have never returned and no doubt if I did so I would be totally disillusioned. Nevertheless, my resolve to return at that time provided the initial impetus to the events that are described in this book.

CHAPTER ONE

PREPARATIONS

SOME months after my stay at Shimoni, at the end of my
Army service, I returned to England. I was just in time to
begin the new Michaelmas term at Oxford. My immediate
reaction to this rather strange world in which I suddenly found
myself was to want even more to go back to Africa. Accordingly
I joined the Exploration Club, which seemed to offer the best
opportunities for such a journey.

The Exploration Club was founded in the 1920's with the
object of assisting undergraduates to go on scientific or adventurous expeditions to various distant parts of the world during
the long summer vacations. The club had no funds and little
equipment: it offered advice, guidance, contacts and prestige
to those expeditions it approved. I went along to a club
meeting and announced that I intended going to Africa. My
proposal was greeted with encouraging enthusiasm. I was
requested to decide where precisely I intended to go in Africa,
how I hoped to get there, where I thought the money would
come from and what I would do once I got there. Having decided all these things, I should lay my plans before the senior
committee in a year's time.

Africa is a very large place. It is also a long way away. I had
no money and no hope of getting any. Also I was as useless as
a dodo. At school I had picked up the rudiments of Latin and
medieval French history. In the Army I had acquired a
smattering of Swahili and an imperfect knowledge of company
imprest accounts and obsolete weapons. I had little acquain-
tance with any of the "ologies" which seemed as essential a part
of the modern explorer's equipment as pith helmets and spine
protectors were in the past. I pored over maps in my draughty,
low, oak-beamed rooms, discovered a hundred rivers leading
to a hundred unknown tribes, embraced the whole world with
my conjectures and came to no definite decisions. Autumn came,
then winter. The sun became cool and pale, raw wet mists
crept out of the Isis, the geraniums were put away in the college

potting shed and I crouched over my inadequate gas-fire. Africa seemed even more remote and desirable.

The term ended and we all went home. An examination loomed like a large and ugly gasometer on a bare horizon and I struggled with my books, trying to follow Alfred's campaigns in Wessex and Aeneas' wanderings in the Mediterranean, lost in the mysteries of Greek drama and the complexities of Anglo-Saxon grammar. On the last day of the vacation I turned to a map of Africa by way of a change. I drew a circle round every island off the African coast and looked up in the encyclopaedia each island I had marked. I have no idea why I did this, but it was very fortunate, looking back, that I did so. Snow had fallen, I remember, and the world was cold, black and cheerless.

Africa is ringed with many islands. I began in the north-west, worked south, rounded the Cape of Good Hope and worked north. Madeira and the Canary Islands, the Cape Verde Islands, São Thomé, Ascension, St. Helena, Tristan da Cunha, Madagascar, Réunion, Mauritius, the Comoro Islands, the Seychelles, Zanzibar—I looked them all up in the encyclo-paedia. They all sounded immensely pleasant, but there seemed no obvious reason, no excuse, for an expedition visiting them with even a vaguely scientific intent: they had been adequately explored and many large books had been written about them. There was only one island left: an island with a completely unfamiliar name: a red dot off the coast of Somalia labelled Socotra (Brit.). I turned to it in the encyclopaedia and couldn't find it. I went away and had tea. It is very strange, I thought, that I have never heard of this place and that it is not mentioned in the encyclopaedia. I returned and found it spelt with a K.

Sokotra, I read, was an island in the Indian Ocean, part of the Aden Protectorate. It was 500 miles from Aden and 130 miles from the African coast at Cape Guardafui, situated along the main shipping route to India. It was 72 miles long and 22 miles wide and had an area of between 2,000 and 3,000 square miles. It was a rugged country, with an overall limestone plateau averaging 1,500 feet in height, through which projected a central mountain range, the Haggier Massif, reaching nearly 5,000 feet. These mountains constituted one of the oldest land surfaces in the world and had been an ark of refuge for many strange and primitive forms of plants and lower animal life, found nowhere else. Frankincense, myrrh, dragon's blood, cucumber and pomegranate trees grew there. 10,000 people lived on this island and they were of two sorts: on the coast were a mixed lot of Arabs and Africans; in the mountains lived the true Sokotri, who were aboriginals isolated on the island "from time immemorial", living in caves, talking a unique language that nobody knew, subsisting on dates and milk. Not much more seemed to be known about the island, no Europeans lived there, and the last scientific expedition had left in 1899. As I read this brief account I became interested and then excited. Nobody had been there since 1899. That in itself was sufficient justification for my going. And there appeared to be many mysteries still unsolved. Where did the Sokotri come from? What was this language nobody knew? How did they live? How many unique and primitive plants and animals were there left to discover? I decided immediately that Socotra was the place I had been looking for.

In the next few weeks I tried to gather more information about the island. There seemed to be hardly any books written about it. I learnt that the first scientific expedition had taken place in 1880, when Professor Balfour went there and spent six weeks looking for plants. Afterwards he wrote:

"What has been done by this expedition is but a fragment of what there is to be accomplished. . . . It happens that on this island within but three weeks' journey from England, there dwells a people whose origin is lost in myth, and of whose speech the true relations are undetermined, who, according to received reports, having obtained some degree of civilisation and embraced Christianity have gone back from their advanced position to the lower state in which we now find them and thus present to us a feature of great interest to the history of mankind. . . . There is now on Socotra alone a wealth of material for exploration and investigation which would amply reward the work of another expedition."

I began to make tentative plans. I began to draw up a scientific programme. Most travellers to distant places cannot afford to pay their own way. They must thus propose to carry out scientific research in the country in which they intend to travel and hope that interested scientific bodies will contribute towards their expenses in return for the scientific data and specimens they aim to collect. They are like the tramps who wander the countryside and offer to dig gardens or chop wood in return for a loaf of bread and a cup of tea. The arrangement is of mutual advantage and not at all unethical.

I was told that Socotra was of great archæological importance. It had never been properly surveyed and was believed to have been an important entrepôt for trade between the Far East and the Mediterranean during the years of the Roman Empire. Large stone ruins had been found there that might indicate a vanished culture and a superseded Christianity among the island's past inhabitants. I was put in touch with Peter Shinnie, who had recently returned from the Sudan, where he had been Director of Antiquities for a number of years. Peter was married with two young children, and he had the invaluable qualification of being able to speak Arabic. He became interested in the project and I invited him to join the expedition.

The British Museum, it turned out, would welcome a further collection of plants and animals, particularly as the expedition would be the first to visit the island during the Arabian summer. And it was just possible, they said, that we might find the fossil remains of a giant tortoise in the limestone caves. I was approached by Michael Gwynne, who was doing research work for a Ph.D. at Oxford after graduating in biology at Edinburgh University. He was 23, had been at school in America and travelled in Mexico and Canada. He was obviously a first-class scientist with plenty of experience of field work, and I invited him, too, to join the expedition. The Professor of Botany knew nothing about Socotran flowers, but he suggested we took blood-group samples from the Socotrans, as these might afford some clues to the mystery of their racial origins. I learnt that little was known about medical conditions on Socotra except that diseases were as rampant there as in any other undeveloped country in the East. Somebody in the party with medical knowledge seemed essential, for there was little chance of obtaining outside help once we were on the island, and to run the risk of possible serious infection or accident was more foolhardy than brave. I asked Neil Orr and Richard Lister to come along with us, to combine the work of blood-grouping with care of the health of the party and of the Socotrans themselves. They were both 25 and had been at Cambridge together. They were now at St. Thomas's Hospital in London, on the point of taking their final examination before qualifying as doctors. John Weakley, a friend and contemporary of mine at Oxford, the only other undergraduate in the party beside myself, joined us as quartermaster. A solidly built man, a lover of large and scorching curries, good music, Rugby football and the open air, he seemed ideally suited to the job, and was never happier than when making packing cases out of champagne crates or pushing trolleys laden with stores along cobbled streets, dressed in a bottle-green cardigan that reached almost to his knees.

The programme was decided, the personnel selected, and the expedition began to gather momentum. From the Admiralty I acquired one of the rare maps of Socotra, made in 1835 and marked with vague but beautifully engraved hills, and with little treasure-map instructions: "No water to be obtained in this part of the island than that collected from the hollows of the rocks," "Ruins supposed to have been a pagan temple," "Salt water swamp". I began to work out routes and time-tables. The examinations were over and the summer had come. The Cherwell flowed green and punt-infested into Isis. The hard yellow and grey spires incised deep blue skies. Africa was a long way away.

We were faced with many problems, the greatest being the question of transport. How could we get to Socotra? The great snag was the south-west monsoon which, unleashing itself from the southern Indian Ocean, hurled itself northwards, veered east and fell upon Socotra like a bull on a tea-cup. During the period of our expedition, between August and October, the island was effectively sealed from the rest of the world by gale-force winds and raging seas. During the rest of the year the only ships calling at the island were native dhows. There was no ordinary sea or air service to the island. There seemed no way of getting there till I learnt that there was a rough natural-surface airstrip on which aircraft occasionally landed.

I knew that in the past the Royal Air Force had often transported government officers, troops, supplies and sometimes private individuals—travellers and scientists like ourselves—to parts of the Aden Protectorate that were extremely difficult of access by any other way. It seemed to me that they might be willing to help transport our own expedition to Socotra. I therefore wrote to the man I thought most likely to help us—Air Chief Marshal Sir Basil Embry. He was a man of an adventurous disposition (his escapes from German hands during World War II are well known) and he was a Patron of the British Schoolboys Exploration Society. Some days later a reply came from the Headquarters of Allied Air Forces Central Europe: "Obviously," Sir Basil wrote, "the only way for your expedition to reach Socotra during the south-west monsoon is for the members to be flown in, and I support the idea that the Royal Air Force should come to your help . . ." When we read this the world became suddenly radiant. Sir Basil would make a few enquiries to see what could be done to help us. He would write again in three or four weeks' time.

We waited anxiously for a reply, for everything depended on it. After four weeks Sir Basil wrote as he had promised. He enclosed a letter from Air Marshal Sir Claude Pelly, commanding the Middle East Air Force, who had been in touch with the Air Officer Commanding, Aden. It appeared that periodic routine training flights were made to Socotra. Provided the expedition was kept small and simple, there was no objection to flying men and baggage to Socotra in a transport aircraft making one of these routine flights between Aden and Socotra.

I shall always be grateful to these officers who agreed to help us in this way. The expedition owes debts of gratitude to many people for many reasons, but I shall always think that the biggest debt of all is to the Royal Air Force, for without them we should never have got to within 500 miles of Socotra.

This seemingly insuperable problem having been solved, I completed the expedition's plans. They were submitted to the senior committee of the Exploration Club and in due course they were approved. This meant that we could now be considered an official project of the University of Oxford and had the full authority and prestige of that institution behind us. We had some paper printed with the heading "Oxford University Expedition to Socotra, 1956", and with this we proceeded to bombard many firms, learned bodies, government departments, grant-giving trusts and private individuals at home and abroad. The whole project began to snowball rapidly. The interest the expedition roused in the scientific world caused me to extend the scientific programme: almost weekly I was forced to increase my original estimate of expenditure: I became so occupied with the minute details of organisation that I had little time for anything else. One afternoon I went to London and met three men who had within recent years paid visits to Socotra: George Popov of the Desert Locust Survey, Don Beydoun of the Iraq Petroleum Company and Colonel (then Major) Ian Snell, at that time Assistant Adviser to the Mahra Sultanate, of which Socotra was part. I fired every possible question at them. I learnt that food would be extremely scarce during the period of our visit so that we would have to take all our food supplies with us. I learnt that there were no bazaars and no shops of any kind so that we would have to take every item of equipment with us, as we couldn't hop back to Aden if we had forgotten anything. I learnt that the only form of transport was camels and that they were expensive. I learnt that the people were peaceful but avaricious.

The second winter came. We compiled long and formidable lists of equipment, right down to tin-tacks and drawing pins, scrubbing brushes and meat safes. We bought a refrigerator in which we could preserve bedouin blood samples; we bought tents, a corkscrew, mosquito nets, Primus lamps and a pair of hair clippers. We went into an ironmonger's and asked for ten dozen padlocks. "Ten dozen, sir?" the ironmonger asked, as though he only sold them by the gross. "Yes, sir, what sort would you like?" We visited the War Office and they supplied us in record time with compasses, binoculars and a Very pistol. We asked if they could spare us a .22 rifle. ".22? What's that, an elephant gun?" No, we told the War Office, it was used by the Army on miniature rifle ranges. "No," they said, "I don't think we've got any of *those*." Many firms provided stores free of charge. From Boots we received nine cases of drugs and surgical equipment, specially selected, packed and labelled with great care. I visited a shoe factory in Essex, the small back rooms of museums and government departments, the Royal Geographical Society and the B.B.C. The latter waxed enthusiastic, said the expedition was another Kon-Tiki, loaned a tape-recorder and twelve hours' worth of recording tape and despatched me into Regent's Park to record the gardener, an American tourist, an old-age pensioner and a colonial student who knew little English. As the weeks passed and our sailing date of Friday, July 13, approached, the college entrance became cluttered up with boxes and cardboard cartons containing free donations of Porage, tea, dried milk, toilet paper, soap, flour and every other conceivable item of food and equipment. Sometimes we made embarrassing mistakes in our obsequious requests for commercial charity. We got a letter from a biscuit manufacturing firm: the letter was headed "Supermeats, mixed squares, terrier, puppy and dog cakes" and informed us that the firm to which we had directed our request for supplies had gone out of business two years ago and that its successor made only dog biscuits. If, however, we would find any use for dog biscuits. . . . We replied graciously, saying that though in the end we might have to eat like dogs we would, naturally, like to do the best for ourselves in the meantime.

Gradually we began to acquire funds. Many learned bodies supported us generously—the Royal Geographical Society, the University of Oxford, the British Academy, the Medical Research Council, Harvard University, and others too numerous to mention. On one occasion Mike happened to learn that all applications for grants from a certain scientific body should be in by 5.0 p.m. on a certain day. To his horror he realized that this was the day and it was 5.30. He went along to the premises of the scientific body. He tried to gain entry to the building and the janitor pushed him out at the end of a broom. So Mike waited till the janitor left and then took out the screwdriver he happened to have in his pocket. He forced the lock and entered the building. He heard typing upstairs and found the secretary of the scientific body still there. He presented his application for a grant to the secretary, who typed it out and placed it on top of all the other applications. A few days later he learnt that the expedition had been awarded £150.

The sailing date approached rapidly. John and I moved into a disused stable and established the expedition head-quarters there. We set up our office and living quarters in the hayloft and piled our accumulating stores in the stable itself. It seemed that the telephone would never stop ringing, the postman or the railwayman delivering, and ourselves frantically hammering, typing, painting red numbers over everything, and at odd hours of the day and night, eating and sleeping. By Sunday, July 8, we were almost ready. By dint of working right through the night John, Neil and myself packed, locked, labelled and listed every package preparatory to driving them down to the docks. There were one hundred and fifty packages of different shapes and sizes, weighing altogether nearly three tons. Some of the scientific equipment was already in Aden, having failed to reach Socotra before the monsoon broke and ended the dhow traffic. We loaded our hired lorry and drove round the streets of Oxford. It was a beautiful evening, warm and pensive, for the summer had started well, though later it was to turn to rain and misery. We drove out to our American friends. "Come and look at the lorry!" we cried. They came out and appraised the cargo we had on board. Then we went in and had tea in the alcove of the garden. There were trailing roses on the trellis, and the scent of flowers, and over the fence came the voices of children, and at the back of the field at the end of the garden an evening mist was coming up. After nearly eighteen months of planning and preparation the expedition seemed almost a reality.

The next day John drove the lorry down to the London Docks. As we were descending a narrow hill, a tanker moving in the opposite direction pulled over to our side of the road, with all its headlights blazing, in an attempt to overtake a long line of Army vehicles that were moving up the hill. The car in front of us had to pull on its brakes to avoid a collision with the tanker. John quickly applied the brakes of our own lorry. But our payload was too heavy: I heard John say, "I've got all the brakes on!" and then we both sat and watched our lorry sink down and down on to the car in front. We smashed into its back, biffing it many yards on amidst a tinkling of glass. Then something hit us from behind. As we gave evidence to the police they pointed out various holes in the fence that ran beside the road. Many lorries had plunged off the road and crashed down the bank, they said. We were grateful that all our precious equipment, the result of months of work and the life-blood of the expedition, had not suffered a similar fate.

The day before we were due to sail we were still not ready: there were innumerable details still to be worked on—a last injection, the final settling of accounts, a call to the Post Office to dismantle our telephone. We just caught the London train, filling a compartment with rucksacks, tape-recorder, film cameras and suitcases. John hadn't got a ticket and the collector wouldn't let him on to the platform. While they argued the train began to move out. "Come on, John! Come on!" we shouted. John dodged a red, irate ticket collector and hopped into the open carriage door.

We assembled in Richard's flat and excitedly opened two

large boxes full of shoes. We all put on identical suede chukka boots. These were our uniform for the next few weeks. In the evening we adjourned to Peter's flat. We ate goulash and drank wine and beer and talked of the island, 3,000 miles away, upon which we were to descend. It was the first time we had all been together.

We got to bed at three that morning. I looked forward to a rest on the boat, for I felt quite exhausted.

CHAPTER TWO

THE BARREN ROCKS

THE next day we set sail from Southampton. The voyage was uneventful: we enjoyed the sun, the rest, the cheap cigarettes and a day in Malta. We did not enjoy the Red Sea in midsummer: it was like sailing through steam, and our bare feet left moist brown prints on the deckplanks.

I tried to find somebody in the crew who knew something about Socotra. Only one man in the whole ship's company had ever landed there, though many had seen it from a wary distance as they sailed towards India.

"Rather you than me," he said.

He had landed on Socotra in 1926, looking for slave runners.

"They'll eat you, if you don't watch out. Usually they only eat themselves, but foreigners go down very well. Once they all sailed across to Cape Guardafui and ate the lighthouse keepers there. It's their idea of living really."

He said we should go well armed.

"They look like Europeans, but they've got no idea of civilization. Actually," he added, "they don't eat women. They keep them to do the work."

He told me that a long time ago there had been nine tribes who had lived in the Garden of Eden, in Arabia. When Eden became a desert eight tribes had migrated northwards and founded civilization, while the other tribe had gone south and settled on Socotra.

"Where they didn't do quite so well," the sailor said.

We reached Aden on July 28. I woke at two in the morning and saw, in my half comatose state, the gates of hell and the eternal bonfire. A red fire burned behind the black and ominous hills as we entered Aden harbour; it glowed sinisterly like a promise of damnation, silhouetting the broken ridges of the hills. It was, I learned later, the waste burner of the oil refinery at Little Aden, but it was a bad thing to wake up to, in a strange country, not knowing what it was.

A grey dawn revealed black hills, a half-moon of bare rocks

where nothing grew and only the buzzards wheeled endlessly. From the town, huddled along the sides of the long-extinct and drowned volcano that formed the harbour, came the sounds of steam-hammers and the honking of a steadily increasing traffic.

> "Be'old, accrowd upon the beam
> And 'umped above the sea appears
> Old Aden like a barrick stove
> That no-one's lit for years an' years."

Only already the unlit stove was getting very hot.

We left the ship and made our way to the hotel. I had just reached the hotel desk when a small and yellow-faced boy handed me a telephone.

"Mister Bottink?" he squeaked.

"Yes," I said, very surprised.

A voice crackled out of the telephone. I could barely hear it because of the faintness of the line.

"Commodore . . . A.O.C. . . . half an hour's time."

"I beg your pardon."

"Vice-Marshal . . . half an hour's time."

"Who is that speaking, please?"

"The Air Commodore."

"Oh—I'm sorry, what did you say?"

"A.O.C. . . . at the hotel . . . 10 o'clock."

I had just finished breakfast when the Air Officer Commanding, Air Vice-Marshal Sinclair, arrived in his staff car. Sitting in the austere brown hotel lounge we discussed the expedition's airlift to Socotra in a few days' time, while bare-footed white-turbaned waiters brought us coffee. He was helpful and most interested, and by the time he left, half an hour later, we had sorted everything out to each other's satisfaction. He told me that a Valetta had made a satisfactory trial landing on Socotra a few weeks previously, as there had been some doubts about the condition of the airstrip there.

Later in the morning we were taken in hand by Nigel Groom of the Secretariat, who referred to a fat dossier labelled, somewhat to my embarrassment, "The Botting Expedition to Socotra". He was most helpful and arranged, among other things, for the loan of a Land-Rover from the Government Guards, thus saving us the great expense of hiring taxis, the only other form of transport in Aden. That evening he took us

The Sultan of Socotra on his return from his pilgrimage to Mecca. On his right is Abdulla, his chief executioner.

Part of the expedition's camel caravan leaving the airstrip en route for the capital.

A roof-top view of Hadibo, the capital of Socotra, dominated by the spires of the Haggier Mountains.

A typically uncrowded street in the capital.

to Government House, a new building like a cross between an ornate fortress and a rajah's palace. Here, sitting in wicker chairs on a curving, stone-flagged terrace, we talked quietly of this and that, while our glasses were filled and a slight breeze rustled through the garden. At a discreet distance a sentry stood at ease with his rifle, beside an ancient cannon pointing out over the harbour approaches. It was a pleasant evening; the air was cool and there were stars shining clearly; it was difficult to believe that we were here, and that only a few miles away was desert, and five hundred miles across the sea was Socotra, in the middle of the fierce dry monsoon that we could not feel now.

The next days were hectic and my memory of them is blurred. I have a confused recollection of stooping in and out of jeeps, in and out of banks, offices, the Secretariat, Khormaksar Airport and the R.A.F. Headquarters; of being driven rapidly from one part of the port to another, barely conscious, in my pre-occupation with final preparations, of the life of the town around me, the new town of rising buildings of concrete and steel, garages, oil storage tanks and blocks of flats, the old town of high dark wooden houses with leaning fretwork verandas and traditional markets, where wailing Arab music drifted out of dim, scented interiors and followed you down past the stalls of sweetmeats in trays, of beads and *qat*, bales of bright cloth, stacks of clay amphoras, buckets and hurricane lamps and two delicate, beautiful gazelles tethered in a doorway.

The Labour Commissioner had scoured all the streets for unemployed cooks and sent them to the hotel one lunch-time. They crowded together inside the entrance, all shouting at once and thrusting their tattered chits and references in my face. When I mentioned Socotra a number of them drifted away, and after I had explained to the rest where Socotra was and what I thought it was like, most of them drifted away too. From those who were left—the ignorant, the needy and the opportunists— I chose two of the opportunists: a Somali in white trousers and a canary yellow pullover, who spoke good English and looked capable and honest, and another Somali, who was his friend and related in a vague oriental way, a tall, wild-looking man with a deep gruff voice and pieces of cloth wrapped untidily round his loins, neck and head. These two excellent gentlemen, I learned, were called Abdullahi (Abdi for short) and Ali, and

c

during the following months they were to serve us unflaggingly and very competently in our greatest needs.

Peter had not yet arrived. He had been held up by bad weather at Asmara on his way out from England by air. It was the sort of thing I had dreaded happening, but Nigel Groom informed me, to my relief, that the Sultan of Socotra would be flying to the island after his return from Mecca, and I was able to arrange for Peter to fly in his plane, four days after the rest of us.

The last day came, the last dinner, the last sleep between sheets. The last evening was a bad one and I didn't get much sleep. In the middle of packing, writing letters and working out accounts I collapsed on my bed at two in the morning. The coming day would bring what it would bring. . . .

I woke at four and it was still dark outside. I had gone to sleep in my clothes with the light on and when I woke the light hurt my eyes and my mouth tasted rough, the way it does when one sleeps for only a short time.

I got off the bed and turned down the electric fan regulator. I opened the shutters of the veranda. The air felt wonderful, cool as on top of a mountain. I felt I could cup my hands and gather up the air and pour it over myself like cold water. The world looked wonderful. There was a lightening round the edges of the hills where the dawn was coming. You could see the dawn coming as you watched. It was coming up green behind the hills, like a light seen through water, suffused. You could see the street lamps and there were some lights in the black harbour, disembodied. I couldn't hear a thing.

I packed and wrote a few more letters and then I went down to breakfast. It was to be our last civilized breakfast for some time, but we did not appreciate this: we were in too great a hurry. Pineapple juice, bacon and eggs, toast and marmalade, coffee: we gulped the lot and went out to the taxis with our baggage.

The aircraft were due to take off at 6 a.m. We left the Hotel at 5.50 and half-way to the airport I remembered our guns and ammunition were still in the police station. Richard went back for them in the second taxi and the rest of us drove up to dispersal and saw the two Valettas and their crews waiting for us. We felt very stupid because we were fifteen minutes late.

I got out of the taxi and went over to one of the crews.

"I'm sorry we're late, but we're having a spot of trouble getting our guns out of the police station. Won't be long, I hope."

"Are you the Oxford party?" an officer asked. I wondered who else we could have been. We were all immaculate in pressed white shirts and identical suede boots.

"Yes, we're the Oxford party."

We loaded our personal baggage on to the aircraft we were to fly in, and after nearly half an hour Richard arrived with the guns.

The Flight-Sergeant was a very experienced pilot and he had landed on Socotra a few weeks previously. He called the young Flying-Officer, the pilot of the second aircraft, over to him.

"There's a fair old wind blowing out there," he said.

"Ah."

"Follow me in and watch me carefully. The strip is firm enough, but the wind's quite something."

The Flying-Officer bit his lip and said "Uha".

"Just watch it."

"Right."

We clambered up the steps into the aircraft and sat behind the piles of crates, kerosene cans and collecting boxes. First one engine and then another roared and died. We taxied gently down to take-off. The engines roared again in unison, increasing in pitch; one could almost feel one's brain straining to absorb the tremendous noise. The plane trembled and then we were speeding down the runway, gathering speed and power with an angry sort of intentness. Mike told me that the Valetta has a low fuselage and I had seen that this was so. The fuselage almost scraped the ground. Mike said this was a dangerous feature of the design. In a high, gusty wind on a rough old air-strip that sloped upwards you would have to be ready for anything. As we rose gently off the ground I anticipated our ultimate landing on Socotra with a serene fatalism. *Finito, kaput, fini, khalas, kwisha*: I thought of all the different versions of *finished* that I knew. For eighteen months Socotra had been lodged in my mind as an idea excluding almost all other ideas, a kind of glorious conception, a goal, a fulfilment, a pin-point of light at the end of a tunnel: anything beyond the end of the tunnel was a vague abstraction of perpetual possibilities: I wanted only to reach the light. Now, as we turned ponderously over the airfield, with Socotra only four hours distant, I felt I didn't mind what happened so long as I saw the island and landed there in some sort of corporeal shape.

As we wheeled slowly over Khormaksar I could see the half-moon of black rocks that hedged in Steamer Point, and the sun glittering on the steel machinery and metal roofs of the oil town at Little Aden. Then we were over the sea and flying directly eastwards along the shore of Southern Arabia. We climbed to 7,000 feet and the air was cool and pricked in our nostrils. Abdullahi was asleep. Ali stared transfixed out of the window. I don't think he enjoyed being so high in the air.

Soon we were flying over the mountains of the Hadhramaut. They were grey, like flint, and dry and powdery-looking. They looked old and dead and you might think a gust of wind would scatter them and dissolve them in a cloud of dust. But they overlook whole cities buried beneath sand.

We flew past Mukalla, a white blur on the shore line, some miles away to our left: we had to look carefully to see it. We landed at Riyan at 8.15. Riyan is an R.A.F. outpost on the edge of a desert, a cluster of white huts and an airfield, serving Mukalla, 15 miles away. Already it was very hot on the edge of the desert. We drove in a jeep to the Officers' Mess and someone handed us cups of hot drinks, coffee that tasted like tea. Then we took off again and flew straight out to sea.

From Riyan to Socotra is about 370 miles and the journey by air takes about one and three-quarter hours. As we flew out farther and farther across the ocean I could see that the surface was becoming more and more troubled. It was flecked with white; the flecks twinkled like stars and more and more appeared. This is what the monsoon does to the sea, but I suppose we were high above the wind, for we flew on smoothly.

After an hour or so the co-pilot came up to me and beckoned me to the cabin. I sat in the co-pilot's seat with the control column moving about slowly in front of me. He tapped on the cabin window in front of me and I looked through the window and saw Socotra way down there many miles away, all covered in mist. I stared at it as a frog might stare at a snake. It just looked like a vaporous uprising lump of sea, but soon the different elements resolved themselves. There was the sea, there was the land which was misty, and there were the clouds over the land. Many clouds piled over the land. The plane began to bump badly. Now you could feel the wind. We came down lower. The sea was rough and thrashed by the wind, and the plane was buffeted by the wind, bumping up and down so badly that sometimes I was squashed into my seat as though someone was pushing down on the top of my head, and then I would be standing with the seat gone away from under me. In the compartment Richard became quiet and pale and was sick in a little brown paper bag which he took to the Elsan and disposed of. John joined me in the cabin, bumping his head against a roof of rubber-cushioned dials, switches and plugs. He tried to speak to me, shouting above the noise of wind and engines; but only the upper register of a few words came through to me, shrill, harsh, unintelligible squeaks.

We had been thinking about Socotra for varying lengths of time and now here it was. We came in over the north-west coast. There was the salt water creek I recognised from the map. The land was all yellow and barren. It looked inhospitable. I looked for signs of vegetation, but I could see none, and no signs of habitation. Just yellow and desolate rocks. Then we flew over Hadibo. I presumed it was Hadibo because that was about where it would be, recalling the map. Hadibo was white and clean-looking but very small, and there were patches of green where the palm trees grew. Behind Hadibo were the mountains, grey and scored by steep watercourses that were dry now. Everything looked dry. Dry and bare, with nothing growing and a fair old wind blowing and blowing and the sea impossible to navigate, and over all the mountains, heavy in cloud. It was rather formidable and very impressive.

We pulled up short of a high hill, turned around and went back along the coast the way we had come, circled the airstrip and landed after only two circuits. I thought our fuselage would hit the ground but it didn't. We landed without incident and stepped out on to Socotran soil.

CHAPTER THREE

BY THE PINK ARABIAN SEA

WE stepped out of the aircraft into a howling gale. The wind came over the hills behind us and raced across the plain and into the sea, taking with it uprooted scrub, rusty oil drums, my handkerchief. Dust and sand blew in our faces and our hair streamed out to one side of our heads. Sudden violent gusts would make us stagger and stop talking and lean into the wind, and we had to shout into each other's ears in order to make ourselves heard.

There were a number of natives and one or two camels at the side of the airstrip. They came up to us, milling around us like the frenzied eddies of the wind and just as noisy. They screamed at us above the wind, demanding baksheesh and biscuits, taking us confidentially by the wrist and rubbing their stomachs to signify their need for food. Some of them were making a motion with their right hand as though they were pouring peanuts into their mouths at a cocktail party, and this, too, we learnt, signified their need for food. Surprisingly, only a few old men looked thin and undernourished; the rest seemed to have adequate flesh on them, though I wondered where they got their food from, for the sea was too rough for fishing and nothing seemed to be growing for miles around but inedible camel-thorn struggling up between the flints and gravel that covered the plain.

Our first contact with Socotrans was tempered by the slightly suspicious curiosity of a tabby cat sniffing an unknown Manx of doubtful potential. They seemed very friendly people, very small and rather polyglot. They all wore tartan-coloured *futahs* or loin-cloths, and some of them had torn and faded shirts; they were barefoot and walked on the razor-edged stones of the plain without difficulty. Some of them had ugly-funny faces, some had striking hawk-like faces, a few were beautiful. More and more of them appeared from nowhere and after some argument we managed to persuade them to help unload the aircraft. In a short time everything was piled in confusion

at the side of the runway, the two aeroplanes taxied down
towards the sea and with a roar and a leap in a cloud of red
and yellow dust took off and disappeared westwards.

I paid the porters some shillings and presented some letters
to one of the Sultan's representatives.

My principal concern at this time was to find water. It
seemed almost conventional to think about water in this dry
place. I hired a camel and a camel-boy and left the others
struggling with a small green tent at the side of the airstrip.
Ali, our spindly, gruff-spoken cook, was holding one of the
poles to which part of the tent was attached. I set off eastwards
and when I looked back I could not see Ali but only a tall
swaying mass of flapping green canvas, as though the tent had
roman-candled like a parachute. It occurred to me that inside
that tight envelope of tent was Ali, still holding on loyally to
the tent-pole

The airstrip is situated on the Northern Coastal Plain at its
widest point, at Ras Karma. It looks particularly desolate
because of the ruined buildings in the R.A.F. camp. During the
war it must have been quite a large camp, but now, ten years
after its abandonment, the roofs have all been stripped and the
walls of ready-made cement blocks are falling down. All around
the camp are stacks of rusting oil drums and sardine tins, the
skeletons of two bombers and a fleet of gutted trucks. There are
more vehicles at the edge of the sea, already drifted up with
sand.*

All along its length the plain is skirted to the north by the
windswept, shipless sea. It slopes gently down to the sea and
the gravel gives way on the shore to sand and crusts of sea-salt
and foul-smelling patches of seaweed. Behind the plain, away
from the sea, there are worn, rounded hills which rise higher
behind one another until they reach the thick limestone cap of the
plateau composing most of the interior of the island. Farther

---

* During the war several squadrons (South African, Dutch, Canadian, as well
as British) were stationed on Socotra to counteract German and Japanese sub-
marines operating in the area. A submarine was successfully sunk (and the
pilot awarded the D.F.C.) but not before one of them had systematically
machine-gunned a dhow off Qalansiya : it had drifted into the port after several
days, the survivors too shocked to move the dead and dying who lay as they had
fallen. Ten airmen who were killed in air mishaps on the island are buried on
Cemetery Hill, a little to the west of the airfield. Companies of Aden Protectorate Levies, Somaliland Scouts, Indian and French West African troops
were also stationed on the island during the war. Probably Socotra had never
seen such a time since the coming of the Portuguese 400 years previously.

away one can just see the principal peaks of the Haggier Mountains and, looking westward, a range of blue hills covered in cloud and sometimes obscured by haze. To reach Qalansiya, the principal port of the island, one must cross these hills.

I rode beside the taciturn camel-boy along a narrow track that twisted between the box trees and camel-thorn. Soon the others on the airfield were hidden from sight by a rise in the ground and everything became blissfully quiet. My sense of the uniqueness of this occasion was still strong: only a few hours before I had been eating bacon and eggs among the civilized comforts of urban Aden; now I was in a strange country among strange people, keenly aware of my isolation from most of my own kind in the outside world, sensitive to the most trivial aspects of my new circumstances—the curious rasping sound with which my companion encouraged his camel; the roughness of the hide of the camel's sides between my knees and the ship-like rocking of its walk; the indefinable and barely perceptible scent which the heat of the sun was dragging from the dry earth and stones; the idea that I should be going in search of water on an island in the Arabian Sea. Looking back, it is strange how quickly we became accustomed to the incongruities that filled our lives in the months that followed, and how soon our perceptions became dulled.

After an hour we entered a plantation of fruitless palm trees that were bent into bows by the wind. We stopped beside two large wells and the camel-boy muttered *moiya*, which I had learnt meant water, and went off in search of some water-skins. I sat down on the parapet of a well and a number of small children gathered round me and stared at me silently and with apparent awe as though they expected that suddenly I would explode or fly away over the palm tops or turn green like a chameleon. I felt like a clever and enormously funny monkey and wished I had learnt some tricks. Some women, pale-skinned and even-featured, came up to me and offered some water in a little goat-skin bucket. They said things to me which I could not understand and one of them showed me her leg, which was covered in a fungus growth, scaly and cracked, unpleasant but not painful. The women were dressed entirely in black, in the Muslim way, and I was surprised they were so forthcoming in the presence of a European male.

My camel-boy returned with two goat-skins, dry and deflated.

He turned them inside out, soaked them in water and trampled on them with his bare feet. Then he filled them with water drawn from the well in the little goat-skin bucket. When the skins were full he loaded them on to the camel and we set off back to the airfield.

The others had succeeded in erecting the tent within the sheltering walls of a now roofless R.A.F. building. Late in the afternoon the wind died and it was as though we had stopped banging our heads against a wall. The sky was cloudless at this time and the sun was not so hot; the hills looked beautiful with the sinking orange sun on them. We used a little of our water to wash the dust out of our eyes and ears and when the sun went down we lit the lamps.

Our cooks prepared a special supper to celebrate our arrival on Socotra. They worked quietly opening tins and boiling and cooking over the red wood fire, and when it was all cooked they came and asked where the table-cloths were. We had no table-cloths and the cooks were not pleased. Richard, the gastronome of the party, had written out a menu:

> ### DINER CHEZ BOTTING
> *Menu le Premier Août*
> *Consommé de poules avec nouilles*
> *Curry avec riz bouillé et cruets divers*
> *Fruit de pin avec une sauce formidable*
> *Fromage execrable de l'Angleterre*
> *Café*
> ### BONNE VACANCE CHERS ENFANTS

The dinner was much better than Richard's French. Afterwards I twanged my guitar, but it sounded thin and puny in the middle of the wide, still plain. The guitar, untraditionally, was not a great success on the island and a camel demolished it before we left.

Before turning in I went for a short walk in the darkness. There were many stars out; the Milky Way was splashed across the sky like a soda spray and a large yellow star hung over the plateau. I thought I saw the light of several fires on the slopes of the foothills and sometimes I heard the whisper of the waves on the shore. For a moment I seemed to be living in a fantasy; listening and watching in the darkness, surrounded by the Indian Ocean and 500 miles from anywhere, I experienced a

peculiar sense of unreality and disembodiment until I struck
my big toe on a stone and was brought back, by the mortification
of flesh, to the realities of the present.

I woke later that night with sand in my eyes and a chill
draught in my sleeping-bag. Dust was swirling and the tent
cracking like a gun. The wind had got up again.

The next morning I went with Abdullahi to the village of
Mouri, half a mile from the airfield. The village consisted of a
score of small, oblong, mud-and-coral huts built close together
so that there was nothing that could be called a street but only
a space between one hut and the next. The huts were roofed
with palm branches and turtle shells and covered over with a
deep layer of earth and stones; some of them had roofs of
corrugated iron fetched from the R.A.F. camp, and a number of
houses had walls and courtyards constructed from rusty oil
drums, so that much of the village had the appearance of a
shanty town. Around the edge of the village were numerous
conical mounds of fish-bones and shells; a few white Egyptian
vultures waddled on the flat rooftops, waiting for carrion—
sewage and the disposal of refuse was no great problem in
Mouri.

We were ushered into a courtyard of oil drums. The wizened
old village head-man, bald and bird-like, scurried out of his
hut and welcomed us; he offered us an aluminium bowl containing water that tasted plainly of animal excreta; we sipped
a little, for politeness' sake, and followed him into the house.
He beckoned us to sit on two dirty woven mats which were
very old and curled up at the ends. There was little else in the
room. From the roof hung a broken hurricane lamp and a
round clay pot. The only light came from the door, a gap in
one of the walls of the hut. A number of children began to fill
the doorway and a very small boy suddenly started screaming
with his eyes shut; he fell heavily on his bottom and was jerked
into silence, and then his mother came and picked him up and
took him away.

I asked the head-man whether I could hire some camels with
which to transport some of the expedition stores to Hadibo,
the capital of the island. He listened very attentively while
Abdullahi translated my question and then got up, without
replying, and began to rummage in a sack at one end of the

room. He came back holding something on the end of a string.

"Would you like to buy a fish?" he asked.

He showed me the fish, about a foot long and very dry. It was a dull sooty colour and looked as though it had lain in dirt for a week in the sun. I did not trust the fish and said I did not want to buy it.

"*Talata shilling*," the head-man suggested, holding up three fingers.

"*La*," Abdullahi said, "the *sahib* does not want fish, he wants camels."

"Aaah," said the head-man, his voice trailing away in a sort of sympathetic understanding, as if I had told him I was the chosen son of the Prophet. He turned to another wizened old man and began an earnest discussion with him. Abdi could not understand them as they spoke Socotran. Soon other people joined in the discussion and came and sat down, and after a while they were all talking at the same time. A woman was shouting from the doorway in a hard high voice, the children were jostling and laughing among themselves, and I got the idea that there were too many people in the room, especially as they were all spitting on to the ground around me. Though they covered the spittle with dust with a deft, almost subconscious, movement of their feet and hands, nevertheless I did not like too many people spitting near me—and in any case I wanted to know about the camels.

"What about the camels?" I asked.

"*Ismah*," Abdi said, "the *sahib* would like camels."

"*Kam shilling*, how much?" the head-man asked

I was to hear and speak the words *Kam shilling* many times on most days in the following months. One could not avoid it. The Arabs of Socotra talk principally of two things, money and women, and as they have enough of the latter but little of the former, they talk mostly of money. Sooner or later you would ask "How much?" or be asked "How much?" I suggested five shillings for one camel for one day, the head-man suggested twenty shillings, and eventually we settled for ten. They hurriedly discussed the firm offer and agreed to provide two camels to take me and a companion to Hadibo to discuss with the Sultan's deputy the question of raising a caravan of many camels to transport the expedition from the airfield.

Later that afternoon the wizened old man came up to our

camp and said that they all greatly feared the Sultan and were afraid to give us the camels they had promised in the morning. All the camels, apparently, belonged to the Sultan.

Shortly after the old man left, disconsolate with his fears and his regrets, we were visited by a man who was obviously of high rank. He was dressed in a white robe, and when he stood in the wind the robe was wrapped around him like a white cotton boiler suit. He wore a white *kafia* wound about his head like a turban, and carried the string of yellow beads which Muslims tell in odd moments. He was taller than the average Socotran and had an aloof, unsmiling, hatchet face, with a little beard struggling out of his chin. This man's name was Ali bin Selme, and he was head-man of the village of Qadhub, four miles to the east of the airfield. He said he was the Sultan's right-hand man, and jingled a bunch of keys as if to prove it. I did not much like the look of Ali. He had an annoyingly contemptuous manner and a loud complaining voice, and it turned out he was a bad-tempered, scrounging old rogue. But we asked him to sit in one of our green camp chairs and offered him a cup of tea and a cigarette. We produced Forbes' *Natural History of Sokotra* and showed him the life-sized colour pictures of centipedes and spiders. We asked him if he knew these, but he looked at them very disinterestedly and started holding a conversation with cook Ali. I told Abdullahi to tell him that I wanted a number of camels to take the expedition to Hadibo. It turned out that there was no possibility of getting camels without the authority of the Sultan or the Sultan's deputy, the Little Sultan, at present in Hadibo. I was tape-recording this discussion and when Ali saw the microphone he at once mistook the recording machine for a radio set and wanted to talk to his Sultan in it. (The Sultan had just returned from Mecca to Aden, where he was living with his retinue in a back-street *pension*, waiting for the plane to bring him back to Socotra.) When it was explained to Ali with difficulty that he could not speak to the Sultan, but that this machine only caught his words on sticky paper, he said that we had better write a letter to the Little Sultan, asking for camels. As neither he nor I nor Abdi nor cook Ali could write in Arabic, this might have proved difficult had not one of the men of Qadhub come along, a *karrani* who could write beautifully, and who for a small fee would willingly write a letter as dictated. So the letter was duly dictated and the *karrani*, a pleasant and above all polite and soft-voiced young man, sat out of the wind holding a small piece of paper upon which, with infinite pains and much licking of the pencil lead, he wrote the graceful Arabic words that look like shorthand notes. When the letter was written he said he would find someone to take it to Hadibo, for a small fee, and there did not seem to be much else I could do but await the pleasure of the Little Sultan, whoever he might be.

Ali was, among other things, a hypochondriac. He complained to Richard of backache and tummy trouble. Richard could find nothing wrong with him so he rubbed him with tooth-paste and Ali was immediately cured, expressing satisfaction, comfort and happiness. He drifted away and we had tea.

Early on the fourth morning a large number of camels and men began to assemble near our camp. They had not come for us—the Sultan was due back that day by air from Aden, and his camels, camel-men and household were gathering in anticipation of his arrival. Every half-hour some of them came over to us and demanded to know when the Sultan was due to land. They told us that the Little Sultan was with them. I was interested in meeting him and about mid-morning I went over to pay my respects.

There was a great crowd of burly Africans in red fezzes and violet waistcoats with mother-of-pearl buttons, and some rather superior-looking Arabs in their best and brightest clothes. But it wasn't obvious which was the Little Sultan.

"Which is the Little Sultan?" I asked Abdullahi.

Abdullahi made inquiries. Then he stepped through the crowd and stood in front of two youths sitting cross-legged on palm mats.

"This," he said, tapping one of the youths on the head as if he were exhibiting a piece of furniture, "is Little Sultan One. And this," tapping the other youth on the head, "is Little Sultan Two."

The two royal youths, indistinguishable in dress, features or demeanour from the retinue that jostled round them, did not seem to mind Abdi's rather ungracious approach. They hardly moved, said nothing, only looked up at me with large yellowish eyes and smiled wanly. They were very docile, slight, innocuous aristocrats. I said "how do you do" and shook their hands, tried to make conversation with them, failed, and left. Looking back, my first introduction to the upper crust of Socotra was typical—it was a very strange crust.

At midday the Sultan's plane arrived. All the inhabitants of the neighbouring villages seemed to have turned out and there was great excitement among them and much washing of faces and straightening of *futahs*. As the plane taxied up the airstrip the crowd formed up in a long line. A very large African began to fire shots into the air with an old rifle and then the long line advanced towards the aircraft, Ali bin Selme at the head of them. The door of the plane was swung open, there was some jostling in the doorway—I was relieved to see Peter's face peer out momentarily—and then the Sultan trod gingerly down the steps and crossed over to the line of his chattering subjects. The wind wrapped his long white robes tightly round him. He was a short, slight, rather yellow-skinned man. His *kafia* was encircled by an *agal* of gold cords with black thongs, and on his feet he wore short purple and yellow socks and black patent leather shoes. A curved dagger was tucked in his belt and he clutched a symbolic sword in a jade green case, a present from the Saudi Arabians. He was followed closely by Sheikh Ibrahim bin Khaled, his first Wazir, dressed also in white, with a red thermos flask hanging from the crook of his arm and a white umbrella and string of yellow beads held tightly in his left hand. Behind Ibrahim was Sheikh Issa, the second Wazir, and one or two others of the royal retinue. The Sultan's wife, a scurrying little black-veiled figure, was led away and I never saw her again. The Sultan began at one end of the line and worked his way slowly down its length. He was greeted by everybody, each in turn ceremoniously grasping his extended hand and kissing his wrist, while Ali bin Selme and my *karrani* of the previous day, his head wrapped in a magnificent golden turban, stood by in attendance. When he had worked his way along the line he sat down with his Wazirs. Immediately the line broke and everyone crowded round him, squatting in a circle several rows deep, babbling loudly and jumping up and down. The Sultan began speaking. He seemed to be relating his adventures of the last few months, during his pilgrimage to Mecca, and every so often he made a symbolic gesture—one of these gestures was a chop. Everybody seemed very pleased that their Sultan had come safely back to them.

Peter was last out of the plane. He brought news from the

outside world—trouble over Suez, the results of the Test Match. He had acted as interpreter on the flight and had seen the Sultan's reception at Riyan. A guard of honour was drawn up of Aden Protectorate Levies in red turbans and Hadhrami Bedouin Legion in red and white checked *kafias*. When the Sultan got out of the plane arms were presented and bugles blown, and the Sultan stood at a rather half-hearted salute, a little out of his depth, clutching an umbrella.

I had sent a telegram to Peter before he left Aden. It had reached him in garbled form:

"All well please ask Shinnie to bring one gross matches, eye water jerrycans or equivalent, two chairs, one coin money, books, one spade on Sultan's plane. Also Mukalla interpreter have got one case of slight utentant cater RAF."

The message had mystified him considerably. He was un-certain whether we wanted a jerrycan of eye-wash and whether a case of slight utentant cater was a rather rare disease (it referred in fact to a Flight-Lieutenant's suit-case which had been off-loaded on Socotra by mistake). Eventually he trans-lated the message, bringing with him a jerrycan, because we needed something in which to keep our water; two deck-chairs —the first time we sat in them the canvas split irremediably; one money-box, containing £500 in one shilling pieces tied up in sacks; and a spade, because as archaeologist he needed something to dig with.

Peter and I went to meet the Sultan to discuss with him the possibility of obtaining camels for the next day. We found him surrounded by henchmen and baggage—an extraordinary miscellany of kitchen utensils, funnels, buckets, kettles, bottles of orange syrup and a bundle of black umbrellas—and after greeting him we asked him about the camels. He was very diffident and sour-faced and avoided looking directly at us. He would not speak Arabic and Sheikh Ibrahim had to translate Peter's Arabic into Socotri. The Sultan's executioner, Abdulla, a very large, very black negro, stood by in attendance. He had a bald, shiny head and a tuft of wiry beard on his chin. He suffered from elephantiasis and had a scrotum the size of a football

Rather to our dismay the Sultan began by demanding twenty-eight shillings per camel per day. This was a fantastic price and we began to haggle, bracing ourselves against the wind, Ibrahim inscrutable behind his green sun-goggles, the Sultan disinterested and aloof in his purple and yellow stockinged feet, mumbling incoherently in Socotri.

After a while Peter turned to me.

"Ibrahim says that as a special concession the Sultan is prepared to let us have camels at eighteen shillings a day!"

The Sultan was already walking away . . . he was scrambling on to the back of a camel . . . he was riding off. . . . It was eighteen shillings, take it or leave it.

It was a terrible price to pay, but it seemed we had little alternative if we didn't want to rot on the airfield for the next few weeks. We hastily arranged for camels for the following day and watched the Sultan's caravan disappear eastward over the plain.

The Valetta took off and we watched it as it gained height, sped out to sea and became an infinitesimal dot in the north-west. The villagers drifted away and we found ourselves alone in the middle of the bleak, windswept plain, severed from the rest of the world by many miles of unnavigable sea.

The next morning early, the camels arrived. There were nearly forty altogether, kneeling in a circle round our camp with their backs to the wind, opening their jaws in impotent bad temper and letting out a liquid burbling growl from the backs of their throats, like a lot of testy old men gargling, baring their bad teeth, exhaling their bad breath, urinating arbitrarily into the wind. The camel-boys added to the confusion, shouting to each other among the camels and rummaging excitedly between the piles of boxes and champagne crates. We had our first experience of their loading methods. Their plan was to rush in a body towards our stores, waving their arms and shouting; then, amid much squabbling, they selected the very lightest packages they could find, hurriedly placed them in long panniers of woven palm leaf, slung the panniers on either side of their camel's false hump,* and led the camels some distance from the camp to where the barely loaded animals assembled preparatory to the start of the caravan. We did our best to ensure that each camel carried a full load—on one occasion we

---

*This false hump is an unusual feature of Socotran camel practice. It is made by laying a number of *shamlahs* (rugs) and thick wads of sacking across the actual hump. They are then forced up into a high ridge along the camel's back by means of a rope tied tightly round them. The object of this false hump is to elevate baggage and rider above the metayne trees which cover much of the plains and foothills.

The mosque in Hadibo—the largest in Socotra.

The door of
the wazir's house
in Hadibo.

Bedouin from the interior receiving treatment from Dr. Richard Lister in the expedition's clinic at Hadibo.

Local medicine—a negro boy in a mud-pack intended to cure his fever.

caught a one-eyed African leading away a camel loaded only with an empty biscuit tin and a broken guitar—but there were only six of us and forty of them, and their plan of campaign had been well thought out and was ably directed by, of all people, Ali bin Selme. By the time the entire caravan was loaded and ready to start, there were so many heavy boxes left behind that I had to order another twenty camels for the next day—which was exactly what the camel-men (on instructions, I imagined, from a certain higher authority) had intended. John volunteered to stay behind to look after the remaining stores and the caravan finally set off at 8.30, after we had made sure that the ammunition box containing the £500 in one shilling pieces had been loaded on to a camel.

The long line of camels slowly crossed the plain, passed the wells and the fruitless palms at Kedah, and after an hour and a half reached the foot of the *aqaba*. Here, in the shadow of a large rock, was a small domed construction of stone and mortar, like a little Muslim tomb, with a cement basin inside containing cool water. On the ledge of the basin were set large sea-shells from which the thirsty wayfarer could drink. The trough was filled daily by the women of a neighbouring village.

The camel-men halted round this little edifice, a *siqaya*, and tethered their camels. Some even began to unload them. We sat down on the step of the water tank, on the shady side because already the sun was very hot. We fetched a jerrycan from the donkey that carried it and drank the warm, chlorinated, amoebaless water in tin mugs while the camel-men in turns drank the cool, sweet water of the tank from sea-shells. Then Ali bin Selme began to speak in his grousy, camel-testy way:

"*Ya sahib!*"

"*Naam?*" said Peter.

"*Ya sahib*, we want half our money now."

"*Leish?*"

"Because we want to go into the village to buy food."

A quarter of a mile away, at the end of a long stretch of white sand, beside the green and sprayblown sea, was the off-white, tumbling-down village of Qadhub. It was the third largest settlement on the island, with 200 inhabitants engaged principally in fishing between October and March and disengaged during the rest of the year. Most of our camel-drivers came from Qadhub, and I imagined the unexpected prospect of pay made

D

them over-anxious. We refused to let them go into the village, refused to let them have half their pay, and told them to un-tether their camels and go on. "It's a try-on," we assured ourselves. "If we let them go we won't see them for the rest of the day." Having told them to go on we waited half an hour till the argument (a dozen men at once at the tops of their voices—perhaps the constant wind blowing at them all their lives made them talk in shouts) subsided and they untethered their camels and moved off. All except Ali. He said he was going no further, but that a relative would go in his place. He also demanded a day's pay for his work as muqaddem of the caravan. This led to another argument and Peter, who as Arabic speaker of the party bore the brunt of the conversation, became annoyed.

"These people," he said, "are noisier and more avaricious and unpleasant than any I have met."

This was an objective, almost clinical statement, reflecting only a small part of the waning of our tolerance in the sun. It was a first impression and we all agreed with it. Later we modified our views—the people remained extremely noisy and extremely avaricious, but on the days when they lapsed and were neither of these things we found, to our relief, that they were extremely pleasant.

After a while Ali condescended to rejoin the caravan that was now toiling up the initial slope of the *aqaba*. He was by now thoroughly disgruntled and for the rest of the journey, through-out the heat of noon, he, like his camels, never stopped grousing.

The *aqaba* of Ras Hebak is a rugged spur of the Haggier Mountains which undulates down from the higher peaks, yellow and scrub-covered, to fall into the sea in rocky confu-sion. It extends for only a few miles along the coast but quite effectively separates Hadibo from the western part of the island. It is crossed by one of the worst camel-tracks in the island, a track so bad that most Socotrans prefer to go by sea from Qadhub to Hadibo, though during the summer the south-west monsoon makes this impossible.

We began to climb up a steep, boulder-strewn slope. The entire caravan was straggled up this slope, each camel pausing while the camel in front of it was pulled and pushed by its driver over some particularly difficult part of the track. Once we had topped this abrupt initial slope (which rose to several hundred feet) we followed a barely discernible track over rocks worn shiny and slippery by the feet of generations of men and camels. This track led between enormous burnt boulders and a Walt Disney landscape of cucumber trees—short squat trees which covered the hillsides like strange, grey, bloated, motionless fingers thrust out of the hard ground—and candelabra euphorbias and green fleshy shrubs like prolific runner beans gone wild. Sometimes the track ran beside the clear green sea which lapped in the whorls and caverns of that eroded shore; sometimes it ran high above the sea. When it is wet, camels occasionally fall from the heights of the *aqaba* into the sea, but at this time the going was good and we were constantly amazed at the performance of the camels which clambered slowly and surely over everything in their way. Sometimes the track was so narrow that the camel's baggage got caught between overhanging rocks, so that two camel-men had to ease it through, one man pulling on the camel's neck-rope, another pushing at its hindquarters. Or a camel would be defeated by some particularly massive boulder that lay in its path and then the camel-men would stand on rocks above the camel and gently lift it over the obstacle by pulling on its tail and neck-rope. The beast carrying the money-box had the worst time. Its load was probably the heaviest and certainly the most awkward of the whole caravan, the box strapped right on top of its hump. It sat down several times in difficult places and the box was constantly slipping off the hump and dragging the creature sideways. In fact, the Socotran camel is a remarkable animal altogether, wonderfully adapted to the exigencies of the rough and precipitous terrain of the island. It is strong, but without the stamina and thirst-endurance of the true Arabian camel— it has to be watered daily in the drier parts. It is as sure-footed as a mountain goat and can climb from sea-level to a 3,000-foot pass over the mountains without too much difficulty. Only in the wet does the Socotran camel let you down. Then its broad, squashy feet (like squeegies) cannot grip the mud and slippery rocks. Weeks later, when some heavy rain had fallen in the mountains, we saw a camel that had slipped and broken its neck. We threw a stone at it and the stone bounced like a rubber ball off the taut, inflated stomach. Shortly afterwards the camel burst and you could smell it half a mile down the valley.

At noon we were still toiling along the *aqaba*, climbing up and down. The sun was very hot and overhead, there was no shade and the wind could not reach us. We passed a tiny cove with a beach of white sand and could not resist paddling in the water. I took some sips of salt water and felt better for it.

At one o'clock we came over a rise and saw a gently curving bay and a wide plain before us. At the near end of the plain, at the edge of the sea, we saw a small village of white houses in the middle of a green plantation of date palms. We could see quite distinctly the white minaret of a mosque rising above the palms.

"Can that be Hadibo?" someone asked.

"No, that can't be Hadibo. It's too small for Hadibo."

"Ali, is that Hadibo?"

Ali, disgruntled, growled inaudibly.

"It must be Hadibo. On the map there's no other place between Qadhub and Hadibo. It's very small for a capital."

We passed the *aqaba* and found ourselves at one end of an amphitheatre of hills, a flat plain backed by a group of fantastic mountains to the south and the blue, foam-flecked sea to the north. Two miles away, at the edge of the sea, the white houses of Hadibo reflected the brilliant sun through the enclosing date plantations.

We began to cross the Hadibo Plain, going on ahead of the camels, aware only of our considerable thirst, the heat bouncing off the stone-covered earth, and the grey, jagged mountains that rose steeply on our right hand. We passed by a cemetery and some gardens with nothing growing in them and the fences blown down by the wind, and then we entered Hadibo. We were in a kind of square outside the mosque. At first the streets were deserted. We caught brief glimpses of African women dressed in black peeping from behind the doors of houses. Then they were on us. As we sat in the shade of a house in the square the children appeared and stood watching us—large-eyed, pot-bellied boys in *futahs*, and little woven caps or ragged cloth turbans wrapped right round their faces as though they had mumps or toothache. Soon they were joined by some men, then up came the camels and the noise began again, the frenetic conversations and the shouting. Ali bin Selme became more and more trying. No, he did not know where we could go. No, Ibrahim the Wazir could not see us. He never saw anybody before such and such a time. Peter became more annoyed and at the point of pungent words drove the wretched man to fetch Ibrahim.

We sat in the shade of a house with the camel-men milling around us until Ibrahim appeared, looking very cool and suave and immaculate in white. He propped his green sun-glasses on his forehead and said we could perhaps stay in the askaris' house till tomorrow, when he would find a house for us. The visitors' house had collapsed in the last rains and was no longer usable.

He led us down some streets between small, limewashed, one-storey houses. The streets were floored with sand mixed up with the droppings of many generations of goats. He stopped and knocked at a wooden door that was falling off its hinges. No one came, so he knocked again and called out, and the door was opened by a young man with womanish features and black glistening hair that fell over his shoulders. Smiling, he beckoned us into a courtyard and shook our hands. He was one of the askaris. Another askari with long hair came out of the house into the courtyard, followed by the wireless operator, with short hair. We went into their house out of the sun and sat on the raised concrete end of the room while Abdi brewed two pots of tea. We drank cup after cup of hot sweet tea, drank some lemonade and then went back to drinking tea again.

The askaris' property consisted of a walled courtyard, a grass thatch shed for an electric generator, a well, a palm tree, an aerial and an oblong one-roomed house where they lived, slept, and tapped out messages three times a day on the American naval transmitter-receiver which occupied one corner. There was also a small dark adjunct where the askaris kept their things and sacks of peanuts, flour and weevils.

The askaris had been on Socotra several months and they didn't like it. For one thing, they had run out of cigarettes some time ago; for another, the wireless operator confided to us, "The Sultan is a thief"; for another, they had nothing to do. They were askaris of the Hadhrami Bedouin Legion, with 25 rounds of ammunition and two Lee-Enfields between them, garrisoning the Government wireless which was the only link between Socotra and the rest of the world. They kept their uniforms in boxes, and never wore them except once when I went to photograph them. Then they put on their long khaki kilts, scarlet sashes round their waists, leather ammunition belts and red and white checked head-dresses with a silver badge in the middle. The wireless operator, a rather older man, had found himself a wife in Hadibo. The two younger askaris, with the long hair and the womanly features, had no wives either in Hadibo or Mukalla where they came from; they just killed time lying in their room combing and oiling their long hair and falling ill from time to time. In the first few weeks there was a sort of bond between the askaris and ourselves because we were all foreigners and in the same boat together; and they were grateful for our cigarettes.

Later in the afternoon we went down to the sea through the palm grove around the town. The sea was beaten by the wind so that as the waves came, like rank after rank of plumed cavalry, the plumed tops of the waves were caught by the wind and blown sideways in hard, sharp spray.

In the evening we sat in the courtyard of the askaris' house under a palm tree and a mast with a sagging aerial. Mike and I felt rather sick because Richard, in an excess of enthusiasm, had tipped a bottle of chlorinating tablets into the askaris' well and the medicated water lay thick and oily on our stomachs, like gas. The askaris wondered for days afterwards what had gone wrong with their well. It smelt like a swimming-bath. Somewhere in the town was the noise of drumming and singing. The drumming had an insistent rhythm. It sounded like a railway train chugging endlessly over the plain behind the town. The singing was the same simple tune that went on and on without stopping or changing. The people had begun creating in this way at three in the afternoon to celebrate, they said, the safe return of the Sultan. They would sing the same song for seven days, stopping only between six in the morning and three in the afternoon.

After dinner we discussed for a long time ways of erecting our mosquito nets so that they would not be blown down in the wind. Presently we found that the fittings had been left behind at the airfield and that there were no mosquitoes. Peter and Richard went on to the roof to sleep and the rest of us lay down on our camp beds inside the tent we had erected in the courtyard. At that time we thought it might rain.

In the middle of the night the wind blew the tent down and we struggled against the wind and swirling dust in the darkness, sleepily hammering wooden pegs into the iron-hard ground. In the town the drums were beating a slow heavy beat and some people were singing without enthusiasm. Away at the airfield John was sleeping alone on the ground among the boxes.

CHAPTER FOUR

IN THE CAPITAL—1

In the morning Sheikh Ibrahim accompanied me on a tour of the houses to let. He led me down narrow streets that were painfully bright with the sunlight reflected from the dazzling limewashed walls of the houses. From end to end the town was no wider than an average English suburban street, but I quickly lost my sense of direction, for each street appeared bewilderingly the same as the next, an accidental space between the decaying houses. It seemed a remarkably tiny and ramshackle capital; the palm rib fences of the small garden plots had been blown flat by the wind; certain houses had collapsed and lay in ruins, mounds of coral rubble; the only signs of life were the chickens and the goats and the hesitant children who scrambled through doors half off their hinges, and the faces of women who peered momentarily between wooden shutters and through the iron grills of glassless windows. One or two houses were larger and more splendidly built, with two storeys, parapets decoratively fretted and castellated, and nail-studded teak doors carved ornately in the Arab style. These, I was told, belonged only to the Sultan and his Wazirs, or to wealthy foreign merchants now passing the monsoon months in their residences abroad. I recalled a story I had heard of an elderly American couple who wished to break their round-the-world tour on Socotra, which they saw so exotically situated in the Arabian Sea; they wrote to the Aden Secretariat asking for details of the best first-class hotels on the island and in due course received a reply politely informing them that not only were there no hotels of any sort but that there were also no restaurants, no shops, no roads, no food, nothing. I could understand the Americans' misconception, for the capital itself is marked on some maps in print quite disproportionate to its size and importance.

We came in time to the square in front of the mosque, the largest building and the only landmark in the town. It was a simple, unpretentious mosque with a main dome and two

55

smaller satellite domes and a small minaret like a lighthouse, where a muezzin called out the hours of prayer. Ibrahim led me into a house opposite the mosque; it consisted simply of two rooms which formed two sides of a walled and empty courtyard; there had been a third room, but it had recently collapsed in the rains, and the well was stagnant; two small adjuncts seemed to be suitable for a kitchen and larder, and there was a hole in the roof, discreetly enclosed by a low cubicle wall, which I was told was the domestic latrine. The house seemed ideally suitable as a home for the expedition, and we fixed on a rent of forty-five shillings a month and fetched women to sweep and dust the place with twigs.

During the rest of the morning we moved in. Kerosene cans, parachute hampers, champagne crates, an enormous turtle shell and the bare frames of our unfortunate deck-chairs were stacked against the courtyard walls. The largest room was selected as a store-room and surgery, and in the living-room we rigged up two aluminium tables, stacked our books in alcoves, hung a mirror on the wall and over the door suspended an inverted meat safe full of sour limes and oranges which a precocious bedu boy had brought from the hills and sold to us at an exorbitant price. We bought a kid and a chicken and let them loose in the courtyard; they made the atmosphere quite domestic until the day we ate them.

By the evening we were comfortably settled in our new home. From the roof we could see over the houses to the sea, blue and hazy between the swaying palms; behind us rose the grey mountains. During the day the mountains had been covered in a thick pall of cloud but now only a few drawn-out wisps clung round the topmost peaks and the sun shone at such a low, oblique angle that we could see every line and wrinkle in the island's old face; each crag and fumera and chasm was revealed quite distinctly and separately by the delineation of light and shadow. It was as though a lump of solid granite had been planted in the middle of the island, and the wind and rain had come along with cats' claws and reached up and scratched at the rock face and over the millennia torn it into the rough shape of a gothic cathedral with many spires.

Just before nightfall, as the wind-borne, oscillating duet of two muezzins reached out from opposite ends of the town, Ibrahim called and asked if a doctor would go and see the

Sultan, who was unwell. Neil and Richard went along with him, accompanied by Peter as interpreter and myself as "official observer". Somewhere in the town the drums were beating again.

The Sultan's palace was a long, one-storey, almost window-less building, fronting a patch of waste ground. A battered rusty oil drum incongruously adorned the approaches and outside the door squatted an old black crone like a watch-dog, a bony hand held over her eyes as she peered across the vacant lot.

We entered and found ourselves in a large, cool room. The ceiling was supported by beams coloured alternately red, yellow and green, like a child's nursery, and there were a few mats and some attractive carpets on the stone floor, and cushions in the alcoves of the walls. Ibrahim invited us to sit down on some roughly-made wooden chairs round a crude wooden table covered with a dirty cloth. After a few minutes the Sultan came in and we all stood up and shook hands and mumbled greetings. We sat down again and waited in silence while a slave set glass tumblers in front of us and poured out some orange syrup. We drank the thick, deliciously cool syrup, hoping that more would be poured out. But the glasses were taken away and the Sultan began to talk.

He said he had a cough and a pain in his chest; he said he was breathless in bed, couldn't sleep properly and woke up tired in the mornings. A simple explanation at once crossed our minds, but the doctors played their part and began to ask him questions, giving the English to Peter who translated into Arabic for Ibrahim, who translated into Socotri for the Sultan, who understood Arabic perfectly well but wouldn't speak it in our presence. Did he vomit? Did his bowels move satisfactorily? Did he at the age of twelve suffer from pains in the joints? The answers came back the same devious and polyglot way that the questions had gone.

He was a small, yellowish man with a narrow fringe of beard round the edge of his jaw and a thin moustache above sensuous lips, set in a permanent sneer of disdain. When he took off his shirt and head-dress in order to be medically examined he looked pathetically puny and insignificant, sitting crouched in his chair, mumbling incoherently in the incredible Socotri language.

After the examination Richard made the following report: "Looks utterly fed up. Bored and pre-occupied with himself. Fit, lean-looking, not anaemic. Breath sounds faint, but other-

wise normal. Diagnosis—lack of work and interest. Hypo-
chondriacal. Cough and some degree of chronic bronchitis."

We gave him some strychnine and sleeping tablets and as
we went out of the palace we could hear the tumultuous
thumping of drums—the people honouring their Sultan, keeping
him awake at nights.

The Sultan seldom lived in Hadibo, preferring his remote
residence in the hills, where the air was better for his bronchitis. We never saw him again, though from time to time he
sent runners to us with broken gramophones to be mended.
I imagine we proved a beneficial distraction, but often
wondered how he spent the majority of his days, for the processes of Socotran administration are pretty basic and can
hardly take up much time.

He is a despot in the grand traditional manner. He listens to
complaints, tries law-breakers, exacts taxes and dues and
occasionally, and reluctantly, confers with the British Government officers whenever they visit the island. He is both revered
and feared by his subjects, and it would never occur to any of
them to question his authority or the justice of his rule. His
supreme power is accepted as being in the right and natural
order of things, and if anything untoward happened to him it
would be regarded as a calamity affecting them all. His justice
is severe, his fiscal system extortionate; during their recent
pilgrimage to Mecca both he and Ibrahim were given presents of
large sums of money by the Saudi Arabians, but the Sultan
immediately took Ibrahim's share into his own safe-keeping and
never returned it. It seems most unlikely that much of the
money we paid for transport and labour facilities during our
stay on Socotra ever went into the money-belts of the people
who worked for us.

The ruling class of Socotra, headed by the Sultan, is drawn
from Mahri tribesmen, the Ahl Saad of the Affrar, who have
been domiciled on the island for eight generations and whose
supremacy there is founded on ancient right. The system of
succession to the Sultanate is unusual, for it passes from first
cousin to first cousin, or to the oldest surviving male relative.
In this way it alternates between the Issa branch and the
Tu'ari branch of the Affrar family. The present heir to the
reigning Sultan Issa is the Little Sultan, also called Issa, a shy
and callow youth who sometimes drove a camel for us, chided

by the other camel-men for his inadequacies. He was suffering
from osteomyelitis of the jaw when we met him, an ailment that
could ultimately prove fatal if unattended.

Sultan Issa is ruler not only of Socotra but of the Mahra
territory on the Arabian mainland opposite. This territory,
with its principal towns of Qishn and Sahoot, is a poor, bare
area, inhabited by tribesmen who speak a unique and ancient
language related to Socotri and who are themselves of an
unusual racial stock similar to that of the bedouin of Socotra.
There has always been a strong political connection between the
two countries, and as long ago as the first century A.D. we read
that Socotra was subject to the "King of the Frankincense
Country" of which Mahra was then part. In the year 1482 the
Mahri Arabs appear to have begun a systematic colonisation
of the island, driving the bedouin into the interior in fear of
their lives. This conquest was interrupted for a few years by the
establishment of a Portuguese garrison on the island, but when
an English merchant seaman, one William Finck of the East
India Company, visited Hadibo in 1607 to take on water and
supplies, he found a son of the Mahri Sultan of Qishn firmly
established there. Thus was founded a régime and a method of
government that has not changed to the present day.

Finck, the first Englishman ever to visit Socotra, gives some
interesting details of the people at this time. "The Arabs", he
writes in his journal, "are in manner slaves to the Sheikh and
all soldiers. They are all forced to wear wooden knives or
crooked daggers. They are tawny, industrious and civil in
gesture . . . They love tobacco but are loth to give anything for
it." The women were "some of them reasonable white, much
like to a sunburned country maiden in England . . . very dainty
to be seen, yet scarcely honest". They were all so heavily
adorned with silver that they could not stir but made a noise
"like Morris dancers".

Other English merchantmen called at the island during the
next few years. Sir Harry Middleton, master of the *Pepper
Corn*, seems to have had much the same experience as ourselves
in matters of commerce with the Socotrans, and his first
encounter with them parallels our own dealings on the airfield.
Sir Harry, anchoring off Qalansiya, ". . . earnestly desired to
speak with some of the inhabitants in hope to have procured
some goats or other refreshment for our people, but none, as it

seemeth, durst come to us for fear of the King's displeasure . . .
it seemeth he would have none of his people to do with strangers
but that all intelligences, allowances for fresh victuals and
prises must come from himself, as afterwards I found. . . ."
When he came to bargain with the King he found, as we did,
that prices were inflationary, and noted wryly : "Wood is 12d.
a man's burthen—every particular is a very dear pennyworth
and what else this island may yield I am yet to be informed of,
but rocks and stones. . . ." One detects a certain disgruntled
note in Sir Harry Middleton's voice.

Captain John Saris, landing on February 16, 1611, in the
hope of obtaining fresh food for his three ships bound for India,
found himself at the wrong end of a bad bargain and noted
indignantly: ". . . for goats they charge one ryall of eight apiece,
which though it be dear, yet are most of them not man's meat,
being so vilely and more than beastly buggered and abused by
the people, so that it was most loathsome to see when they were
opened."

Sir Thomas Roe, who visited the island four years later,
confirms that the Mahri Arabs had gained control of the island
as a result of a recent conquest: ". . . the old inhabitants of the
island, but not the eldest, are called bedwines, that have long
dwelt there; they dwell in the mountains and are very populous.
With these the King hath had a war, as the Arabs report, but
they are now at peace on condition to live quietly and to breed
their children Mohomatens, which I perceive they do not,
having no manner of conversation with the Arabs."

Little happened in the next two hundred years to modify
the established government on Socotra. But in 1800 orders were
sent to the commander of the British fleet in Indian waters to
occupy the island. For reasons best known to the commander
himself this order was not carried out, but knowledge of the
intention must have caused the Socotrans some alarm. At the
same time there appears to have been a change in the government of Qishn and its island dependency—the Affrar family
came to power. The new, and possibly insecure, ruler was thus
confronted with an immediate threat of occupation on part of
his territory. It is probably this combination of circumstances
added to the inherent aloofness of insular people that originally
motivated what is by now a traditional attitude of suspicion
and unco-operativeness towards foreigners who visit the island.

And events in later years did not help to ameliorate this attitude. In 1834 Lieutenants Wellsted and Cruttenden of the Indian Navy carried out the first exploration and survey of Socotra. Their favourable report on the country and its inhabitants led to an attempt by the British Government to take over the island as a coaling station for ships on their way to India. They offered to buy Socotra from the Sultan of Qishn. But he would have none of it. "As sure as there is but one God and He is in heaven, I will not sell *so* much," and he made a span with his fingers. "It was a gift of the Almighty to the Mahras and has descended from our forefathers to their children over whom I am Sultan." He remained courteous but firm and Captain Haines, who was conducting the negotiations, was unable to move him. As he left, the Sultan called to him: "God in heaven is my witness, we have both endeavoured to fulfil our duties, you to your government and I to my tribe. Farewell!"

So the British Government occupied the island with Indian troops.

The lack of harbours and prevalent strong winds made Socotra a bad coaling station. When Aden was occupied by the British in 1839 further occupation on Socotra was unnecessary and the garrison withdrew uneventfully, sadly depleted by malaria. Not until 1876 was a treaty with the Sultan successfully completed. In return for an annual subsidy the Sultan agreed to protect the cargoes and passengers of ships that might be wrecked on the island, and never to cede the island to a foreign power or allow foreign settlement without the permission of the British Government. In 1886 the island was formally made a Protectorate and Dependency of Great Britain, and since that time the Sultan of Qishn and Socotra has always resided on the island.

It's a funny set-up, the Affraria Government; unhelpful, unsmiling, almost pathetically comic-opera. It seems not unlikely that it has sniffed the spirit of self-determination that has drifted across the Middle East and is anxious for complete independence; certainly it does not exactly co-operate with the Aden authorities. What it hopes to gain by such independence is uncertain; it has no army, no alliances, no money, very few subjects; it could not stand alone in the modern world. Nor can it complain of oppression by British colonialism. There is no interference in internal government, and Socotrans may not see a white face from one year to the next, unless it is people like ourselves, come to double their annual income. In years of famine the Sultan can rely on the Aden Government to send in food supplies; if an epidemic of disease breaks out he can be sure that medical facilities will be hurried across to him; soon, no doubt, the benign arm of colonial development will be stretched across to him and his people. On the other hand, Socotra's strategical importance at the entrance to the Gulf of Aden makes it unlikely that the British would be very willing to let the island slip from their grasp. The present arrangement seems, in theory, to be of mutual advantage.

After we had left the Sultan's palace Ibrahim asked us if we would come and see his small daughter. She had been sick for two months, he said, and nothing he had done had cured her. We followed him through the darkened streets and entered his house after he had made sure that there were no women in the front room. We sat on palm mats in the dim yellow light of a hurricane lamp and the daughter was brought to us. She was an enchanting little creature of eleven years and, though obviously nervous at the presence of so many Europeans around her, carried herself with a remarkable dignity and composure. I think she will grow up to be the prettiest little aristocrat in all the island of Socotra. She had been suffering from head-aches and vomiting but the doctors could find no symptoms of a definite illness, only a slightly raised temperature and a general unlocatable malaise. Probably her trouble was something to do with her age, approaching puberty, though it proved impossible to enquire into this. When Richard came to examine her he found that she had five burn marks on her stomach and seven on her back, and Ibrahim told him that his wife, failing all other remedies, had branded the child with a red-hot iron.

This was our first introduction to a common practice in Socotran folk-medicine. Hardly anyone we met in the following months seemed to have escaped the *na'ar*, the fire treatment; even babies had been branded by their mothers. Often clay had been rubbed into the burns and not surprisingly some of the burns had turned septic. This primitive custom at first struck us as unnecessarily barbaric, merely substituting one pain for another, until we came to realise that people without medical knowledge are compelled to do *something* to alleviate suffering, make *some* protest against the invisible and inexplicable courses of pain and disease. The fire is no good, Socotrans admitted to us, but what else can we do?

We were to meet other examples of local "cures". One day an obnoxious little negro boy, always the most vociferous in the general clamour for sweets and biscuits, came to us strangely subdued. He had been covered from head to toe in a thick mud pack which had dried rough on his skin. Only his baleful eyes indicated the presence of a human being beneath that grotesque crust of clay, for otherwise he looked like an animated plaster-cast. The mud had been applied as a cure for fever and, since he returned a few days later as noisy and irrepressible as ever, it seems that it had been an effective cure—perhaps the only one in the entire Socotran repertoire.

We were often mystified by the custom of some Socotrans of wearing a piece of cloth over their mouths, hanging down from their ears on a length of string. If they hadn't a cloth they would put their beards into their mouths instead. This, we were told, was to prevent them swallowing a dreadful fly peculiar to the island and capable of inflicting certain death if it entered their mouths. We noticed that old men did not wear the cloth, apparently because they had, over the course of years, learnt to recognise the buzz of this fly and were thus able to close their mouths in time.

One morning the Affraria Government came into our surgery in a state of considerable agitation. In their midst was a small man completely swathed in clothes. They all started jabbering at once while the little man unswathed in the most melodramatic manner—to reveal the local pearl merchant. After a prolonged effort and noise enough to fill the Tower of Babel, Richard discovered that the pearl merchant had swallowed the fly. Further strenuous activity failed to determine in exactly what part of his anatomy the fly had lodged itself, and after a while the Government departed, taking with them the trembling little merchant. They had promised to return when Peter was present to interpret properly, but they never came back, and the merchant was still alive the next day. As far as I can tell this fly is a mythical beast and may possibly constitute a local explanation of pneumonia.

There was little we could do for Ibrahim's daughter, and after

the doctors had finished their examination of her Ibrahim
complained that he himself was not well. He explained how his
eyes twitched and his skin itched and how he woke up in the
nights once or twice a fortnight with vague presentiments of
fear. He had a great respect for Western medicine and displayed a morbid obsession with vitamins. He had brought back
from Aden a bottle of Vitamin B tablets and I watched him, as
he sat cross-legged in the half-darkened bare room, neurotically
discussing the possible miraculous benefits the consumption of
these tablets might bring, and the vitamin contents of various
foods. His little embroidered cap was perched as far back as it
would go on his round, un-Arab head; he wore a white lawn
scarf round his shoulders and green plastic sandals on his feet,
and the pocket of his white shirt was stained with the ink that
leaked from his fountain pen. From time to time he would take
a cigarette paper and a black, foreign tobacco from his little
plastic purse, and as he talked he would roll a very thin, very
loosely-filled cigarette with his delicate hands and smoke
it in a refined way, holding it primly between finger and
thumb.

Although of slave origin (his mother was a negress) Ibrahim
had, by training and personality, attained the rank of Prime
Minister on Socotra. At an early age he had been selected and
trained for an important position in the Socotran hierarchy;
when he was still a boy he sat at the feet of the Naib of Qalansiya,
the high-ranking and almost independent head of the chief
port of the island, learning all he could of administration and
Socotran affairs. During the war his contact with the R.A.F.
and the military garrison gave him a useful knowledge of the
ways of Europeans and the British administration. After the
war he sailed on dhows to Arabia and Africa, acquiring knowledge of commerce and the outside world. As a result he has
added to his inherently considerable intelligence an experience
and knowledge of affairs exceeding that of any other person on
the island including, probably, the Sultan himself. Most Aden
Government representatives find themselves dealing with
Ibrahim rather than with the Sultan. We ourselves dealt
almost exclusively with him in our day-to-day business on
Socotra. He is highly intelligent, speaks perfect Arabic (comparatively rare on Socotra, even among the coastal inhabitants),
has picked up a little Swahili and is anxious to learn English,

of which he knows a few words. He is so well mannered as to make one feel clumsy in his presence, and he has the unnerving ability of putting forward the most outrageous demands with the most urbane courtesy, a bland smile on his face, a self-deprecatory note in his voice. Undoubtedly he is a clever schemer and probably he is consistently one jump ahead of his victims. In our own dealings I formed the impression that he was in the difficult position of wanting to help us but being obliged to look after the interests of his Sultan, himself and the people (in that order); so that, when it became obvious that the expedition constituted a large and unexpected financial windfall, Ibrahim was bound to make the best of it at the risk of antagonising ourselves. Money matters apart, he was helpful; though in retrospect there seem to have been few matters not connected with money.

He was helped in his affairs by Sheikh Issa, the other Wazir, a very different sort of man, lean, frail, apathetic, his face thin and semitic, lengthened with a black pointed beard. He spoke rarely and we never dealt directly with him, though he often accompanied Ibrahim on his visits to us. The two of them directed an administrative system consisting of four principal Muqaddems, or head-men, administering four principal tribal districts, and thirty to sixty lesser Muqaddems administering the sub-districts. The Muqaddems were limited in power and acted mainly as mediators between the Sultan and the people. Among the bedouin of the interior there was still a patriarchal social system, the heads of families being responsible to the heads of clans, who were in turn responsible to the head of the tribe to which they belonged. The remarkable thing about this administration was that it was practically invisible, either because it was so smooth and secretive or because it was so simple and perfunctory.

Ibrahim was unfortunate. We were unable to diagnose his daughter's illness or his own neurosis, and a few days later his small son came to us suffering from measles. Everyone on Socotra falls sick sooner or later—the dust, the flies, the bad water, the food crawling with bacteria, the mosquitoes which come out in thick clouds when the wind drops at the change of the monsoons, the unbalanced diet, the weakness to resist. Even during our short stay we found that our tiny scratches developed into large running sores which refused to heal or

E

respond to treatment and were clustered with flies like wasps round a jam pot. And so day after day in the following weeks an endless procession of men, women and children with enlarged spleens and yellowish anaemic eyes, coughing with bronchitis, eyes gummed up with conjunctivitis, skins covered with sores and fungus diseases, crowded into our small surgery and filled us almost with despair. The doctors, frustrated and irritated at one moment, at the next were full of admiration for the stoicism and dignified resignation of these people, some of whom had tramped four or five days over rugged country from the farthest ends of the island, drawn by the widespread reputation of the Christians' miraculous medicine, hoping for a sudden end to the sickness that had plagued their years. Their favourite form of treatment was the *ibra*, the penicillin injection, which had curiously gained fame as an aphrodisiac. Another favourite was a large, luridly coloured and highly explosive pill called Cathartic Co, guaranteed to shift the most refractory of bowels. When a patient had swallowed his Cathartic Co he was led hurriedly away before he detonated, much to his satisfaction.

The Aden health authorities are well aware of the crying need for medicine on Socotra and have selected and trained a resident of Hadibo to carry out simple treatments and health measures. His name is Thani bin Ali, a black, cheerful, helpful, little man, with a high, rather whining voice which at first unfairly prejudiced us against him. When he first appeared before us he wore a forage cap and a creased and starched khaki uniform, his bare squashy toes poking incongruously out of the ends of his trousers—a sight so unfamiliar to Ibrahim that he was overcome by it and could only chortle incredulously "Thani! O Thani!" while Thani looked embarrassed and shuffled from foot to foot. Thani's job was to tour the island treating the sick, and twice yearly he sprayed the houses of Hadibo with insecticide, marking the walls of houses thus treated with crosses, which reminded me sinisterly of the red crosses chalked on the doors of London houses during the Plague, so that I half expected to see "God have mercy on us" inscribed also, *Allah yisallimna*!

In Thani's neat, grass-thatched clinic, with its shelves full of aspirin bottles, Flit-guns, fly-swats and hot-water bottles, I came across the more startling realities of traditional Socotran justice. In a jar of preserving spirit on one of the shelves was a severed human hand, like an old wrinkled brown glove. This hand, Thani explained, had once belonged to a bedu from the hills. One day he had stolen a goat, and the owner had complained to the Sultan. The Sultan, after hearing the case, decreed that the bedu should be punished for his theft, and so all the inhabitants of Hadibo gathered together at the place of execution and the executioner, Abdulla, was summoned to administer the punishment. From Thani's account the removal of the hand seems to have resembled a surgical operation. First the bedu's wrist was dislocated. Then Abdulla sawed methodically through skin, tendons and bone with a bread knife and plunged the bleeding stump of the wrist in boiling fish oil in order to cauterise it. Apparently the bedu had smiled broadly throughout the operation. Sometimes, Thani confided to me, hands were chopped off with a sword made from a rusty barrel hoop.

The severed hands are usually displayed on frequented tracks, suspended from a tree on a piece of string. There they remain until they rot, warnings to other would-be transgressors. The subsequent fate of men who have been punished in this way is doubtful. According to Thani, some are deported to Muscat and Mukalla, an even more devastating punishment for the extremely insular bedouin, few of whom could survive transplanting to an alien society. During a recent famine the Sultan ordered a mass punishment as a result of a wave of livestock thefts. Forty bedouin from each of the four principal tribes of the island were selected at random and immediately deported, without redress and without hope of return. Some bedouin who have their hands removed apparently return to the hills, though I never saw or heard of any there. I imagine many of them must die of shock or infection of the wound in such a climate.

I asked Thani what would happen if a man was caught stealing a second time.

"*Bass,*" he replied, "he would have his other hand chopped off. There are many bedouin in the hills with no hands at all. No hands at all!"

He was very indignant when I asked if the Arabs were punished in the same way as the bedouin.

"Only the bedouin steal. They are like birds in the corn. It's their nature."

Murder is extremely rare on Socotra and again seems to be confined to the bedouin population. In this case the punishment is made to fit the crime—a strangler is strangled, a cut-throat has his throat cut. A few months before our arrival a public execution had taken place just outside Hadibo. Apparently a bedu got angry with his wife one day and strangled her. Her kinsfolk objected to this and asked the Sultan to intervene. He sentenced the husband to death and the man was duly garotted in front of a large audience and buried immediately. His grave stands on the plain, at a place where the track forks.

Prostitution is rather more common. I have heard that half the prostitute population of Mukalla consists of deported Socotran women, and on three occasions we were offered women at a price—once by a foreign merchant, once by a bedu, and once by a relative of the Sultan. There was a house in Hadibo which we called the brothel. This was because it always seemed to be full of negresses hanging out of windows and leering at us, and men were constantly going in and out. The punishment for prostitution is characteristic. The offender is stripped to the waist and whipped through the streets. She is then thrown into a dry well for the night. The next day the sap of the euphorbia tree, a thick white lactic sap, is applied to her hair, eyebrows and eyelashes. This sap destroys the hair follicles and makes the person treated in this way go bald. If the sap gets into the eyes there is a danger of blindness. The woman is then deported.

An interesting feature of judicial cases on Socotra (and on the mainland as well) is the ancient practice of trial by fire and compurgation (a method of testing the veracity of an accused person which was once used in England, under Anglo-Saxon law). Trial by fire consists of passing a red-hot knife or spoon twice across the tongue of the accused. If the accused is unharmed he is considered to have passed the test and to be speaking the truth, otherwise he is guilty of perjury. This trial is carried out by a special tester who has inherited both the post and the "power", and it seems likely that the tester uses his red-hot spoon according to his personal convictions in the case—if he is sure that the accused is guilty he will make certain that the tongue is burned. Such a practice is obviously open to abuse, but it may well be that the tester is a good psychologist with an ability to detect whether a man is lying or not.

All that can be said by way of comment on Socotran justice is that although the punishments inflicted on criminals are barbarous by any normal standards, they seem to be very effective deterrents to law-breaking. A police force of only a dozen or so Africans armed with old rifles is sufficient to police the whole island, and many more civilized nations would envy the rarity of serious crime on Socotra.

CHAPTER FIVE

IN THE CAPITAL—2

THE daily pattern of our lives in Hadibo arranged itself spon-
taneously and without conscious planning. We usually slept on
the roof, where the air was cooler, and at one in the morning
we would be awakened by the wind roaring lustily after its
evening lull. It blew steadily at about 40 m.p.h. and sometimes
gusted up to 70 m.p.h.; often it would tip us out of our camp
beds, and one morning Peter found himself lying on the bare
canvas of his bed, his sleeping-bag blown off him like a glove
peeled from a hand. On another morning I clambered out of
my sleeping-bag and sat on the edge of the bed, slipping my feet
into sandals. When I turned round I saw that the sleeping-bag
had vanished, blown away over the rooftops in the space of a
few seconds. A thorough search failed to find it and thereafter
I had to sleep in locally-made blankets of goats' hair which
smelt strongly of goat and, the others exotically suggested,
camel urine. Only long afterwards did I discover a clue to the
fate of my sleeping-bag. One day, in a particularly lonely part
of the mountains, a man by the name of Seiyid Ali, a step-
brother of the Little Sultan, pointed to Neil's sleeping-bag and
asked me how much it had cost to buy. I told him 150 shillings
and he made an appreciative clucking sound and then said:
"Ibrahim has got one just like that."

We rose soon after dawn. Our latrine on the roof had been
banned on the grounds that it was insanitary, for the dejecta
fell into a small enclosed space next to the larder, so we would
hurry down to the beach, a hygienic communal latrine where
we could spend a few pleasant minutes in the cool of the early
morning, scanning the bare horizon and listening to the squeak
and rattle of pastel-coloured pebbles as they were dragged into
the sea by the green waves that lapped on the shore. Coming
back from the beach we would meet various people. Peter told
me that on these occasions the appropriate greeting is "*Shifitum?*
Is it removed?*" to which the correct reply should be "*Shifitum
Allah!* God has removed the obnoxious substance!" But Arabic

is only a second language on Socotra and the only reply we
ever received to our cheerful *"Shifitum?"* was an uncomprehending "Uh?"

Breakfast was eaten round a table in the courtyard while
there was still some shade. We started with Porage, a surprisingly successful tropical dish, and passed on to fish served
up with slices of bitter lime, when we could get either of these
fresh foods. Sometimes we were lucky enough to have eggs.
The eggs were small and rare and expensive: sometimes they
would ask two shillings for an egg, and if we offered less they
would go away and eat the egg themselves. A small boy called
Hamet brought us eggs secretly. I think he poached them
because his manner was so secretive and he accepted biscuits
instead of shillings in return. He was a shy child and rarely spoke
above a well-mannered whisper; if anyone spoke a harsh word
to him, even in jest, his eyes would fill with tears. He was
inseparable from his friend, a handsome and more robust
young boy who, had he had the mischance to fall into the hands of
a film mogul, might have been publicised as a second Sabu.
It was difficult to think that either of them would grow to be
like their elders, mentally enervate and physically sluggish
except when roused to febrile clamour at the possibility of
financial gain.

The sun rose quickly and was already hot before nine. We
would go our various ways, hoping to steal a march on the heat
which by noon would evaporate our energy like a shallow
puddle. The doctors would visit the sick in their houses or tend
the patients who crowded the surgery. Peter and John would
vanish over the plain looking for archaeological remains, while
Mike would wander up the wadi Hanefu, collecting grass-
hoppers. I would do a little filming, walking down the streets
looking for suitable cinematic subjects and followed by a small
baggage train hung with cameras, tripods, light-meters, tape-
measures, microphones, a tape-recorder and trailing wires.
At first the Socotrans were apprehensive of my cameras, which
resembled guns with sawn-off barrels, but in time their nervous-
ness gave way to curiosity and in the middle of some carefully
arranged shot an urchin would come and peer through the
other end of the camera lens, while the others crowding round
me would detect a certain asperity in my demeanour and tell
each other "His work is *pictures*", as though that explained

everything. Only Ibrahim fully understood what I was doing—
he had been to a cinema in Aden. To the rest of the population
my work must have seemed as incomprehensible as our other
activities: Mike assiduously collecting lizards and scorpions
("Does he *eat* them?"); Peter spending hours in the sun,
scratching at old mounds and handling bits of ancient and
hopelessly shattered pots with loving care; the doctors asking
strange questions ("How old are you?") and giving medicines
free; John, fiery-faced, his chin already bristling with an
embryo beard, performing feats of superhuman strength. . . .
We must have seemed a strange crowd, rich and unpredictable
and probably omniverous.

The afternoons were trying in Hadibo, for flies and the lack
of shade in our courtyard made rest impossible. Sometimes we
would go down to the lagoon at the edge of the date plantation
and stretch our sweating bodies along the prickly grass of its
banks; we would wake, after a few minutes, to a circle of a
score of little, black, pop-eyed faces. We were glad when
evening came. Evening was the best time. The sun sank quickly
behind Ras Hebak and left a sky of fading green; the stars came
out when the velvet fell and the wind dropped to a fluttering
warm breeze; the bats scurried over the courtyard in a lunatic
and twisting flight and you could hear their almost ultra-sonic
twitter, and the braying of the donkey next door, the chatter
of the women and children passing outside, the sea breaking
on the shingle on the beach and the wireless tuned to Aden
Radio in a house down the street. The muezzins called from the
mosque tops and their high, unnatural, undulating holy wail
was carried towards you on the breeze, undermining reality,
seducing the senses, reminding you of Ali Baba and flying
carpets and podgy Sultans sitting on tasselled crimson cushions
wearing rubies in their turbans and clapping their hands for
honey and pomegranates. Hearing the muezzin in the white
minaret calling to the faithful in the now darkened town, you
remembered Hollywood's Orient and whatever you had believed
in childhood.

We sat in the courtyard with the sounds of the town in our
ears and a little whisky in front of us. While we waited for
dinner Mike would tell us many remarkable scientific facts—
so many I can't remember any of them—and produce insects
to amuse us. Like the jumping beetle. If you pressed its bottom

it shot two feet up into the air and landed with a ping on the metal table-top. We all took turns pressing the beetle's bottom.

Then the cooks brought dinner. Always it was a big dinner and every night we had a different dish prepared from the same tinned ingredients. The best meal was the one with the fresh crayfish. It was the only crayfish we ever had and the man who brought it had asked a prodigious number of shillings for it. We looked at the crayfish with the colours of the sea still on it, delicately inlaid like a Chinese ornament, in blue and red and pink and green and violet—and we said, Hell! Let's buy it. So we bought it and that evening sat ecstatically sucking the pink legs, and afterwards fell on our camp beds and lay watching the stars and the falling shooting-stars that fizzled out like fireworks so many million light years away. We were like lords, and we felt like lords over all we could see. Twenty square yards of gravel and goat droppings surrounded by two mud and coral walls and two mud and coral rooms with the lime plaster decaying and one of the doors falling off. We felt very fine in the evenings.

One morning in Hadibo I came across a small boy sitting in the middle of a street. He hardly looked at me when I went up to him, and said nothing. He sat almost motionless except for a feeble movement of his right hand between his mouth and a fly-covered ball of dates he held in his other hand. His legs and arms stuck out like twigs from a pear-shaped body that gradually expanded from his fleshless shoulders and reached its maximum width at his stomach, grossly distended with malnutrition. His skin was covered in a thick, grey-white crust of dirt and salt and he had the grossest conjunctivitis I had ever seen. His eye-lids were almost gummed together by the pus that oozed from his eyes and he didn't seem to have sufficient strength to brush away the flies that clung to them in a black seething mass. The other boys crowding round him knew all about him. He was not a stranger in the town, though I had never seen him before. "He's a bedu," they said. "*Mafi baba au mama.* He has no mother or father." Another bedu boy, like a little wild antelope, sleek and well-fed, took hold of the starveling's head and forced it upwards. "*Esh ismak?*" he shouted. "What's your name?" The starveling stared at him weakly through pussy eyes.

"*Esh ismak? Esh ismak?*" the other boys joined in. They were pleased to find somebody worse off than themselves.

Later in the evening there was a faint knock at the door of our house and when we opened the door there he was, standing outside in his dirty rag. He came in and sat down on a champagne crate against the wall of the courtyard. Richard bathed him in the canvas bath, treated his eyes, and gave him some vitamin tablets. Then some Porage and fish were cooked for him and Ali gave him his best *futah* without saying a word and Musa said he could sleep in his own house. The boy ate the Porage and fish slowly and completely and then sat silent and motionless in the darkening courtyard. After a while he made a faint sound and Musa came and led him away to his house for the night. Thereafter he came each morning and evening to be washed, treated and fed, and it was heartening to see him gather strength each day. His eyes improved and after a few days he had sufficient strength to brush the flies away. Then he began to speak—not much, a few childish, indistinguishable words—and his face began to register expressions. Soon he could walk quite firmly. We learnt that he was not really an orphan but had a mother who herded three goats in the hills and had sent him into Hadibo to beg during the worst months of the summer monsoon. Evidently she thought his prospects would be better in Hadibo than in the hills, but he had not made a very good job of begging.

There were several other bedouin begging in Hadibo and most of them seemed to be doing quite well. The summer months on Socotra are lean and hungry months. No rain falls on the island and the wadis are full of sand. Many of the wells dry up and many small coastal villages are abandoned by the inhabitants. The grass is withered and invisible between the hot stones of the plains, and the cattle, goats and sheep are lean and have little milk. The bone-dry soil in the small garden patches is cracked and the shoots of the vegetable plants are sparse and stunted. The date harvest is over and all around the coast of this exposed island the winds of the south-west monsoon prevent the fishermen putting to sea or the dhows from East Africa bringing in maize, the island's staple food.

The people of Hadibo and the more prosperous coastal villages usually had enough food to last them the summer, their goat-skins packed tight with soft dates from the last harvest and with maize hoarded since the last import. For this reason a proportion of aged bedouin, women and children moved to Hadibo to beg a livelihood during the lean season, and since the duty of the *zakat* (the voluntary setting aside of part of a man's property as alms for the poor and needy) is one of the five pillars of Islam,* these bedouin beggars do reasonably well so long as there is anything to give them. Some of them are adopted by coastal Arab families, who not only feed them but clothe them also and shelter them in their own homes.

Normally, heavy rain falls during the north-east monsoon between November and February, bringing out the grass and leaves on the trees, filling the wadis with raging torrents, nourishing the sprouting vegetables, the date palms and the small grain crops. In gardens in Hadibo and other coastal villages and in the fertile wadis of Gow and Fahr to the east of the Hadibo plain, pumpkins, beans, onions, cowpea, sweet potatoes, melons, tomatoes, coriander, tamarisk, a little millet and a little maize are grown. The milk yield of the herds of cows and goats increases and fish and shellfish are caught in the sea. But the cultivation is on such a small scale that only a small proportion of the population benefits, and the quantity of dates produced by the poorly tended date palms and of fish caught in the sea is barely sufficient in a good year. A large part of the population must exist very near a border-line of starvation, and there is no natural famine reserve—even dates must be imported. The result is that when the rains fail one year, and there is no relief between one dry summer and the next, the precarious balance of the Socotran economy is upset and famine ensues. When this happened in 1844 the island was almost depopulated. Ten per cent of the bedouin died of starvation in 1942-3, and many of those who managed to survive by stealing goats had their hands removed. A similar disaster in 1954 was averted by the prompt action of the Aden Government, which sent a relief frigate laden with grain.

Not only does the soil of the island produce insufficient food for their needs, but the Socotrans are hard pressed to purchase from abroad sufficient of the grain that forms their staple diet. The island is poor; no oil has been found there; its natural products are exotic but unremunerative and exported in only

*The other four pillars are, briefly: *Shahada*, profession of faith; *Salat*, ritual prayer; *Hajj*, pilgrimage to Mecca; *Sawm*, Ramadan—the month's fasting.

small quantities. The principal export is *samn* or ghi, a clarified butter made by the bedouin and reputed to be the best in the whole of the northern Indian Ocean. A very small quantity of dragon's blood, aloes' juice, lichen, ambergris, civet musk, dried shark, pottery, pearls, rugs, skins, tobacco and mother of pearl is exported, in return for maize, rice, cloth and a few oddments like pots and pans, fish hooks and groceries. There is a two-way traffic in dates and some visiting dhows take on salt from brine evaporated in pans at the village of Neht on the south coast. No incense or tortoise-shell is now exported, nor is any commercial use made of the peculiar wood of the metayne tree, the Socotran Box, a slender, bare tree that covers much of the lowlands of the island. Its wood is very close-grained and almost as hard as lignum vitae; it sinks in water and is used by the dhow sailors to make pulleys and other hard worn fittings for their ships. During the war it was subject to a rigorous test to see if it might make a satisfactory substitute for steel ball-bearings; it wore down only a fraction of an inch under great pressure, but had to be discarded.

It is surprising that the island has always attracted merchants to come and carry on trade there, men from the Hadhramaut, the Yemen, Saudi Arabia and the Persian Gulf, some of whom have settled down in Hadibo and lost their former nationalities and bred a first generation of Socotrans who will grow up to speak the language and adopt the customs of the country. One such man was Rashid, a small man with staring eyes, gnome-like and most hospitable. He had something wrong with him that required a penicillin injection and was delighted when he got better. Whenever we went near his house he would pop his head out behind the grilled window and ask us in for tea—hot, sweet, neat tea in little glasses or Japanese coffee cups. He was not fond of Socotra. "If you want to do something," he said to me, "what can you do here? If you want to go somewhere, where can you go? Socotra is like a prison. There's nothing to do and nowhere to go." When I asked him why he stayed he explained that he had happened to marry a Socotran woman and had inherited some goats and date palms and now all his property was here and his children were little Socotrans, so he couldn't very well go away, could he?

Some of the traders from the Persian Gulf live on the island for half the year, travelling round the country purchasing their goods from the bedouin and selling them to the dhow captains during the trading season. One such man was the man of Dibai. Sometimes he came to our surgery and sat against a wall telling his yellow beads or reading a sort of Penguin edition of the Koran from which all the pages were falling. He spoke an Arabic that was almost incomprehensible to Peter. None of us had ever heard of Dibai. "It is a great town," he said, "with hundreds of English soldiers in it." We didn't believe there was such a town. Then we asked him what he did on Socotra and he said he bought and sold things. He bought things on Socotra and sold them in Dibai, and every year his motor-boat came and collected him and his goods. We didn't believe he had a motor-boat. We asked him all sorts of things because he was very affable and worldly-wise, and some of his answers we could not understand and the others we did not believe. We were very disbelieving but very polite. We asked him whether there were any incense trees on the island and he said: "No, none at all, none anywhere." And then after a pause: "Except in the Qalansiya valley, where there are *thousands*." Then he told us that in Hadibo they grew pumpkins the colour of the sky which were as big as this—and he stretched out his arms as far as they would reach. After that he took out his pocket Koran and began reading it and we thought he hadn't got any more fisherman's stories to tell us.

The majority of the inhabitants of Socotra live in considerable poverty but they have their own humour, dignity and self-esteem. Material poverty is usually a comparative thing—one's poverty can be measured in strict ratio to one's neighbour's wealth. On this island where almost everybody is poor, and there are as yet no foreign standards to shame and disturb them, poverty is accepted without degradation. It is unlikely that they will ever be richer than they are today, but the conditions of living can be greatly improved. There is no reason why, in the future, disease cannot be reduced and the production of agriculture, fishing and livestocks greatly increased. It seems unlikely that in these days of increased consciousness of backward areas the programme of colonial development which has been in operation for several years in the mainland territories of the Aden Protectorate will not be extended to this remote and hitherto untouched island as well. I hope whoever will be in charge of such a programme, that

can so easily and disastrously change the whole mental balance
of a country, will have read these words of Harold Ingrams,
who has himself spent many years of his life grappling with
similar problems, first in establishing the Pax Britannica,
the Peace of Ingrams, among the warring tribes of the
Hadhramaut, and then in attending to their welfare and
development:

"Socotra's circumstances and history seem to set the problem
of its development in a proper perspective, both as regards
the tempo and the amount to be applied. Plainly a community
like this cannot absorb much at any great speed without
injury. Development of any kind—economic, social or political
—is not an end in itself. Behind it always lies the development
of human personality, and the important thing is that in
developing his personality the individual shall be free to decide
how best to do it himself against a background of security.
Thus a sympathetic approach to the problem of applying
development is necessary. It is essential to see things through
the eyes of the Socotrans themselves.

"It is difficult to do this without a much closer study of
them. Their language, and therefore their mode of thought,
is still largely unknown. Anyone living outside Socotra can
hardly get into the skin of a Socotran and see things from his
point of view and with the limitations which Socotran life
imposes on him.

"There is an admirable opportunity for carefully thought out
planning."

Already progress has begun, first with Thani bin Ali and his
clinic, then with the despatch of six Socotran boys to the
Bedouin School at Mukalla. The Aden authorities had wanted
to send the Little Sultan there, but his mother, a matron of
considerable wealth and remarkable authority, had refused to
allow him to leave the country, so that he had to make do with
a Socotran education.

At present there is hardly any formal education on Socotra,
and almost all the inhabitants are illiterate. Very early every
morning you will hear the shrill chanting of the schoolboys in
the two schools in Hadibo. When I paid a visit to these schools I
discovered a remarkable state of affairs. In the first school, in the
room of a house next to ours, I found two boys sitting in the
corner reciting the Koran at the very tops of their high voices.

They were both obviously bored stiff and fidgeted incessantly. Neither of them looked at the tattered books on their laps and both were reciting parrot-wise different parts of the Koran. In the middle of this chaos slept the schoolmaster, flat on his back, an arm over his eyes, snoring very quietly. He woke up after ten minutes and scolded the boys for something. This was the "advanced" school, where apparently the older boys went. I left and went on to the next school. At first the schoolmaster, a ferrety little man, wouldn't let me in. Then he said he would let me in if I paid him three shillings. "It's not that I want the money," he explained, "but the boys could do with it." I wondered with what altruistic self-denial he would divide 30 cents between 11 boys. Thani bin Ali who was with me, a sort of chaperone in my wanderings among the institutions and industries of Hadibo, browbeat the schoolmaster and told him that he was shameful, so I was admitted to the school at a reduced fee. It was a pleasant little school, situated in a brightly limewashed courtyard under a grass thatch roof. All the boys sat on a long, clean strip of palm matting, their old torn copies of the Koran resting on flat cushions on their knees. They were all in their very best clothes, bright yellow vests, white shirts, scarlet *futahs*, finely embroidered caps—one boy even wore long baggy white trousers which, apart from Thani's, were the only indigenous pair on the whole island. The schoolmaster sat down in front of the line of boys and said something like "Ready, steady, GO!" They were off immediately, shouting and screaming in their hard, high voices, rending the holy words with sublime indifference to the sensibilities of Allah, throwing back their heads and baying like cayou dogs, their *suraigu* voices trembling as the teacher had taught them to tremble, going on and on till they stopped for a desperate gasp of air. The remarkable thing was that each boy was reading a different part of the Koran. I was amazed, and Thani looked at me and grinned sheepishly. As soon as the boys had started, the schoolmaster lost all interest and sat with his head sunk between his shoulders and his eyes closed. A number of children, who didn't seem to belong to the school, appeared from nowhere and sat round the walls of the yard. The boys went on for ten minutes till I asked the schoolmaster if I might ask him some questions. He seemed to wake with a start. He silenced the boys and peace reigned again in Hadibo.

I asked him what all the other children were doing sitting around the walls of the courtyard.

"Their parents are poor," the teacher replied. "They can't afford to send their boys to school."

Only the sons of rich men went to school in Hadibo. The fees were two shillings a month and forty shillings for every book of the Koran they got through. One boy had already got through thirty books, and another had read twenty. This represented a considerable sum of money on Socotra.

"Do they learn anything else besides the Koran? Do they learn arithmetic—you know, one and one makes two?"

"No, only the Koran."

And that was the extent of Socotran education, the Koran learnt parrot-wise in sporting competition with the boy sitting next to you.

While their more fortunate contemporaries are being taught in the school, the poorer negro boys learn the rudiments of navigation in the shallow lagoon that meanders through the date plantation to the sea. They play with toy boats, some of them simply palm-leaf ribs with the feathers of an Egyptian vulture stuck into them to catch the wind, others more elaborately carved from lumps of wood made to resemble a small dhow, with a mast, a lateen sail, a rudder and, curiously, an outrigger. There are no actual boats fitted with outriggers on Socotra, so this alien feature of the model boats must be due to a tradition handed down from their slave ancestors with memories of the craft of their native East Africa. When they grow up these negro boys will be sailors and help to sail the island's dhows to Muscat, Abadan, Mukalla and Zanzibar.

The Africans constitute the working class on the island. They are descendants of slaves imported from East Africa during the nineteenth century.* They are freedmen now, though they are often still referred to as slaves. "Oh, it's only the slaves," you will hear the Arabs say as the African community begins to

*Some of the younger generation of African Socotrans are the offspring of French West African troops stationed on the island during the war. There was considerable lamentation on the beaches when the soldiers embarked for Africa at the end of their service : their wives came down to the shore with babes in arms, while their erstwhile husbands loaded sacks of cowrie shells (a valuable form of currency in their homeland) on to the rafts that were to take them to the troopship : but it was found that the rafts were sinking under the weight and orders were given to jettison the shells : for the soldiers it was like pouring diamonds into the sea.

kick up hell's delight in the streets of an evening, banging drums and singing. Their hooliganism embarrassed the Arabs.

There are about 2,000 descendants of slaves living on Socotra, most of them in the three principal villages along the north coast, or at Suk, the African colony, or at the residences of the Sultan or Little Sultan. Many of them still live in round African grass huts. They were still being imported as slaves round about the turn of the century. In 1902 a Portuguese cruiser caught a fleet of Arab dhows at the mouth of a river in Mozambique and after a sharp fight captured the vessels and released 725 slaves on board capturing 150 of the Arabs. Between the wars there was still some slave-running and Royal Navy ships kept up a patrol of Arabian waters to intercept slave-ships. There are still some Africans on Socotra who have been freed in their own lifetime and can remember when they were brought to the island. One day one of them knocked at the door of our house in Hadibo and demanded to speak to the "Christian who knows Swahili". He was very black and old and wrinkled. His head was covered with a hoary white bristle and he had a white goatee beard. He was a retired member of the Sultan's household and he hadn't done too badly, by the look of him: his *futah* was new and smart, his vest clean and without any holes in it. He was infirm on his legs and walked with the help of a stick.

"*Jambo, bwana!*"

"*Jambo.*"

"You are the one who understands Swahili?"

"Yes," I said, "I am the one."

His face was radiant when he heard the musical syllables of the language of his birth—was it fifty or sixty years ago? He spoke the language rather gutturally and remembered his native land with regret, but without bitterness at the circumstances that had forced him to leave it.

Did he know Mombasa? Yes, he knew Mombasa, he had been there in the Sultan's dhow. Did he know Zanzibar? Yes, he knew Zanzibar. Did I know Pemba? No, I had never been there.

"Pemba is a good place," he said. "I was born there. I lived there till I was six. Then the Sultan came and brought me here to work for him. I came without my baba or mama and I have never been back. I was a very little boy but I still remember it. . . ."

F

He frowned with the pain of remembering the country he had never returned to.

"Do you know *ndizi*?" he asked.

Yes, I knew *ndizi*, bananas. Many bananas grew in Pemba, and paw-paw and coconut, he said. It was a country full of fruit. It was a beautiful country. One day he would like to go back, just to see. . . .

I asked him how he liked Socotra after all these years.

"It's all right," he replied. "Most years Socotra's all right." He didn't enthuse.

He spoke for a long time, digging up shadowy, transmuted memories. He was unwilling to go. Richard treated him for his infirm legs and after a while the old man went out leaning on his stick.

"*Kwa heri!*" he said. "With good fortune."

"*Kwa heri!*"

I never saw him again.

Most of the Africans on the island have never known any other place but Socotra or any other languages but Socotri and Arabic. Many of them are of mixed African-Arab blood, like Ibrahim and his brother Ali, and now they constitute an essential part of the community. Some of them are in positions of responsibility. The blacksmiths and silversmiths, most of the sailors and pearl-fishers, the house-builders, the carpenters and menders of boats are African. In day-to-day domestic life it is the African women who do the bulk of the work. They sweep the streets outside their houses with twig brooms first thing in the morning, fetch wood and water, carry the babies to their toilet on the rubbish dump at the seaward edge of the town, dampen each struggling plant in the small dry gardens with *burmas* of water, weave blankets and grind corn into flour. In the streets of Hadibo you will usually see only the African women. They are not kept in such strict seclusion as the Arab women. Most of them are remarkably ugly but they flatter themselves unreasonably—if any of them suddenly confronted one of us unexpectedly coming around a corner they would utter a shrill scream, drop everything, even the pots of water balanced on their heads, and scurry away in their long awkward black dresses. Then they would peer out at us through a door slightly ajar. What was it, we wondered, that made the women run from us—had we the evil eye? In time it became an irritating habit, especially as the women, once at a safe distance, would begin to giggle with mock coyness. Peter had a burning desire to photograph some of them, a passion spurred on by the elusiveness of his subjects and difficult to account for in view of their uniform ugliness. He used to wait round certain street corners, like a clandestine bookie, with his camera aimed and cocked. As soon as a woman, any woman, came round the corner he clicked the shutter. Sometimes also he photographed them through the cracks in the door of our house as they scuttled unsuspectingly down the street towards him. As a result of this dedicated work we now have a splendid series of views of street corners, distant and out of focus, adjacent to which are sil-houettes of vaguely female shapes caught at the moment of surprise, like sniped soldiers.

Not all the women were like this. The women in the house-hold of the termagant, for example. The termagant was a terrible woman. She was big and middle-aged and had a face like a Chief Justice with dyspepsia. There were two other wives in this household, and also a husband, a small man with a piping voice and no control whatsoever. The termagant ruled the lot with a voice like thunder dragged over serrated moun-tain peaks. You could hear it all over the town, a terrible sound, very loud, wheezy and bass. I went to her house one morning to film the grinding of the corn. The maize is ground with a rotary quern, a primitive but effective device consisting of two hard, flat round stones, one on top of the other. The maize is dropped through a hole in the centre of the topmost stone and ground into flour by turning the stone with a wooden stick fitted into a slot at its edge. The flour falls out on to a large round mat. As the women grind the corn they sing tradi-tional songs, breathlessly. I started by shifting the entire corn-grinding apparatus to the other side of the courtyard, out of the dark shadows into the sunlight. This created a rumpus and attracted a large number of men and boys who began to pack the courtyard several rows deep. Through cook Ali I explained that I would like to record the work songs of the women and film them as they ground the corn. At this juncture the terma-gant came to the forefront. She wanted two shillings. I agreed, to avoid the endless wrangling that would ensue if I refused. While I set up my camera, the termagant and the youngest wife gave the rotary quern a few turns. My apparatus was barely prepared when the termagant said *"Khalas!"* in her sub-human voice. "Finished!" "But," I said, "I haven't taken any pictures yet!" *"Khalas! Khalas! Khalas!"* The voice like worn-out thunder boomed round the crowded yard. Thani bin Ali became abusive, the husband made conciliatory gestures, cook Ali grunted. "All goats, all goats," he said. The small boys began to play and the men sat down round the walls while the sun rose higher and higher. The youngest wife sat beside the quern and tittered. She had such wide shiny nostrils that I thought for a long time she wore silver rings in her nose. It was nearly an hour before order was restored. When I did begin filming and recording, the stick that turned the quern-stone broke, so I left, as the sun was now too high for satis-factory photography.

These women make attractive blankets of goat's hair and sheep's wool, weaving the strands by hand on primitive looms in their houses. The blankets are made in strips six inches wide and six feet long. These strips are then sewn together to make a blanket of any required size, usually about four feet by six, though once a visiting naval officer bought one fifty feet long. They are black and grey for the most part, but decorated with stripes and borders of coloured wool. They sell them in Aden for up to twenty-five shillings and use them locally as rugs, blankets, or saddling for donkeys and camels. Between us we bought about thirty altogether.

There are two silversmiths in Hadibo; one a white-haired old man, living amidst a litter of empty baby-food tins, coffee pots, converted petrol cans, knick-knacks and Crawford's biscuit boxes; and the other, a younger man, who makes better silver-ware. They both import larger, more ornate and finely wrought silver ornaments from Muscat, for sale to special rich people, but most of the products they sell are of their own simple work—ear-rings, bracelets, armlets, pendants, rings and thorn-pullers. The Socotran women wear a great deal of jewellery—as many as nine ear-rings suspended from nine holes in each ear, a silver chain hanging from each ring; a necklace of Maria Theresa dollars; eight bracelets on each wrist, five rings on one hand, and two bangles round both ankles. All the silverware is hammered out of Maria Theresa dollars which are often skil-fully tapped out into a fine wire. These large silver coins are imported from Aden and Muscat and are of considerable interest. They are still manufactured in England bearing the date 1780 and the effigy of Maria Theresa, Empress of the Holy Roman Empire, Queen of Hungary and Bohemia, Archduchess of Burgundy and Styria. They are imported by bullion merchants in Aden who distribute them along the shores of Arabia and into the interior, where they are still used as currency. The dollar is a face-value coin and it therefore fluctuates in value, depending on the supply and demand and the world price of silver. Sometimes it is profitable to mint new coins, sometimes merchants have gone to the extent of buying up thousands of them and shipping them back to England to be sold as bullion.

Not much else is manufactured in Hadibo but crude iron implements. In a thatch penthouse at one end of the town is the blacksmith's. The blacksmith is an old African who is helped by his wife and a younger assistant. The woman squats against the wall and all day works the goat-skin bellows which keep hot the charcoal fire. The blacksmith and his mate hammer rough bits of scrap iron, raw material left behind by the R.A.F. after the war, into nails, door hinges, crowbars and the knives the bedouin use, the blades set in handles of hard metayne wood.

They are a musical lot, the Africans on Socotra. On several evenings of each week you will hear the sporadic thump of a tambourine or drum as the villagers prepare for an evening's entertainment, warming the skins in the fire to tauten them. Then they will begin, gingerly at first, a tambourine all by itself, a singer all by himself, until the band gathers impetus, more people join it, and the sound of drum-beats like a railway locomotive puffing up a steep gradient echoes over the darkened town. Such occasions are of no particular significance, celebrating nothing, simply an amusement for those taking part. The men squat in the dim yellow light of a hurricane lamp in a street, banging the well-worn, warped tambourines, while a soloist, the leader, chants impromptu verses from the Koran and leads the rest into a chorus, rising on his knees and exhorting them in a loud voice. There is also usually a leader of the band, a man who bangs a big round drum decorated with red crosses. Sometimes three of the tambourinists rise to their feet and stand in a line in front of the leader, while another man on their right performs a dance as he beats his tambourine, slowly revolving, hopping and jigging. Then another dancer joins him and the two revolve slowly and sinuously round each other in time with the accentuated rhythm of the tambourine beats, always keeping the same distance. It is a strange sight, the dancing curiously restrained and unadorned, simply the jigging motion of the upright body, the raising of one foot and then the other, while the same monotonous song is repeated over and over again, accompanied by the unchanging syncopated thumping on tambourines. *One-two-three, one-two-three, one-two-three, BANG!* Usually the same song goes on for about twenty minutes and only ends when the leader tires of it or, as happened once when I watched them, a drummer puts his fist through his instrument. During the interludes women and young girls flit among the shadows like bats, bearing little cups of coffee and halves of coconut shells full of balls of tobacco and glowing charcoal. The men pass round a couple of crude hubble-bubble pipes, gourds or hollow coconut shells half-full of water, with an upright stem projecting out of the top and another stem projecting out of the side. They put a pellet of tobacco in the tray at the end of the upright stem, place a lump of glowing charcoal on top of it and draw out the coarse, thick, sweet smoke through the stem at the side. They inhale once or twice deep into their lungs and then pass the hubble-bubble on to the next man. Then the burnt tobacco and the extinct charcoal are removed and the pipe is filled again from the shells the women bring. This is the height of the ordinary Socotran's pleasure, the singing for no reason at all but the joy of it, the few whiffs of tobacco in between songs, the women quietly attentive, bringing coffee. They forget the inclemency of the season, their own poverty, the disease and periodic hunger. "All I want," says the poor man in the Chinese proverb, "is just enough food for my belly, enough raiment on my back, and a beautiful landscape to look at—and then I will be the richest man in the world." "Ah," say the gods, "these are the riches of the gods alone, they are not for ordinary mortals." The Socotrans, on occasions like these, are as near to the condition of the gods as they will ever be. The beating of the drums and the nanny-goat songs go on for a few hours, till the wind rises and the town is deserted and the streets are full of dust and fury.

These are the "Songs of the Koran", and they all sound exactly alike. The other songs, the "Songs of the Sea", are more tuneful to the European ear. They have a fast, exhilarating rhythm and a catchy, lilting tune. Almost always these songs and dances take place after nightfall, but one day I returned to our house after a filming session in the town, very hot and thirsty and looking forward to some tea, to find the surgery crowded with the most elegantly dressed Arabs, including the entire foreign community, the Affraria Government and many others I had never seen before. I was rather puzzled.

"Do you want medicine?" I asked the Naib of Qalansiya.

"No," he said, "I have come because of the *ngoma*."

"What *ngoma*?"

"This *ngoma*," he said, pointing through the door and down the bright white street. At that moment a great crowd came flocking around the corner at the end of the street, preceded by many small boys and girls, twirling and jigging and hopping towards us, their faces split by delighted grins. The drums had started and three drummers with large skin drums round their necks advanced side by side beating out the loud, insistent rhythm. Behind them came a large crowd of gleeful slaves waving sticks and dead palm fronds, and in the middle of them was the *muqaddem* of the *ngoma*, the leader of the dance, a big, surly man waving a walking stick like a band-leader's baton. The performers settled down and for two hours played two tunes alternately. They stood in a wide circle round one or two "couples" hopping and gyrating in the middle. The dancers kept their bodies erect and their hands by their side and they danced with dead-pan faces, simply hopping and turning, while the crowd around them sang the incoherent words of the songs and sagged at the knees in time to the rhythm of the drums. Later they all formed up into two circles and went round and round waving their sticks and palm fronds. It was like "Here we come gathering nuts in May". One old African, with a white beard, popping eyes, and a stick, gave a special performance all by himself, an improvised dance which was patently a throw-back to the dances of his native Africa. It was a war dance and he was a warrior. He advanced with slow undulating motion towards me, holding his stick like a rifle. When he came within shooting distance, about two feet away, he screamed, aimed his rifle and fired. "Gow! Gow!" he yelled. Everybody thought he was dotty. Ibrahim tittered and Thani poked him in the navel with the end of his umbrella. Then the dotty warrior pretended he had been shot himself and during his death throes, a most agonising business, he watched me out of the corner of his popping eyes to see if I was looking. Then he came up and asked for baksheesh.

The next morning, perfectly sane and normal, he came back to the house. I asked him if he had ever been an askari and he said he had never been one, he was a sailor.

"Where did you get that dance?" I asked. "In Africa?"

"No," he replied, "it was in my head. It came out like a river in spate and I couldn't stop it. Now it's all run away."

CHAPTER SIX

THE DRAGON'S BLOOD COUNTRY

A few days after our arrival in Hadibo we began to reconnoitre a suitable site for a base camp in the mountains, where most of our scientific work was to be done.

Wednesday, August 8th. This morning Neil and I, and two donkeys and Thani bin Ali and a guide whose name I do not know, set off across the plain and into the mountains. We wanted to look for a suitable site for the mountain base camp which we must establish soon. Last night we asked Ibrahim for two donkeys and a guide, and when the guide came this morning he asked us where we wanted to go in the mountains. We weren't sure, so we looked at our map and mentioned a few places at random—Gow, Redahn, Grunhin. The guide, a pleasantly quiet, good-humoured, sensible, middle-aged man, knew none of these places. He did not know where they were and there were no roads to them, he said. We detected a note of desperate illogicality in his argument but said nothing. We were not particularly bothered where we went so long as it was in the mountains where the bedouin lived. We wanted our mountain camp to be near a bedouin settlement so that we could study them and take blood from them when the time came. I remembered the name of a place which had been glowingly described by a previous visitor. Did the guide know Adho Dimellus? Adho Dimellus? Adho, Adho? Yes, he knew Adho. Were there any bedouin at Adho? Oh, no there were no bedouin at Adho. There were no bedouin in the mountains at all. He didn't know where they were but they were certainly not in the mountains, Yes, he knew who the bedouin were. But they were not in the mountains. I got the idea that the guide did not want to go into the mountains, and Thani, who last night willingly agreed to accompany us, this morning seemed most surprised when we asked him if he was ready. "Ready for what?" he asked. "For the journey to the mountains," we said. He was very loth to come with us. It seems the custom of this island that decisions reached after hours of discussion on the previous evening are completely forgotten by the next morning, so that one has to begin all over again. Eventually they both agreed to take us into the mountains, for the agreed fee of nine shillings per donkey. We pay for the donkeys and not for the men.

We left Hadibo about seven and crossed the plain in a south-east direction towards a great split in the mountains where a wadi comes down and crosses the plain to Suk. This wadi is the only way up into the mountains on the north side. When we were out of Hadibo the guide suggested that we might like to ride on the donkeys. We tried this but found that our legs trailed along the ground and were scratched by the thorn bushes. So we got off and walked humbly behind Thani and the guide, who sat comfortably on the donkeys.

After an hour and a half we came to the foot of the wadi. It stretched upwards in front of us, its upper reaches hidden in cloud and driving mist. It was an impressive entrance to a lost and unknown world. The wind blew cold and strong down the chasm and drops of rain fell on us. We felt very intrepid as we started up the mountainside, following a vague track on the right of the wadi. This wadi has cut deeply into the mountain over the millennia, so that now a narrow stream-bed falls precipitately down to the plain between steep mountain-sides. The path often led high above the wadi, which appeared to be dry. Sometimes we saw what we thought was a waterfall, tumbling over great slabs of rock in the wadi bed, but when we came close we could see that it was only a kind of white chemical stain on the rocks, glistening in the sunlight. Probably limestone from the dried-up stream, precipitated on to the rocks. As we climbed slowly up the track, picking our way between the large stones, slowly winding between the huge slabs of granite that seem to have been flipped all over the wadi-sides, we became more and more conscious of the lowering temperature, and of the cool blustery wind that blew down the gorge. All around us towered the spires of the Haggier, very grey and gnarled and majestic. The lower peaks had no clouds round them, but when we looked up the wadi we could see the clouds hanging about at about 3,000 feet and not coming any further northwards, so that all the bottom of the wadi and all the lower peaks had the sun on them. There were a lot of trees on the mountainside; I wish I knew the names of them, but they were mostly leafless, and the track wound between them The plain lay below us like a relief map, criss-crossed with wadis green in the dirty yellow of the plain, and we could see the heat bouncing off it, like dust.

Thani said "*Shuf.*" We looked where he was pointing and saw a man sitting on top of a huge round rock some distance away, his legs curled behind him. He looked like the mermaid that sits on the rock at the entrance of Copenhagen harbour. He watched us as we went past. "Bedu", Thani said, in a confidential tone. We were pleased to have seen a bedu. When we looked back the man had vanished from the top of the rock and after that I had the distinct impression that we were being watched by unseen eyes all the way up the mountain.

Thani said he wanted to pray. It was about midday and Neil and I reclined in the shade of a large tree and ate raisins and drank the warm water from our Army water bottles. Thani and the guide went down among the bushes towards the wadi bed, to find water to wash themselves with when they prayed. I caught a glimpse of Thani bumbling about among the bushes. He had changed into a *futah*. He thought long trousers were irreligious. I lay back and slept for a few minutes. It was very peaceful and there were pigeons flying among the trees, very small and coloured grey-green. I woke up when Thani and the guide came back and we went on up the mountain.

We came to a pool of clear water with orange and purple crabs in it. We had to stop beside this. We drank handfuls of cold water, very fresh and sweet, filled by running mountain water coming from a narrow wadi full of rushes and grass and trunkless palms. It was very cool and I let down the sleeves of my shirt. The boys caught a chameleon and played with it delightedly till we moved on.

We were now at about 2,000 feet altitude and the mountains still went on higher and higher before us. This was the dragon's blood country. The dragon's blood trees only start growing at about 2,000 feet. They grow everywhere from here on. They are shaped like umbrellas blown inside out. They have perfectly straight trunks which branch suddenly in all directions. The branches are short, not more than about one foot long, and from each branch sprouts another branch of the same length, so that there is a very fine and complicated mesh of short grey branches surmounted with a cover of spiny green leaves. They are very strange trees and they grow in extraordinary places: on sheer walls of rock, narrow ledges, projections and cornices. The sky-line is made freakish with them, dotted along it like a massing army or like the Red Indians that always appear suddenly on the horizon in the cowboy films at that inevitably crucial moment when the stage coach, loaded with gold and heroines, enters the narrow pass. There are whole hillsides covered in them.

In between the stones on the track grew Alpine-like flowers— yellow pimpernels, tiny mauve violets, blue campanula, and some aloes.

Always before us was what looked like the top of the mountain. When we reached one top we saw another one stretching up above us. "*Wen* Adho?" we persistently asked the guide. "*Karib*," he always replied. "Near." Adho remained near for half an hour or more and then we reached it. We did not know we had reached it until the guide sat down with the words "Adho." "*Wen* Adho?" we asked incredulously. "*Hina*," the guide replied. "This is Adho." We could see nothing at all but the grey bare sides of the mountain, and the peaks all rotting and craggy around us, with wisps of cloud streaming round them, and stretching before us an expanse of dim hills vanishing into mist and a mêlée of winding wadis. Between the walls of rock the wind thundered like a railway train and blew cold in our faces and on our goose-pimply arms.

"*Lakin, wen bedui?*"

"*Mafi bedui. Ana kalamtuk!* I've told you—there are no bedouin."

"Good Lord!"

I had fully expected to find bedouin here. I had expected to find a thriving village with people going about in the streets, a bazaar perhaps, and crops sprouting in the fertile soil. But there was nobody here, nothing. Adho apparently means a pass. So that this place is the Dimellus pass over the mountains. It is the watershed of the mountains, and a low wall of stones marks where the mountain goes neither up nor down. The mountains lead up to the wall on one side and down on the other. All around is green grass, short and wiry.

Thani and the guide, looking rather doleful, stretched out in the lee of the low wall out of the wind, and let their donkeys graze on the grass, while Neil and I went down the other side of the wall to look for bedouin. Neil explored the right-hand side of the pass while I explored the left. Neil disappeared over a rise and I squatted among the bushes. When I stopped moving I could hear nothing but my own breath and the sporadic roar of the wind along the walls of rock that stretched up on our right and left. And the scream of an occasional bird, wheeling out into space. Before me the mountain sloped steeply down and lost itself southwards in the tumble of hills and valleys. I do not think I shall ever forget the strange sensation I had then, silent among the bushes, of living in a past and depopulated world. I felt intensely that I was living in a world so old that man had no place there. Some people have a vivid sense of the past. It is an obscure, hyper sensitive mental process, like nightmares when you're awake. It goes further than merely *imagining* the past—going into the Tower of London and deliberately conjuring up in one's mind images of Anne Boleyn and the Princes and all the kings and people. It is *being* in the past, suddenly oppressed by the dungeons, losing touch with reality, sinking back into the stream of human history. Only at Adho Dimellus I had sunk beyond even the beginning of the human race. I had a terrified feeling of being completely lost and alone, without kith or kin in the whole world, not because I was, in fact, lost and alone, but because in the presence of these incredibly ancient rocks and the primeval dragon's blood trees and the screaming birds and the wind roaring and nothing else anywhere, I felt I was treading on the threshold of the world. Humanity had no place in these terrifying, watching, silent and animated mountains. The mountains were alive, watching me. I was like a strange, newly-evolved flea on the giant's back. Where had the pterodactyls got to, I wondered?

I heard a loud scratching noise. It sounded like a man crawling among dry leaves. Now and then the scratching stopped, as though the man had stopped crawling and was watching and planning. I had an irrational moment of panic. The loud scratching began again. I located the direction of the noise and after listening carefully found what was causing it. A small lizard just behind me was eating a large insect, part of which still hung out of its mouth. It is a measure of the monastic silence of the mountains that one can hear a small lizard chewing a fly.

Neil and I went back to where the boys were sleeping. The

sun only occasionally shone because the clouds mostly obscured it. It was quite cold. There was no water at Adho Dimellus and we had to find somewhere to stay the night.

We set out again, following a track that led eastward along the shoulder of the mountain. We crossed over a stream and followed the track through a wood of short trees, stooping to avoid the branches. We passed by an orange tree. There were two bright little oranges at the top of the tree and at the foot of the tree was a pile of orange peel. I felt like a hunter coming across the spoor of an animal I knew was near but could not see. Beautiful scents came out of the shrubs, and we went along pinching the leaves of all the bushes and smelling our fingers to see which bush was fragrant, and what the smell was. The air was pervaded with the smell of lemon-scented thyme. There were sweet-wooded myrrh trees, like small spreading cedars.

We came out of the wood and found ourselves in meadows of grass. The meadows sloped down to our right where there were little walled fields. Some white vultures were eating a dead cow in one of the fields. We saw some people in front of us, watching us coming. I thought they would run away but they came towards us, a man and two boys wrapped in brown cloth, looking shy and amiable. When they came up to us they held out their hands and we touched hands lightly, then they put their curled hands to their noses and we did the same, a graceful, curving gesture all in one complete movement. We said *salaam*, and they muttered something shyly, and we watched them while they spoke to Thani, talking in quiet voices, hardly opening their mouths, talking in vague monosyllables which seemed to seep out of their mouths like smoke and drift away in the wind, their meaning lost in the air and half-caught by Thani. We went on and saw where they were living—in very low houses of stone, built into the corner of a field, roofed with earth in which the grass was growing. They lived there like Puck of Pook's Hill. We went on while the mountains became dull in shadow when the sun vanished behind them until we came on a group of young bedouin, sitting on rocks. They shook our hands the way they do and then sat around watching us. They were all dressed in two pieces of brown cloth, one round their middles and the other slung easily around their shoulders or draped over their heads. They were all young, with delicate, beardless, un-Arab faces, close-cropped hair (except for one who had long hair like a woman), small noses and light-coloured skin. They showed us where we could find water, leading us to a small pool at the bottom of a large rock. Thani did not think a great deal of them, because they were bedouin, and when he spoke to them he made it clear that he was doing them a favour. But they were pleasant and shy, their faces registering surprise and kindness and laughter like unselfconscious children. Thani said they were what was left of a settlement that had gone further down the mountainside.

Near the pool we found a place where we could sleep the night. There was a huge rock with some flat earth at its leeward side. While Neil filled the waterbottles I cleared our bed space of stones and cattle dung. The night began to come on and the bedouin disappeared with a concerted movement like a flock of birds, bounding goat-like over the rocks and up the hill-side, till they merged with the rock and were gone. Thani and the guide made a fire.

On our left was a steep wadi, its sides covered in dense undergrowth. There was a 1,000-foot drop to the bottom of it, and it stretched southwards out of sight. On the other side was a grey peak of mountain, and the wadi ended in the hills behind us. A kind of buttress projected out into the valley, its edges ringed with stones piled on top of each other, and here a boy was herding his cattle, calling to them in the twilight. As his voice rang like a shrill bell between the mountain-sides in the now still and cold air, I again felt myself losing touch with reality. Pinch yourself, prod the fire, get some food inside you, don't pay any attention. The cows wandered across the buttress and I turned to Neil and said: "This is a lost world, you know." The boy's high voice came up to us and we watched him till he disappeared with his cows and night fell.

We boiled the water in the cans on the fire and drank hot lemonade. We ate some dates the boys had given us in return for biscuits, and some raisins and barley sugar. I had squashed some Christmas pudding, left over from yesterday's dinner, into a tin can and we ate some of that. Then we went to sleep in our sleeping-bags on the ground wearing our sweaters, ourselves on one side of the fire and the boys on the other. We slept in that strange place without disturbance.

Thursday, August 9th. We were woken at first light by the shouts of some bedouin galloping down the hillside towards us.

Some of them were already watching us with great interest as we lay in our sleeping-bags with the hoods over our heads. We felt rather ridiculous as we stared back at them, our strange, white and alien faces poking out of our quilted cocoons. After a quick breakfast we had a long discussion with Thani and the guide as to our route. We wanted to go to Gow, which we believed was in the next wadi but one. But Thani and the guide said they did not know Gow. They said there was no way across or along the wadi gorge that barred our path, that the only road in the whole region was back to Hadibo the way we had come. Regretfully we retraced our steps to Hadibo and arrived there in the early afternoon. It was hot and soporific after the coolness of the mountains.

We had been resting only a few minutes when Mike and Peter came into the house and told us that the refrigerator was now on its way from the airstrip where, too heavy for camel, donkey or porter, it had remained under the surveillance of a man of Mouri. We went out on to the plain to watch the triumphal entry of the machine and saw a camel coming in carrying it right on the top of its hump. It was moving quite quickly, an extraordinary sight, and entered Hadibo at six. The refrigerator is the first to be seen in the town.

I learnt in the evening about the epic of the refrigerator. It was an amazing performance. Shortly after Neil and I left for the mountains on Wednesday, John and Richard set out for the airstrip with some camels. They reached the airstrip at 9.30 a.m. and uncrated the refrigerator, vacuum containers and meteorological instruments, which had all been looked after by the man of Mouri. After they had sorted out the equipment, they had an argument with the head camel-boy, who maintained that none of his camels could possibly carry any of the stuff. Richard and John became abusive, with gratifying results. The met.-box and vacuum cases were loaded on to one camel and the refrigerator on to the top of another, secured by a bowline. The party set off unsteadily, the camels and camel-men refractory because of the awkward loads. The refrigerator had to be re-roped twice because it slipped down off the hump and dragged the camel sideways. When they reached the foot of the *aqaba* near Qadhub the camels and their drivers rested, and John and Richard began to carry the refrigerator up the *aqaba*, not resting until they were out of sight of the camel-men.

A dwarf Socotran cow in the doorway of Mesna's house at Suk.

Arab boy from Hadibo.

Sheikh Ibrahim (centre), the Prime Minist[...]
discussing camel prices with the author.

African dancer in Hadibo.

Arab woman of the coast.

They took it in turns to carry the front part which was the heaviest—without the door and accessories the refrigerator weighed the best part of 150 lb. At 5 p.m. they dumped the frig. well off the road and returned to Hadibo before dark.

Early next morning Mike and John returned for the refrigerator and slung it between two wooden tent poles, securing it with a strap. After a while they were joined by Peter and Richard and they all took it in turns to carry the thing, carrying it with the poles over their shoulders, a quarter of an hour at a time. They struggled on for two and a half hours till they came to a sandy cove. Here they bathed in the green sea and ate bitter oranges and slept and smoked, and at three Peter and Mike left for Hadibo, to get a camel to carry the frig. from the end of the *aqaba* across the plain. And that was when Neil and I met them.

It is a remarkable achievement because it is terrible carrying such a heavy and awkwardly shaped thing in the heat over such a difficult track, with no shade and not much to drink. I think they were spurred on by local scorn and incredulity. They met many people on the way also struggling under heavy loads of water-skins and firewood, and it would not have done for the refrigerator party to have broken down or appeared exhausted in front of them. The camel-men whose camels had had to carry the frig. were sullen and unhelpful. From time to time they were encouraged with the words "Sultan—heads off!"

Friday, August 10th. Our survey of the Northern Haggier Mountains was not very conclusive. In the two days we spent there we met no more than eight bedouin, so this morning John and I set out on another reconnaissance in the direction of the Wadi Gow—Wadi Fahr system, some miles to the east of the Hadibo Plain, which traverses the island as far as the south coast. These bedouin must be somewhere.

We left Hadibo at 9 a.m. with two donkeys, camp-beds and rations for two days. We crossed the plain eastwards until we entered the dense date plantation at Siriyahun. There is a small scattered village here, the houses built in the African style, either entirely grass-thatched and circular, or with square mud walls and thatch roofs. One of the donkey-men suddenly sat down here in the shade of a palm tree and, losing all

G

interest in the donkey which was supposed to be in his charge, began to pick at the sole of his right foot. He said he had a thorn in his foot and produced a pair of tweezers which he carried especially for this emergency. The donkeys wandered off through the plantation and one of them suddenly became awkward and ran off, pursued by John. I got hold of the other one and tied it to a tree. I couldn't see John anywhere, nor the donkey, while the donkey-man still picked at his foot, helped and encouraged by a small boy. I shouted for John and went right through the plantation and climbed to the top of a slope, but I could see no sign of John or the donkey. When I came back, the boy was picking at the donkey-man's feet while the donkey-man lay on his back in the shade. The other donkey I saw wandering away down the path to Hadibo, so I ran after it and tied it again to another tree. It got very hot—the wind didn't seem to be blowing much this morning, I think the monsoon is dying—so I rested under a tree. The donkey-man and the boy came up to me and showed me a half-inch thorn that had come out of the donkey-man's foot. The boy was very pleased and I made adequately interested noises, but the donkey-man was a half-wit with a face like a vaguely anthropoid ape and a senseless look and with skin on his feet that must be very thick indeed—a quarter of an inch at least. After a while I asked the donkey-man where he thought his donkey had got to and he pointed to the one I had tethered to a tree. I told him that when he started out he had two donkeys and he said "Oh, *tamaam*," and was only going to sit down again under the palm tree when I told him rather abruptly to "bloody well *shuf* for the thing. *Shuf humar!*" He went off into the palm grove with the boy, and presently John came back and said he couldn't see the donkey anywhere. As it had been carrying our water and food there wasn't much point in going on, so we returned to Hadibo with the donkey that hadn't run away. We got back about 12.30, having spent three and a half hours getting two miles in the right direction. Later the half-wit donkey-man came back with the lost donkey. Ibrahim wanted to charge us for the lost donkey and for the expense of looking for it.

The refrigerator is not yet working. Something is wrong with it. It is much hotter inside the refrigerator than outside.

Saturday, August 11th. To-day John and myself again set out for the main wadi system. Two donkeys had been arranged for 6 a.m., but none turned up and eventually I had to send for Ibrahim and ask again for two donkeys to be sent for us. At last we set out late with the sun already very hot.

After an hour's slow journey across the plain we passed a small group of people sitting in the shade beside a well. The rear donkey-man decided to pass the time of day with them leaving the two donkeys in the charge of the other donkey-man, who was none other than the half-wit of yesterday. I can't think how we came to employ him again. He, a few minutes later, leaned on his stick and waited for his colleague, and the donkeys jogged on placidly by themselves. We followed them till they disappeared round a bend in the track and were hidden by the metayne trees that grew very thickly on both sides of the path. We hurried after them, but when we came round the bend there were no donkeys in sight. We didn't know whether to collapse with laughter or anger at the ludicrousness of this situation. We found one of the donkeys all right but the other donkey was completely lost, the perverse little beast; I bet it was the same one as yesterday. The donkey-men ran off and we could hear them shouting among the trees, while we sat on a stone, drank a little water and controlled our rapidly flagging tempers. After a while one of the men came back with the baggage the donkey had been carrying—our sleeping-bags and two packs—and gave them to us like a peace offering. But now that it was apparent that the donkey was completely lost we became very angry. We told them to put everything on the remaining donkey and they protested that the donkey could not carry such a load. So we put the packs on their backs, and they took them off and threw them on the ground. We became angrier and angrier, though I think we could both have howled with laughter if we had not decided to be angry instead. It was all too much like a pantomime. We swore at the men and forced them to go on carrying the packs. After a few minutes we sent the half-wit back to Hadibo and went on with one donkey and one donkey-man, carrying a pack ourselves in turn. Hopeless.

We crossed the plain and passed the Little Sultan's palace, glistening white among the trees. We passed Jebel Hawari that dominates Suk and followed a path leading between two low scrubby hills till we came to a kind of amphitheatre formed

by a circle of low hills enclosing a dry, tree-filled plain. We saw
some date palms on our right and struck down a track till we
came to the hamlet of Kam among the palm trees. It was
midday and very hot. We came to a stagnant pool covered with
a green scum and beetles skimming over it. There were some
men and a small girl and boy lying beside a pool, all prostrate
and immobile in the heat. When we arrived they turned their
heads towards us but otherwise remained prostrate and
immobile. We had come all the way from England and probably
we were the first white people they had seen for years, but all
they did was momentarily turn their heads. We gave them each
a barley sugar and they spent a long time trying to get the
paper off. We ate some biscuits and Marmite and drank some
of our hot water from the jerrycan. John put a handkerchief
over his head and went to sleep with his head against the
stones they pile at the bottom of their palm trees to prevent
them being torn out by the wind. I photographed the men
of Kam who winced when I clicked the camera shutter but
otherwise did not move. One of them lay with his head against
a palm tree trunk, with his arms flopped out over the ground
like hosepipes and a bare knife lying across his stomach. He
remained like that all the time we were there. I gave the
advertisement leaflet out of a packet of biscuits to a small boy.
On one side of the leaflet there was a picture of a baby and on
the other a picture of a dairy-maid clutching a wheatsheaf and
smiling. The boy was delighted to have it and held it upside
down while I photographed him. There was a small girl there
in black with coloured beads round her neck. A pretty little
girl, destined to grow old at 25. I suppose no one minds growing
old at 25 here. If they had our expectation of life would they
appreciate it in this place, another twenty years of daily
tribulations and prostration from heat, malaria and lack of
food?

We pushed on down the wadi Ma'abath and turned inland
round the Batageber, a high hill about 1,800 feet high. It is
also known as Fedahan Delafonte. *Fedahan* is Socotri for hill,
but I believe Delafonte is a Portuguese name. The donkey-man
was quite affable, as though nothing had happened. The
country is dry, flat and scrubby, with the foothills and arms of
the mountains blue and rolling in the distance.

We came to the hamlet of Garr, a few scattered thatch huts

among palm trees by a dry wadi bed. There were some gardens here fenced off with palm ribs and growing nothing. We entered the property of an old man. He lived in a two-room thatch hut, one of the rooms with its front wall missing, like a garage without any doors. He owned a lot of ground, all fenced with palm ribs. There were palm trees in his front garden and a well, and many metayne trees with goats grazing among them on the odd bits of sparse grass struggling up between the stones that filled his property. The old man was prosperous for this place, because he had quite a lot of goats and two young wives. He came out like a perky, wizened old sparrow and welcomed us. He brought out two palm mats for us to sit on and some dates in a clean platter of woven palm leaf. He offered us some meat and brought it out for us raw to see, but we thanked him and said no. If this had been Arabia the host would have been offended, but I think the old man was glad we did not want the meat. We said *ashkuruk* (thank you) many times and he took the meat away and brought us a bowl of water to wash our fingers in. In the morning he also brought us a bowl of milk, warm from the goat, for which we were very grateful, but I wished he had offered us some of his coffee. He gave the donkey-man coffee in the little cups and filled a hubble-bubble for him with a little tobacco which he kept in a knot of his *futah*. He preserved the trappings of Arab hospitality but spoilt things by asking us for money and patently hanging around for biscuits. I was too tired to talk much with him and was not a deserving guest, but grateful for his kindness.

We slept that night in the old man's stony field, two lonely beds in the middle of a circle of hills and mountains dimly lit by a bright crescent moon and cooled by a slight breeze. There was a movement of goats and the odd noise of the donkeys as they grazed. They were still grazing in the darkness when we fell asleep.

We moved off at six the next morning after a breakfast of bully beef and biscuits. We sent the donkey-man back to Hadibo, retaining only one pack in which we put our binoculars, three cameras, water bottles, biscuits, raisins and barley sugar. We carried the pack ourselves for the rest of the day, an hour each.

We aimed for a village called Deishel which seemed to lie in the direction we wanted to go. For the next three hours we strode across the trackless country as fast as we could force ourselves. It was dreary country. The ground was either devoid of all vegetation, coloured dull brown or red, full of boulders and impeded with lumpy or sandy wadis, or else there were hillsides in our way with no tracks over or round them, covered densely with leafless trees which caught at our shirts or the packs we were carrying. We got very hot and tired and swore at the trees that clutched at us. The wind whirled around us and once it snatched our map from John's back pocket and blew it across the country. I found an unexpected reserve of energy and chased after it over the jagged stony ground. From the top of a hill we saw a small wadi with some goats grazing on the grass. There was a little barely-flowing water in the wadi, going green at the edges and covered with water beetles. We drank some and it tasted of salt. There were some houses near by but no people. The whole place was deserted. We trudged down the wadi and at length found ourselves back in the old man's garden at Garr. We had been gone seven hours and now we were back again having marched in a complete circle, found nothing, seen nobody, and risen hardly above sea-level. We passed the heat of noon in the old man's place, beside his well. Before we went he came down to us and gave us some more dates.

We forced-marched back to Hadibo, racing against the clock, for we had only allowed ourselves three hours to get back before nightfall. We were very tired on the Hadibo Plain and marched back in a kind of cold fury, forcing ourselves as hard as we could. From the top of a rise we saw Hadibo, nestling among its palms, as light was fading. We were very pleased to see the place and when we got back to our house Peter gave us some cold lemonade.

We had marched at a tremendous pace for ten hours to-day over terrible country, for the most part off the track, covering 25 to 30 miles. For each alternate hour we had a pack on our back. I do not think it is possible to do more than this in one day in this country. I felt quite done up at the end of it. One thing is certain, there is no prospect of a base camp in that part of the island. It seems even more depopulated than the mountains, it is hot, and communications with Hadibo are not good. I think we will have to establish our base camp somewhere near Adho Dimellus. Mike at least will benefit greatly there from the point of view of his biological work. I hope there may be more bedouin skulking up there than we think.

CHAPTER SEVEN

SO FAR FROM PORTUGAL

EVERY day during our stay in Hadibo, Peter set off to explore the surrounding plain for archaeological remains.

Before we left England we had been told by various eminent authorities that Socotra was of the first archaeological importance. The theory was that the island had been an important entrepôt for trade between the Far East and the Mediterranean during Roman times—roughly between the second century B.C. and the sixth century A.D.

Round about the year 100 B.C., we are told, a certain Greek helmsman called Hippalus discovered the long-kept secret of the monsoon winds which sweep alternately east and west across the Indian Ocean. He was the first Westerner consciously to use these winds, and thereafter Graeco-Roman merchant seamen found that by entrusting themselves to the wind, out of sight of land, they could sail to India in two months and thus by-pass the long and expensive overland trade route. By the beginning of the Christian era as many as a hundred Roman-owned ships were sailing to India each year, not only tramps and freighters but passenger ships also, running to a regular time-table. Some of them also sailed south, down the East African coast, and Roman trading settlements are being dug up there, as well as in India.

It seems inconceivable that some of these ships should not have called at Socotra. Lying in the mouth of the Gulf of Aden it straddles both the route to East Africa and the route to India. The island was known to the Greek and Roman world as far back as 300 B.C. and was a busy trading post before the Romans ever arrived on the scene. Indian, Arab, Greek, Persian and African merchants went there, while the Socotrans themselves acted as middlemen in the Egyptian-Indian trade. In a shipping manual called the *Periplus of the Erythraean Sea*, written in the first century A.D. by an unknown Greek sailor for the guidance of other sailors navigating the northern Indian Ocean, we find the first detailed description of Socotra ever written. The anonymous author calls the island Dioscorida, a name the Greeks derived from the Sanskrit *Dvipa-Sukhadara*—"The Island Abode of Bliss"—from which the modern Socotra is also derived. "Dioscorida," he writes, "is very large, but desert and marshy, having rivers in it and crocodiles and many snakes and great lizards, of which the flesh is eaten and the fat melted and used instead of olive oil. The island yields no fruit, neither vine nor grain. The inhabitants are few and they live on the coast towards the North.... They are foreigners, a mixture of Arabs, Indians and Greeks, who have emigrated to carry on trade there. The island produces the true sea-tortoise, and the land tortoise, and the white tortoise which is very numerous and preferred for its large shells, and the mountain tortoise which is the largest of all and has the thickest shell, the worthless specimens of which cannot be cut apart on the underside because they are too hard, though those of value are cut apart and the shells made whole into caskets and small plates and cake dishes and that sort of ware. There is also produced on this island Cinnebar (dragon's blood), that called Indian, which is collected in drops. It happens that this island is subject to the King of the Frankincense Country. Trade is also carried on there by those who chance to call there on the voyage from Damirica and Barygaza; they bring in rice and wheat and Indian cloth and a few female slaves, and they take for their exchange cargoes a great quantity of tortoise-shell."

The crocodiles, large lizards and most of the varieties of tortoise have died out, if they ever existed. But it appears from this account that the island was indeed an entrepôt for trade of some sort, and the large quantity of tortoise-shell ware, once highly popular in Rome, would have provided sufficient incentive for Romans to visit the island, just as the author of the *Periplus* visited it.

Peter hoped to find traces of Greek as well as Roman settlements on the island. There is no doubt that Greek *émigrés* lived there during several centuries, and one Arab historian, Idrisi, writing in the ninth century, has a curious explanation of their original settlement. Alexander the Great, returning home by sea after his conquest of India, stopped at the island and was favourably impressed by its fertility and pleasant climate. He remembered the advice that his tutor Aristotle had given him, that if he cultivated the famous Socotran aloe he would become prosperous. So Alexander, who did not believe in half-measures, promptly deported the existing inhabitants of the island and in their place settled a colony of Ionian Greeks, with orders that they should cultivate the aloe. A later historian, Yaqut, accounts for the eventual disappearance of these Greeks in later years by recounting how, when the Socotrans were converted to Christianity, the Greeks refused to marry and so died out.

Not until he visited the village of Suk, five miles eastwards along the coast, did Peter have much success. Suk was once the capital of Socotra, and its very name (*suq* is Arabic for market) suggested that at one time it may have been the principal trading settlement on the island. The present village is inhabited mostly by Africans, living in grass thatch huts and one-roomed, dirty-white, mud and coral houses. A few garden patches are dotted around the village, the palm rib fences blown down in the wind and a few shoots of tobacco plants pushing out of the dry earth. The village is dominated by Jebel Hawari, a low steep-sided projection of rock, with white sand blown up against it from the beach so that it looks snow-capped from a distance. Between the hill and the village is an attractive, shallow, fresh-water lagoon, full of fish and bull-rushes, meandering between grassy banks and the dense date plantation. A wadi comes down from the foothills and feeds the lagoon, but at this time of year the wadi is dry, full of soft sand and date palms which grow more thickly here than anywhere else in the island, though they are wild and poorly tended. Behind the village the plain is covered in a frothy scum of low, green, fleshy-leaved shrubs.

It is a poor, dishevelled village, but its inhabitants were well aware of its importance in the past. There were numerous mounds around the village, covered with occupation debris, and some of the present houses were built on mounds. These mounds probably covered ancient buildings and were a likely place to start an archaeological excavation.

Suk could not have been a very large capital. It must have been smaller than Hadibo, which is small enough with its 400 inhabitants. But it undoubtedly had a great natural advantage. Its lagoon, now much silted up, must once have been navigable by small ships and perhaps, many centuries ago, deep enough for larger ocean-going vessels to anchor in.

By such a creek one would expect to find traces of former occupation. Here, we imagined, came Egyptian incense-traders, Roman sailors, Arab and Indian dhows bringing grain and slave girls and taking away tortoise-shell and dragon's blood; here lived the expatriate Greeks, refusing to marry on principle. Here Peter decided to dig.

He discussed the details of the digging with Ibrahim and Mesna, the head-man of Suk, a stocky, kindly African. He asked for six men and eight boys and one morning set off to trudge the five miles to Suk to begin the first excavation. When he arrived he found all the potential workers standing around and arguing who was to take part in the day's work. The prospect of employment was so unprecedented to the men of Suk that they all clamoured for work. After much shouting in the high wind Peter sorted them out and the digging commenced. To his surprise and horror he discovered that the only tool they had to dig with was a sharpened crowbar. It is normal archaeological practice to allow the workmen to provide their own tools to which they are accustomed, so all that Peter had brought with him to the island was a spade of dubious efficiency. It was therefore a new experience for him to see his team of diggers sitting on top of the excavation site and spearing the earth with their crowbars in a disinterested way while a horde of small boys grabbed the loosened soil in handfuls and put it into little panniers to carry off to the debris dump. It was obvious that any precious old pot or artefact that had lain intact in the earth through the centuries would rapidly become a potsherd before it saw the light of a twentieth-century day. The other unnerving thing about this dig was that the team of diggers changed each day "so as to give every man a chance". The boys worked hard and earned their money, continually shuffling with panniers of earth between dig and dirt heap, funny little African boys, their black skin coated with grey dust. But the men only worked when you watched them, and some of them not even then.

It must have been one of Peter's strangest digs in his twenty years of archaeology. In the Sudan he drove in a jeep to the site where he was surrounded by all the panoply of professional archaeology, where the diggers had proper implements, came back the next day, and didn't think they were digging for gold, and where there were sometimes sunshades and occasional cool drinks, and other pleasant and necessary things. But here Peter had to walk five miles across a flinty plain and sit for most of the day in the broiling sun with no shade anywhere, blown about by the wind, covered in dust, refreshed by dungy water from a dirty clay pot, beset by flies, knowing that if he went away for a moment the work would stop, and that if anything whole lay in the ground it would get a crowbar through it. And then the five miles' walk back to Hadibo.

The first site Peter selected for excavation was a large mound at the top of which the foundations of some building could be seen quite clearly. During the course of a week or so the top layer of earth and debris was removed to reveal the bases of six columns of stone and mortar and a mortared floor. Each column was differently shaped—one was star-shaped, another round, another square and so on. It was a fairly large building and resembled most nearly a mosque, though it bore little relation to the direction of Mecca. Little came out of the earth to identify or date the ruin precisely except potsherds, the topmost of which clearly originated in Stoke-on-Trent and Japan, while the potsherds from lower levels appeared to be medieval in date—glazed Arab ware and some rather lovely Chinese porcelain, thin and delicate, glazed in subtle shades of blue and grey and with some patterning on one or two of the bits. At the edge of this mound he sunk an exploratory trench in order to examine the various occupation levels beneath the one where the foundations of the mosque lay. He found three occupation levels before he came to sand, but all of them appeared to be medieval in date and the usual potsherds came out of them all. Clearly this mound, which was almost the largest, contained nothing of very great antiquity.

Some days later Mesna took Peter to look at some more foundations about a hundred yards from the uncovered mosque. Here were just discernible the outer walls of a large building and one or two interior rooms. The whole foundation was buried in rubble into which two lime pits had been sunk. During the next two months Peter excavated as much as he could of this ruin, and by increasing the number of boy workers to twenty-two he managed to uncover the rough outline of a fortress with a thick outer wall and round towers at each corner. This ruin appeared to be of the same date as the mosque and confirmed Peter's growing suspicion that he had, in fact, uncovered what was left of the Portuguese garrison of 450 years ago. The fort was almost certainly the one the Portuguese had captured from an Arab sheikh in 1507 and occupied for four years, and it was equally probable that the near-by mosque was the one they had converted into the Church of Our Lady of the Victory.*

Socotra was first discovered for the Portuguese in 1503 by Captain Fernandes Pereira. At this time the Portuguese were in the course of establishing their brilliant but short-lived eastern empire in India, Africa and the Persian Gulf. During the course of the fifteenth century a succession of courageous sailors had pushed their little high-pooped ships farther and farther southwards down the west coast of Africa. In February 1488 Bartholomew Diaz became the first Portuguese to round the southern tip of Africa. In the same year another expedition set out and reached the Malabar coast of India via Aden. The seaward route to India had been discovered.

The Portuguese came first to trade and then to conquer. On April 5, 1506, the renowned Portuguese Admiral, Tristan da Cunha, weighed anchor in Lisbon harbour and set sail with 14 ships for the conquest of India. The next morning his second-in-command, Alfonso Albuquerque, set sail with another six ships. They rounded the Cape of Good Hope, but by the time they reached Malindi they found that the season was too advanced for them to attempt the ocean-crossing to India. So they decided to establish winter quarters on Socotra which, according to their intelligence reports, was inhabited by Christians, and from which they could protect the sea-route to India from Arab raiders.

In January of 1507, ten months out from Portugal: "without touching any other land they went and anchored off Çoco [Suk] which is the principal port of that island and where the population lives: and with flags flying from all the ships in holiday trim they saluted the place with artillery, because it was inhabited by Christians. But when Tristan da Cunha saw the fortress which the Arabs had built there, surrounded with a wall and barbican, and with a keep, which was very different to the information which their King, Dom Manuel, had received,

---

*As late as 1800 the Socotrans at Suk were still digging up bits of broken swords and armour, which they exported to Muscat. This may account for our failure to find any Portuguese relics at Suk to confirm our deductions.

he sent for Alfonso Albuquerque and all the captains of the fleet: and he told them that the king his lord had ordered him to construct a fortress in that island and to leave behind Don Alfonso de Noronha as the captain of it, for the guard and protection of the Christians who had lived there since the time of St. Thomas, the king's advice being to extend the name of our Lord throughout all the parts he had conquered."*

The Arab fort, however, was rather an embarrassment. An attempt at a treaty with the Sheikh in command of the fort proved unsuccessful: the Arabs refused to leave or to have anything to do with the Portuguese who had arrived out of the blue. So, in the name of the Lord and in view of the smallness of the garrison, Tristan da Cunha decided to attack the fort. Landing operations were likely to be difficult because a rough sea was running and the beach was unsheltered. Alfonso Albuquerque took a small boat and made a reconnaissance of the shore "and found a creek near a palm grove where the sea was more quiet and although it was a little too far they agreed to land there".

"The great Alfonso Albuquerque ordered his nephew, Don Alfonso de Noronha, to make ready his boat with 40 musketeers and take with him a falconet and powder for it, and cannon balls and two bombardiers, and a cabria (derrick) and two sets of ladders to scale the wall of the fortress, if necessary: and he would go in the ship's skiff with Don Antonio de Noronha, Don João de Lima, Don Geronimo de Lima his brother, and other fidalgos following close upon their track."

The landing party left their ships before daybreak, Tristan da Cunha in the van, Albuquerque in the rear. While they were rowing towards the shore Albuquerque noticed that the surf on the shore seemed much calmer and that it would be possible to land there. He saw the Arab Sheikh and a hundred men come out of the fort and make their way towards the stockade they had built during the night to obstruct the Portuguese landing in the lagoon. Albuquerque therefore ordered de Noronha to land at once, but before this could be done the Sheikh saw them and sent eighty of his men back into the fort while he himself went with twenty men to tackle de Noronha.

---

* This and following extracts are from *The Commentaries of the Great Afonso Dalboquerque* (Hakluyt Society, London, 1878).

"And when these met there was a sharp skirmish with cutlasses and lances and some of either party were wounded. And Don Alfonso de Noronha engaged in fight with the Arab captain and coming to blows with cutlasses had almost overcome him when Alfonso Albuquerque came up with all the rest of his men, and put an end to the Sheikh's life."

When the Arabs saw their chief killed they fled back to the fort.

". . . and when they arrived our men killed eight of them while the others went around the fortress and fled to the mountains. The Arabs who were upon a watch tower, seeing our men close to the wall, began to throw down many corner pieces and stones which harassed them much. And they struck Alfonso Albuquerque on the helmet with a cornice stone so that he fell to the ground immediately in bad plight: but for all this he did not lose his senses and ordered the men to close round and sent Nuno Vaz de Castelo-Branco to bring the shot and the derrick, and the sets of ladders, axes and rams to break down the doors of the fortress. When Nuno Vaz brought the ladder Alfonso Albuquerque ordered them to place it against the wall and our men began to ascend. And the first was Gaspar Dias de Acacere de Sal, who took up his flag, and Nuno Vaz and the standard of Job Queimado and others who followed."

There now began a difficult chase round the parapets and towers of the fort, in which some Portuguese soldiers lost their lives. The Arabs in the fort all fled to a tower and the Portuguese broke through into the fort with axes and rams and sat down outside the door which led up into the tower, waiting for Tristan da Cunha. He had met with some slight resistance from the Arabs at the stockade by the lagoon, but had killed many of them and the rest had fled to the mountains. He now joined Alfonso Albuquerque inside the fort. There were only twenty-five Arabs left out of one hundred and fifty, but they were in an impregnable position as, in order to attack them, the Portuguese had to mount a staircase one at a time and could not retaliate against the Arabs, secure in their tower above them and shooting arrows "with bad effect upon our men". Don Antonio de Noronha was very nearly decapitated by one of the Arabs, had not Albuquerque warded off the blow with his shield. Tristan da Cunha decided to make terms with the

remaining Arabs, as there was not much point in carrying on
with the fight, seeing that the fort was already captured.

"But the Arabs replied 'that they were much obliged to the
worthy chief captain for wishing to spare their lives but that,
in telling them of their captain's death, he had given them a
sufficient reason for declining to receive the favour, for the
Fartaquins [Mahri Arabs] were not accustomed to return
alive to their land and leave their captain dead on the field,
especially as he was the son of their King. Therefore he might
do as he pleased for they were not going to yield.'

"The Chief Captain, at this declaration of the Moors, sent
João Freire, his page, and Nuno Vaz de Castelo-Branco and
Dinis Fernandes, who was afterwards Chief Superintendent of
India, Antonio Dinis de Setubal and Pedralvares, page to the
Count of Abrantes, to ascend to the terrace of the tower and
see if by that way they could get in at the Arabs. And the
first who was up was João Freire, the page, who when leaping
from the parapet of the tower to the terrace was perceived
by them, and they opened the door which led to the terrace
and seeing him by himself fell upon him and butchered him."

Nuno Vaz had a cross-bow and two Biscay palisadoes were
brought up from the boats. Under cover of these, the Portuguese edged up the stairway, well plied by the Arabs with
arrows and lances, and eventually broke into the tower, where
they massacred all but one of the Arabs, who was employed
afterwards as a pilot during the voyages along the Arabian coast.

"The fortress was attacked at six o'clock in the morning and
finally taken at one o'clock in midday. Not much spoil was
taken in it but some supplies and arms were found and a sword
bearing in Latin the motto *God help me*."

Only one other Arab survived—a blind old man whom the
Portuguese discovered at the bottom of a well. "I could see
only one thing," he told them when he was pulled out, "and
that was the way to liberty!" He was set free. It had been an
unexpectedly bitter fight, the worst in the Portuguese experience
up to that time.*

"On the morning of the next day Tristan da Cunha went
with all his men to a moorish mosque: and as it was to be the
principal Church they named it 'Our Lady of the Victory',

*There is a contemporary painting of the Storming of Socotra by Jorge Colaço
in the Museum Militar, Lisbon.

wherein Fr. Antonio de Loureiro, of the order of St. Francis, said mass—not without the tears of our men to behold in a land so remote from Portugal the name of our Lord Jesus Christ reverenced in that house of abomination."

Tristan da Cunha then had a word to say to the Christian bedouin. He told them that his King had sent him and his men to protect them from the likes of the Arabs and they need have no fear. But in return for this protection he asked them to keep peace and friendship with the Portuguese garrison, keep them supplied with food, and learn the true doctrines and ceremonies of the Christian faith which they had long ago forgotten.

The Portuguese then repaired the fort and named it St. Michael. It was committed to the Captainship of D. Alfonso de Noronha with a hundred men under him. On August 1st, 1507, Tristan da Cunha sailed for India: ten days later Alfonso Albuquerque with six ships sailed away for Ormuz, on the Persian Gulf, leaving the garrison to fend by itself till the fleet returned.

Seven months later Albuquerque came back to Socotra. He found his nephew, the garrison commander, terribly sick, four of the men dead and all the rest in bad shape. The Arabs who had fled to the mountains had persuaded the bedouin that the Franks had come only to enslave them. The bedouin had revolted, harried the Portuguese and denied them supplies. The garrison was so hungry that the men had to resort to eating palm rind and wild fruit. The small boats had dry rot and the ships were in need of repairs. Albuquerque shared out what supplies he had and gave the men of the garrison eight months' pay due to them.

In May all available ships in the Portuguese fleet went into winter quarters on Socotra.

"Then Alfonso Albuquerque, with the forces he had brought with him, began to wage war upon the natives, and these after being thoroughly beaten and paying the penalty due for the murder of our men, sent desiring to make peace, and he received their petition on condition of their paying each year to the people in the fortress a tribute of 600 head of sheep, 20 cows and 40 bags of dates."

After the punitive campaign had been satisfactorily concluded Alfonso Albuquerque set sail again from Socotra. In November 1509 he became Viceroy of India. He never returned to Socotra.

Mubarak, the wireless operator, and soldiers of the Hadhrami Bedouin Legion.

Boys reciting the Koran at the school in Hadibo.

The expedition's caravan prepares to leave Hadibo for the interior.

The garrison struggled on for another year or two, and then thankfully withdrew, depleted by disease and undernourishment. After that first stormy winter, when the fleet was almost blown out to sea in the south-west monsoon, the island was not used as a harbour or winter quarters, though Portuguese vessels occasionally called to take on water during the succeeding years. The Portuguese were busy elsewhere—in Goa and Malacca, at Ormuz in the Persian Gulf, at Aden, fighting, burning, accomplishing in their tiny cramped boats, in their steel breastplates and helmets in temperatures such as only India and Arabia know, miracles of naval and military campaigning, establishing their brilliant and rapidly-gained Empire. All that is left of them on Socotra is the mosque, the tumbled fort, oranges in the mountains,* and the name of a hill—Fedahan Delafonte—to the east of Suk. Now, not even a memory in the minds of Socotrans. Standing on the débris of the fort, I thought of João Freire, and the other soldiers who had died here. Their dust was here somewhere. Perhaps in my nostrils or on the skin of that funny little African digger. The place had not changed much. The mountains, the barren plain, the rough sea, the glaring cloudless sky, the flies, were still the same. Only the creek had silted up. I was glad I was not one of those who had to attack this fort in a futile cause in this hopeless place 450 years ago.

Sometimes Richard or myself accompanied Peter to his dig at Suk. In the early morning before the sun was very hot, the five-mile walk across the plain was pleasant, and sometimes we could watch porpoises lying like exhausted, still torpedoes on the sea. At lunch-time we always retired to Mesna's house, and there, sitting on mats and cushions (Peter found it difficult to sit cross-legged, because his knees would not bend that far), Mesna passed us little handle-less cups of black bitter coffee, flavoured strongly with ginger, and deliciously refreshing. Then he would bring a little pannier of soft stored dates, and sometimes bowls of warm, incredibly dirty milk, straight out of the cow which stood diminutively in the doorway like a rather large pet dog. The milk was most refreshing of all. These were the best middays on the island, in Mesna's house. It was not a big house. It had two small rooms, floored with gravel, giving

*The Socotri word for orange is *tanija*, derived from the Portuguese word *larinja*.

on to a small courtyard where the cow stood, shaded with thatch. In the shade Mesna's wife worked, making blankets. She made good blankets and charged us less for them than other people. Not that we ever saw her—we just heard her working outside, and Mesna brought the blankets to sell. There was something wrong with his front door; unless you piled up stones behind it, it swung open letting in a furious belch of hot monsoon air, dust, some goats, a bedu boy and the Village Idiot. The hot air, dust and goats continued out through the other door, but the bedu boy and the Village Idiot remained. The Village Idiot was a well-built, well-featured, amiable bedu, who was, unfortunately, simple. Mesna fed him and sheltered him, together with a slender brown boy who dug for us and looked like an Indian. The boy ate dates quietly in the dark part of the dim, cool room and the Village Idiot was given a hubble-bubble to smoke. He smoked continually, sucking lungfuls of sweet smoke out of the gourd of water, wreathed in blue-grey smoke like an emergent genii till his eyes became blurry and he rocked back on his heels completely befugged. I thought at first that he was drugged with hashish, but always he was the same amiable, inarticulate idiot and he could not be smoking all the time. Mesna was a very generous, stolid, sensible man, quiet and humble: a very good man and the best host far and away that we ever were guests to.

There were the remains of another Arab fort on top of a conical hill called Hasun on the plain outside Hadibo. It had been there in 1615; Sir Thomas Roe had seen it but not been allowed to go near it. It had very thick walls and commanded the entire plain. It would have been impregnable, except that to get water the occupants would have to go down to the plain below. The wind on top of Hasun blew tremendously at 60 m.p.h. and made it difficult for Peter to take photographs or measure the walls.*

Later Peter and John went westwards looking for the inscriptions on limestone rock that Bent had reported seeing in 1897. These were to be found at a place called Eriosh, near the sea at the western end of the Northern Coastal Plain.

They forced-marched there, taking turns to carry their

---

*According to a contemporary Arab account the fort at Suk was destroyed after the Portuguese abandoned it and the Mahri built a new one—presumably on Hasun.

food and sleeping-bags in a rucksack. On the way they stopped at the village of Dihana. "This village of pearl fishers," Peter recounted, "is a real shanty town, the most squalid I have seen in Socotra, many of the houses being built of empty oil drums and roofed with sheets of corrugated zinc removed from the aerodrome. The people, though, were kind and gave us a place to have lunch, very salty water which they heated for us, and dates. For their dates they go right across the island to Nawgeed, the plain on the south coast, where they buy them at one shilling for 2 *rotls*, since they grow nothing themselves. Later they also gave us sweet water, which is brought to them by bedouin from the hills at twenty shillings a *bermil*. Evidently they must make a fair profit during the pearl-fishing season.

"After lunch we were put on our way by our host, Ahmed, who asked nine shillings for all he had done for us (Arab hospitality! but I agreed to it). On the way, passing another village, men came out to greet us and ask us where we were going. Since the way seemed obscure we asked one of them, Khalifa, to take us. After much pulling of each others' beards and good-natured shouting he agreed to take us for five shillings and led us for miles across the plain at what was nearly a run.

"We arrived at Eriosh by mid-afternoon and found there a flat slab of limestone covered with graffiti. Impressions of the feet of men and camels were the most common, but there were also some symbols that looked like the letters of some alphabet, strung together in long snaky lines, interspersed with crude pin-drawings of camels. Near by were ruined buildings which seemed to me to have been huts with courtyards."

Theodore Bent, who visited the island in 1897 (and died shortly after leaving it), considered that the graffiti at Eriosh were almost exactly similar to those he had seen on the steps of the church and on the hillside round Aksum, the ancient capital of Abyssinia. He believed that the inscribed letters were Ethiopic, and since the Abyssinians probably visited the island when they occupied Southern Arabia in the sixth century A.D., the inscriptions at Eriosh probably date from then. The men of Dihana could offer no explanation. Asked whether they thought the footprints were carved on the limestone by Muslims or Christians, they replied: "They are angels' footprints, no human could have made them."

The results of our archaeological work on the north coast of
Socotra were disappointing, but it was not for the want of
looking. If there is anything of great antiquity on the island it
must lie buried deep beneath the sand and accumulated dust of
ages, beyond the reach of one archaeologist working under
unfavourable conditions, with limited time and facilities. But
had we over-rated Socotra's importance in the past? I cannot
imagine that even the most hardy and zealous of traders,
Roman or otherwise, would have found much to induce a
prolonged stay on this inhospitable island, with its lack of food,
considerable disease and, above all, raging wind which then,
as now, cut the island off from all outside contact for six months
of every year. No doubt the survivors of the Portuguese garrison
would have agreed with me.

CHAPTER EIGHT

LIFE AND HARD TIMES

THE move to the mountain base camp "somewhere near Adho Dimellus" was to be in two stages. John, Mike and Neil were to move up in the first stage, with instructions to establish the camp as near as possible to Adho. The rest of us, who still had work to do in Hadibo or Suk, would follow a week or so later bringing the rest of our stores.

The mountain party set off late in the morning of Tuesday, August 14th, at the end of our first fortnight on the island. The camels arrived early in the morning but we could not agree to the prices that were asked, and as the camel-men did not contemplate bargaining they took all the camels away again. After an hour or so they came back and immediately began to demand exactly the same price as before—eighteen shillings per camel per day for the outward journey, fifteen shillings for the return journey. We protested that it was iniquitous to charge us for the return journey when the camels would merely be returning home, without loads, after dumping us at our destination.

"Yes," Ibrahim agreed, "but it's nothing to do with me. These people are very poor and . . . you know . . . simple. In Aden, when you go somewhere in a taxi you're not charged the return fare. But here . . . It's nothing to do with me. These people!" He continued to roll a very thin cigarette, shrugging his shoulders, smiling blandly, dissociating himself from the iniquity he was perpetrating. He said he was only acting as spokesman for the camel-men. He didn't tell me all the camels were his own.

The frenetic, impossible argument went on for another hour. It was hopeless. The camel-men had their orders, they stuck to their original demand, they didn't come down a cent. Then they began to take their camels away for the second time.

A few days previously I had a similar experience of the Socotran's reluctance to bargain. I had asked Ibrahim if he could arrange a dance celebration for the benefit of my movie camera.

Normally the dances are held after nightfall and are therefore impossible to film, so I had to arrange a special performance in the day time. Ibrahim brought along the muqaddem of the *ngoma*, the leader of the dance, a sullen and very uncomfortable African. He spoke to the muqaddem in Socotri and then turned to me, smiling, and said: "The muqaddem says that the fee is five shillings for each man taking part." I had expected to pay something but not that much. I offered a shilling. The muqaddem became more and more uncomfortable. Ibrahim, who was again "spokesman", said the fee was five shillings, nothing less. I refused this price and they both went away and never returned. They never broached the subject again. They preferred to receive nothing rather than receive a price lower than they had asked. This attitude amazed me.

When they began to take their camels away again I became desperate and accepted their price. I didn't know then what I should have done and I don't know now. No doubt after days or weeks of negotiation we might have got a better price. But time was against us and we had to have the camels. Probably we made our big mistake at the very beginning of the expedition, by having too much obviously expensive equipment with us; by putting all our money in one large money-box so that all could judge our wealth, instead of concealing it in small bags amongst our packages; by not standing our ground against the Sultan when first we met him.

Eventually the camels set out, thirty-one of them, and I followed them out across the plain, filming them. Then I left and watched them slowly disappear, a long and impressive line, over the plain.

Three days later I made the following entry in my diary:

Friday, August 17th. Muslim Friday. Our day of rest. Likewise the Arabs'. Peter feeling a little low, but not too low. The flies are terrible. Ali bin Khaled, Ibrahim's shifty-eyed brother, came round in the morning and demanded £80 for the Adho caravan for a three days' journey. It had taken Neil and myself only five hours to get to Adho. We made some demur and said we couldn't understand why camels took two days when one of our parties on foot had made it easily in one day. We also asked if he had brought a note from the others in the mountains, thinking that such a note would explain the situation. Ali became sly and crafty, said the road was very bad and that camels always went more slowly than a man in the mountains and it had genuinely taken two days to get there, and that there was no note for us. So it seemed that there was no alternative but to pay up. The man annoyed us very much with his crafty and insolent manner.

While resting after lunch, a messenger came to the door with a note for me from the mountain party. When asked how it had come he said that Ali had given it to him to bring and that Ali had been given it in the mountains! The letter reads:

"DEAR DOUGLAS,

"It has taken us two days to get to the tree where we had lunch the last time we came. Going is quite a bit slower with 31 camel-men and their camels than we two men and two donkeys. They did 4½ hours yesterday and 3 to-day and pretty hard going to keep them at that. We drove most of the camels ourselves, not to mention the men.

"However, we have found a very fine camp here, sheltered, terraced, water at hand and a grand view down the valley. It takes 35 minutes to Adho and is in easy access of the other valleys. We reckon it would have taken another day and a half to get to Adho and this seems ideal.

"We dismissed the men at 2 p.m. to-day and as I say they have given us seven and a half hours very indifferent service— whatever tales they may tell. We suggest you pay them 18/- for one day and 15/- for the second as arranged. They say it will take them 1½ days to reach Hadibo but I wouldn't pay them that if I were you.

"Best of luck from our rest home in the mountains,

NEIL."

We all felt that the time had come for a show-down with Ibrahim, so when, on coming back from a bathe about 5 p.m., we found him in our house we all thought our chance had come. He, however, clearly sensed how things were going and was at first unwilling to stay and then wouldn't sit down. Before we could make our protest he launched out into a complaint about the three shillings still due to him in payment of the donkey that took John and myself to Garrieh the other day. I only paid fifteen shillings for the two days instead of eighteen shillings because of the way the donkey-men had behaved. This may have been a mistake on my part but I refused to pay any more, whereupon Ibrahim became abusive and lost his temper, while Issa stood uncomfortably by looking rather awkward. This is the first time we have disturbed Ibrahim's inscrutable suavity. Peter asked him not to speak like that, so he turned abruptly on his heel and stormed out, rumpling his skull cap and driving away the patients waiting for Richard's attention in the surgery.

Events have now reached an interesting critical stage. Ibrahim controls all transport and labour facilities. These he can withdraw from us and without them we are useless, our work quite paralysed. We therefore have to keep on the right side of the Affraria Government, but we cannot just sit by and be swindled. Their weakness is that they want our money and this they cannot get if their services are altogether withdrawn from us.

The refrigerator is proving recalcitrant like everything else. Not that Richard gives it a moment's peace in which to quietly make ice—he is continually rocking and thumping it and turning the flame up and down. He has gummed foam rubber round the door for greater insulation, but now the door won't shut unless it is tied up with rope. Peter and I can't master knots so that only Richard is allowed to open the door. The machine's record to-day is unenviable:

  5.30 a.m. Temperature inside same as outside
  9.00 a.m. Temperature in ice-trays 40°F. and ice on cooling tubes
  10.30 a.m. Temperature rising inside
  12.00 p.m. Back red-hot
  12.30 p.m. Still red-hot
  6.30 p.m. Temperature as outside. Full of ants. Ants removed. Kicked and re-started
  7.30 p.m. Ants definitely nesting
  8.00 p.m. Water placed in ice-trays
  9.00 p.m. Water cooking

Saturday, August 18th. Ibrahim withdrew his labour from the excavation at Suk to-day. He had arranged that his Hadibo men should take over the digging from the Suk men, but now, as a result of yesterday's hubbub, he has prevented his men from going over there and sent a letter to Mesna forbidding the Suk men to work for us. They are all terrified of him and we therefore did no work to-day.

I woke up feeling decidedly dicky, but walked to Suk about 10 a.m. Rather violent diarrhoea (beside the green Arabian sea). I suddenly felt shocked and dizzy and went with Peter and Richard to Mesna's house. He gave me some milk and brewed some coffee for the others and I lay down for some time. I think tummy upset, plus lack of salt, plus lack of sleep has caused this. When woken up I felt considerably better. We walked back to Hadibo in the late afternoon and found a wireless signal from the British Agent and Resident Adviser at Mukalla, Colonel Boustead,* in reply to the one we had sent yesterday informing him of yesterday's events. Apparently Ibrahim also sent one yesterday, which was repeated by Colonel Boustead, for our benefit, demanding that Mr. Shinnie should treat the people well as other officers had done before him. Peter is understandably upset by this, especially as the criticism is quite unjustified. Peter yesterday confined himself entirely to translation and expressed no views other than mine. He only criticised Ibrahim for using immoderate language. I have arranged to speak to Colonel Boustead over the wireless at noon to-morrow (voice). He is non-committal, and I do not think he will be able to do much at this distance, but I think he should be informed about what can become a quite unpleasant situation.

The people remain generally friendly, thank goodness, and there is solid ice in the bottom left-hand tray of the refrigerator.

Bed at 8 after two Codeines and two Butobarbitones.

Sunday, August 19*th* ... 12.30 p.m. Spoke to Colonel Boustead over the radio. Reception very bad at first. Had to repeat everything many times. I explained that the trouble we were having had led to an impasse which was prejudicial to the scientific work of the expedition and that Ibrahim's criticism

*Colonel J. E. H. Boustead is a remarkable person. He is probably the only man ever to be publicly pardoned for desertion from the Royal Navy : in 1915, when a midshipman on a cruiser, he deserted his ship in South Africa and joined the South African Horse in the hope of getting to closer grips with the war : not long afterwards he won the M.C. on the western front. After the war he captained the British Olympic Pentathlon Team and was a member of the 1933 Everest Expedition. In 1935 he left the Army for political service in the Sudan, where he had already commanded the Sudan Defence Force. In 1940 he rejoined the Army, raised, trained and led his own Sudanese unit and again campaigned brilliantly against the Italians in Abyssinia, during which time he was mentioned in despatches and awarded the D.S.O. After the war he went to Arabia, where I imagine his place will be difficult to fill on his retirement—there are few men of Colonel Boustead's breed.

of Peter was quite unjustified. Under the conditions of radio reception to-day it was difficult to get the situation across. Colonel Boustead's voice (when I could hear it) sounded remarkably young and vigorous. He said he would send a cable to the Sultan asking him to be more co-operative and if possible to reduce prices somewhat, but added that he had no power to make him do so. "Fall out," he said at one stage. "There's just one more thing, sir," I said, and he replied "Well, er, fall in again." At the end he said: "In all your dealings with the Arabs, in spite of heat, flies, wind and other aggravations, be quiet, very quiet, speak and act softly." This is excellent advice. At least none of us, thank the Lord, has ever offered any physical violence to these people, though in the last few days we have often felt like it, I must say. To get the worst of a straightforward bargain is one thing, but to be cunningly tricked out of considerable sums is quite a different matter. And yet, money matters apart, these people are as pleasant as you could wish.

We arranged to speak again tomorrow.

During the day Ali bin Khaled, Ibrahim's brother, called on us three times: once to be paid for a *shamlah*, once to be paid for the camel Peter takes to Suk, once to be paid for a donkey. In the evening he came again, after I had sent for him. I asked him for camels for Tuesday and he said he would have to ask Ibrahim. He is a small and shifty man, with African blood in him—born of the same father as Ibrahim, but a different mother. His eyes narrow when you talk to him, as though he is scheming something around every word you say, and he only smiles when you give him money, which you always do because he never appears at any other time. Later a note came from Ibrahim saying that if we paid the 3/- still owing to the donkey-man perhaps we would get some camels. We had no alternative but to pay this sum, and so lost this several days' battle—as we were bound to if we wanted to stir out of Hadibo again.

Everybody is very low because of the situation here.

Monday, August 20th. Arranged for camel transport to take us to Kishin to-morrow. Got a letter from John:

"As soon as you have read this letter burn it and swallow the ashes.

"Life here has many compensations—the exhilarating

climate, the superb views and the matchless cooking of the faithful Abdullahi; but should you be coming up in the next few days would you bring: (a) some DDT, (b) some Gemmaxane powder, (c) some more rice, (d) 2 or 3 spoons, (e) a map of Socotra, (f) met. equipment.

"Mike spends busy days collecting and labelling lizards, plants, etc. Neil makes domiciliary visits on mountain tops. I have got my diary up to date.

"We are employing at 4/- a day a local bedu head-man. So far he has stolen an axe, a dixie, a mug, a plate, and Neil's *mushadda*. Fagin done got nuttin' on him.

"Lots of love, wish you were here.

   "Wassammi   Ali   Hassan.

"P.S. Abdullahi wishes me to convey to you all many salaams, and to be remembered with a similar greeting to Ali. He would also like Ali to send up their personal ration of rice and sugar.

        "Hassan (the fat one)."

Spoke with Boustead at 10 a.m. and again at 6.15 p.m. and told him that the position was unchanged. He said he would send a second cable to the Sultan suggesting he reduced prices somewhat. The W/T staff are in rather poor shape with dysentery, urine gone bad and cough. Our cigarettes keep them fairly happy. I keep getting little scribbled notes from Mubarak the W/T operator on the backs of signal forms asking for cigarettes. I got one this morning:

"Mr. Botting pse I am very good from you if you send for me anything cigarettis stop because I have nothing cigarettis in Socotra stop many salaami for all you W/O Socotra Mubarik Obiskohi."

He only lives a hundred yards down the street but prefers to send these messages in his strange telegraphese. As the only English he knows is what he has learnt from sending wireless messages I think he does very well. The garrison have weevils in their flour and are terribly bored.

Dr. Corkill requested information about any epidemics, so we sent a message back: "None but the itching palm."

We had tea with the merchant from the Persian Gulf and his little boy and a friend from Bahrein this evening. Later a wedding started up, with drumming and singing and ululuing from the women. It went on all night and must effectively prevent the marriage being consummated on that night. Perhaps that is the idea. I think the marriage was solemnized in a house during the afternoon and this evening's performance was the general nuptial celebration. I saw the bridegroom, rather finely dressed, sitting in the street with Thani and one or two others. He was about 16 or 17 years old and I daresay the bride was somewhat younger, though I never saw her. At dusk they all gathered inside the mosque and when they came out they assembled in a large crowd and began moving slowly down the street, singing and waving palm fronds, preceded by some drummers. I went out to tape-record them but a negro came up to me and told me in no uncertain terms that Christians were not allowed. "*Mafish ruksa!*" he shouted. "Not allowed!" Later the crowd split up into two groups, one composed of males and the other of females, which proceeded to circum- ambulate the town independently, singing a very fast song very excitedly. This went on till about midnight. On one occasion the female group came down the street in which our house is situated, ululating splendidly, and I was able to record the noise they made by placing my microphone against a crack in the door. Eventually the two groups settled down at opposite ends of the town, still singing. About one o'clock I rose from my bed and crept down the street towards the noise made by one of the groups. I then peeped surreptitiously round the corner of the street and saw the male group singing and dancing. It was a most extraordinary sight, for all the men and boys were jigging round a bonfire, singing. It looked like a witches' congress. I started the tape-recorder and, edging along the bottom of the wall, poked the microphone round the corner. After a few minutes the Hadibo "queer" came up and started jabbering in a high shrieking voice. Normally I think he lives in the Sultan's palace. His oily hair falls down to his shoulders and he reeks of scent. In order to get rid of him I inadvertently strayed round the street corner. Immediately the drumming and singing stopped dead and up came the negro again. "*Mafish ruksa!*" he shouted. I felt a bit of a fool, I must say, standing there in my baggy blue pyjamas and bare feet, clutching a microphone, with numerous eyes fixed upon me.

I have been thinking about the present situation here and it seems to me that Ibrahim and ourselves were complaining and disagreeing about two entirely different things. Ibrahim was not at all concerned about the fraud he had perpetrated whereby we had to pay £80 for the camel caravan to Kishin instead of £50: he was only bothered about the three shillings we owed him (or his donkey-man—same thing). We on the other hand couldn't care less about the three shillings, except as a matter of principle, while we cared much for the £30 we had lost. We have both been doing the other side down in the other side's eyes, but I think both sides will agree that it is we who have been most done down. Anyway, the camels are coming to-morrow, at the same price, and I suppose the matter is at an end.

To celebrate the eve of our departure we shot some red Very lights over the town after dusk. The whole town was alive with chatter afterwards and small boys were rushing out to see the fireworks.

It is very unsatisfactory to leave Hadibo under circumstances like this. Fortunately the ordinary Socotran in the street has always remained friendly towards us.

Tuesday, August 21st. Left Hadibo at 7.45 with 17 camels and 2 donkeys for Kishin where the rest of the party is now established. . . . We did 2 hours over the plain and stopped for an hour at the foot of the wadi where Ali brewed tea on a very small fire in a very high wind in three minutes. Then up the mountains slowly with a stop at 12 for prayers. We were highly suspicious of the camel-men and determined to get them to Kishin this day, so we timed them at their prayers, heathen that we are, though we waited until they had completely finished before telling them to go on. Several times we had to urge them on when they seemed like faltering. Ali bin Khaled is not a bad camel muqaddem, rogue though he is. When we started off after the first break at the foot of the mountains he was first on his camel, exhorting his men like some sort of medieval knight. He sat on top of his camel, stuck his right arm out and made the camel go round in a circle. The camel went round and round in the circle, the radius getting smaller and tighter, until the camel was turning like a top and Ali fell right off the hump. I am not sure what he was trying to prove by doing this, but he reminded me of the oozlum bird. I didn't have much idea where Kishin camp was, and after we had crossed a ridge I asked the one-eyed African camel-boy called Mabruk where

Kishin was. He pointed up the mountain-side and there about a mile away I could just see two green tents, very tiny and lost in the immensity of the mountains. I was very relieved. When we got nearer we could see three pale little figures standing on a huge rock watching us coming. We reached Kishin at 2.30 in very good time, the journey much shorter and less tiresome than we had anticipated. The camp is wonderfully situated and we found tea, whisky-sour, and freshly baked currant buns and bread waiting for us. We are glad to have seen the last of Hadibo for the time being.

CHAPTER NINE

A WALK IN THE SUN

THAT night at Kishin I slept under four blankets and woke only at seven, to find Ali had brought tea. We drank tea, sitting in the veranda of the large tent, reading books and watching the fine rain blow down the valley. The rain, after Hadibo, was delightful, and the air was clammy and cool and pleasantly refreshing. We put on sweaters and took it easy. We lit pipes and smoked them with pleasure for almost the first time on the island.

The camp could not have been better situated. It was sited on a flat patch of grass, on an ancient man-made terrace. The large tent was on the edge of the terrace, with its entrance facing down the valley to the plain, distant and hazy 2,000 feet below, and beyond that the sea. Behind it was our smaller tent, and the whole camp was sheltered from the wind by a vast black rock. Abdullahi had built his kitchen against the side of the rock and a tarpaulin was stretched over it as protection against the rain. We erected the fly-sheet against another part of the rock and put our stores in there, and a smaller tent we set up for Ali and Abdullahi to sleep in.

On our left the hillside sloped steeply up and ended in gaunt crags a thousand feet above us. On our right there was a grassy slope which led to the stream that trickled down the wadi bed. The grey lichen that covers all the rest of the red granite of the mountains does not grow in the stream beds, and there one can see the real colour and texture of the rock of these old mountains. We got our water from a pool in this stream, a hundred yards from the camp, and we could bathe in another pool lower down which John one day had cleaned and deepened. The water was very cold.

On a hillside fifty yards above the camp, under the shade of a huge spreading fig tree, obscured by the dense shrubbery that grows everywhere on the mountainsides, was the privy. Richard had built a thunder-box for the privy, hewn out of a champagne crate. It was an excellent device but bred all the

flies that plagued our camp. A path ran down the hill past the
privy and occasionally a bedu would wander down the path
at an inopportune moment. Early one morning, when Peter
occupied the thunder-box, a bedu called Poor Relation
meandered down the track and smiled vacuously when he saw
Peter still as a stone amid the foliage under the fig tree. He turned
off the path and came up to Peter, said "*Salaam*" and shook
Peter's hand, while Peter, feeling at a disadvantage, tried to
end the interview as quickly as possible without seeming to be
too abrupt. For this and other reasons some of us rejected the
camp privy and wandered over the hillside to find our own
personal accommodation.

The camp was overhung by an acacia and another fig tree,
and under the acacia were three piles of large flat stones. This
was the ablutions. After morning tea we collected bowls of
hot water from Abdullahi and a mug of hot water for shaving
and spent a minimum of time under the dripping tree honouring
the gods of cleanliness. By now some of us had beards. John had
a wild and uncultivated auburn beard; Peter had a distinguished
grey goatee; Richard had a beard like a spade and I had a black
pointed Arab beard, which everybody said was sinister.

We had chupatees for breakfast most mornings, lathered
with butter and strawberry jam, with slices of Abdullahi's
matchless white bread, baked in half a kerosene can. Ali
served us at table and we became endeared to the sight of his
straggly and rather wild black figure in a plastic mackintosh
jumping over guy-ropes with a plate of steaming Porage in
each hand.

During the day we did things, which I shall speak about
later, and before nightfall returned to camp. Some of us bathed
in the cold stream, and we changed into long trousers and warm
clothes, and sat round the table in the verandah of the tent
drinking whisky in the light of a pressure lamp. Then we had
dinner while the moon appeared sporadically between rushing
clouds between the mountain tops, and the only sound in the
wet cold darkness of the mountains was the wind bellowing in
the gullies. We lay in bed at nights reading and slept as the
wind came over Adho and flapped the sides of the tent. Four
of us slept in the big tent head to toe, and if we were all in
camp together, which was not very often, two of us slept in the
small tent, which was used mainly as a laboratory, Mike's

plant presses and preserving bottles and killing jars on one side, Neil's medical equipment on the other, with a table made from the planks of the refrigerator crate.

It was a very comfortable and efficient camp in the mountains, but very damp. Everything smelt of damp and metal corroded. If our clothes were washed they never dried, although they were hung up on a washing-line for several days. Every morning we would find our laundry blown off the line and lying on the mud. Eventually Ali used to go down the wadi to the place where the sunlight started and the rain ended and wash our clothes in the pool and dry them on rocks in the sun, and then bring them back to the camp.

Kishin is normally used as a resting place for camels on the main overland route from Hadibo to the south. It is reckoned as a day's stage in the journey, and the camel-men sleep in the caves behind the rock that sheltered our camp. Or else they go up to Salim's place.

Salim was the bedu head-man whom John employed for a week to fetch wood and water. During that time he stole all sorts of things, aided and abetted by Saad, his nephew. Whenever he was accused of a theft he looked hurt and tearful. A small child would be seen hurrying up the hillside to Salim's cave, and, after a brief interval, hurrying down the hillside clutching a bundle; then a search would reveal the missing articles under a bush. There wasn't much you could do about Salim because he owned the terrace we had camped on, without asking his permission. We just kept a watchful eye on him. He lived in a cave two hundred yards up the hillside and his three sweet light-skinned daughters and his smallest bandy-legged pig-tailed son sat all day on the hillside overlooking the camp, watching us, while his slightly older sons, little Ali and little Hamet, pottered shyly round the tents. Saad lived near Salim, all by himself in a minute rubble hut. For this reason we called him the Poor Relation, and after a while he used to come up and say in delightful troglodytic English "I am the Poor Relation." He was a small man, with only a tuft of beard, and he grinned continually. He had a birth mark on one side of his face, and an enlarged malaria spleen. Salim was a larger man with a beard and a red *futah*, hitched up with a belt of plaited strips of cowhide. He had a way of talking like a child, and the way he pronounced Abdullahi's name was music to

I

our ears, and we hung on the sound, liquid and harmonious with a note of imprecation, and imitated it as best we could. But Abdullahi himself did not think much of either of these two. "They come like *rats*," he said, and made a crawling motion with his hands, his fingers extended like claws. It was a good imitation of a chameleon. "If I catch 'im steal I kill 'im," he threatened. He had a long, sharp-bladed *panga* which he kept by him for this purpose. He was in earnest and I visualised with trepidation the situation that would arise if he carried out his threat. When Salim and Saad stole 50 lb. of our rice and 25 lb. of sugar (the bulk of the cook's rations) Abdullahi wanted us to lend him our shotgun. He waited up several nights hoping to catch them as they crawled down the hillside "like *rats*". Ali, who was a different sort of character, was afraid of the bedouin and did not like the mountains and was glad to return, a few weeks later, to Hadibo and his friend Mohammed and the *harim* which he sometimes visited surreptitiously. He confined himself to more general comments. "These people is all *alimans*," he said, "all goats. They don't know nothing." An aliman, we discovered, was Ali's version of animal.

The day the rest of us moved to Kishin was the end of our third week on the island. We liked Kishin very much, but on the third day after our arrival some of us went down to the plain again.

Peter said he had read that there were charnel-houses at Ras Momi, the extreme eastern end of the island, and he would like to go there and look for them. John, Richard and myself, though not much excited about charnel-houses, wished to have a look at another part of the island, and so decided to accompany Peter on his quest. We discussed the projected trip one evening after a very large meal. We would travel very light, we decided, living only on bully beef and biscuits. We were so replete at the time that we could not envisage how this diet would work out in practice. Our plan was to go to Suk, spend a day there in an attempt to finish the excavation which had stopped because of the trouble with Ibrahim, and then go to Ras Momi along the north coast. We would look for the charnel-houses there and then round the easterly point of the island and travel back along the south coast, finding our way up to Kishin by way of one of the southern wadi systems. We estimated that this would take seven days, a reasonable estimate. We would

take three donkeys, each with a donkey-man, a jerrycan of
water because we believed there was little or no water where
we were going, camp-beds, binoculars and cameras, and nothing
else. We would have to go on foot everywhere, because the
donkeys would be loaded and the country was impassable for
camels.

The next day, a Friday, the four of us went down the mountains again. We passed the Little Sultan's palace on the way
across the plain to Suk, two square, white, unimpressive houses
with a small minaret at the side of one of them. The slaves
came out to greet us. They lived in near-by African thatch huts,
and cultivated the gardens there. We saw dates on the twig for
the first time and examined a ditch that ran from somewhere
near the Adho valley and turned unexpectedly into a metal
pipe that ended in a cement tank near the palace, complete
with an inflow sludge trap and an outflow to the near-by plantations. It was the most impressive water conservation system we
had seen, only spoilt because all the pipe lines were disjointed.
At Suk we rested at Mesna's house and ate some of his delicious
dates and lay on our camp-beds till three. John and Richard
went to Mound 11, an exploratory trench, and chiselled the
dry earth with the sharp end of a ranging pole. They then
removed the loosened earth with the spade, while Peter talked
about Oxford and the Sudan. I rested under the palm trees,
ostensibly to look after our equipment but grateful to be left
alone. There was a little man inside my head beating at the
back of my eyeballs with a mallet, I had a boil on my posterior
as a result of riding a camel bareback between Suk and Hadibo,
and there was something wrong with my inside. The others
came back after digging a chunk out of the mound, carrying a
broken ranging pole. My boil burst with what felt like a sharp
snap and I washed my underclothes in the sea. We ate half a
tin of bully each and some Marmite smeared on lifeboat
biscuits. We made a fire just to see how easily it could be done
but we had nothing to cook but water. It was a very dull meal
and after it we went to sleep on the beach. It was cool, cooler
than it had ever been on the plain, and the flies crawled over
us during the night and disturbed our sleep.

The next day we breakfasted off dates supplied by Mesna
and employed four men and six boys to carry on the dig. While
the work was in progress Thani bin Ali turned up from Hadibo

with a letter from Ibrahim in a brown envelope, headed in Arabic and in English underneath:

"Affraria Government
Geshen, Sahoot, Sokotra."

The letter inside had the same inscription in blue ink, the letters uncertainly printed. But Sokotra was spelt Sakotra this time. The letter was written in ink in a beautiful neat hand, signed at the bottom by Ibrahim, and stamped with a rubber stamp: "Socotra [the third different spelling] Ibrahim Bin Khaled Thkalli". Peter could not read all the words and asked Thani to speak them. The letter said that the Sultan wished to offer us every help and would we call on him if we wanted anything, but keep him informed of our movements round the island and only obtain the services of head-men in the villages. This was a welcome note.

John left for Kishin immediately after breakfast and returned at 1.30, having completed the journey up the mountains and down in seven hours, a most commendable feat which earned him a great reputation among the locals as a strong man among the sahibs. He brought back more food with him, and some things to cook it in and some utensils to eat it with. The previous night's meal had been morale-lowering. He brought rice, condensed milk, Nescafé, Porage, barley sugar, lemonade, two tins of fruit and a bottle of sauce.

We dined well in the evening, after the day's excavations.

The donkey-men the next morning said they did not know the way to Ras Momi. Then after a while they said they knew it perfectly well, as though they were hurt that we should think they didn't. After some more talking and loading the donkeys we started out at 6.30 a.m., having breakfasted on a pint of hot sweetened coffee.

We trudged along the seashore eastwards of Suk, the Jebel Hawari towering above us with sand blown up against it, and in the course of time passed what was left of Sultan Ahmed's palace. Sultan Ahmed was the war-time Sultan, the present Sultan's predecessor. I cannot imagine why he should have chosen to live in such a desolate and isolated position, with not a blade of grass or drop of water anywhere near. We went on over sand dunes and passed inland of Khor Deleisha, an erosion wadi debouching into the sea. The country was brown and burnt, full of flinty stones, dryness and barrenness. It went gently up and down and the path went straight over it. At a

place called Debeni we found a small shelter erected on sticks
and drank water from a pot that stood in the shade of the
shelter. We reached Ma'abath at ten and stopped there to
wait for the donkeys. There were cows lying in the shade of
the oasis and a pool which was stagnant and smelt somewhat,
with banks of tough short grass overhung by palms. We stripped
off and bathed in the pool, which was no more than two feet
deep, and dipped our heads into the water, watching the mud
and algae that we had disturbed float suspended in the browny-
green water while the water drained out of our hair back into
the water of the pool. We washed our clothes in the dirty water
and hung them out to dry on the hot rocks, weighted down
with stones so that the wind should not blow them away. In no
time at all the clothes were dry, and felt pleasant to put on when
the time came. Mesna joined in the general exuberance and
immersed himself at the other end of the pool. We made a fire
in the sand and cooked Porage and coffee and ate biscuits and
Marmite. This was our breakfast-cum-lunch. It was always
better, Peter said, to start as early in the morning as possible,
going without breakfast in order to get as far as possible on the
way before the heat became too great. So the pattern of our
march was an early start after plenty of coffee sweetened with
condensed milk, and a brisk walk to the next water place, and
a stop at between 10 and 11, for food and siesta, and then a
start at 2 p.m. and a brisk walk to the next water place in time
to cook the evening meal before it got dark, at 6 p.m. The
donkey-men arrived an hour after us, rather tired but very
cheerful and friendly. They went at the pace of their donkeys,
neither faster nor slower than was right and natural, and it
was a pleasure to trek with them because they were reliable
and uncomplaining. Mesna we knew of old, an excellent man,
well-mannered and hospitable, as strong and as game as an old
ox. He trotted after us on his short dumpy legs and we always
knew he was there because we could hear the pad-pad of his
bare feet on the flints and the heavy breathing at his extended
effort. His feet went like piston-rods and he had never travelled
so fast in all his life. Really we employed Mesna as a guide while
the other two drove the donkeys, but Mesna did not like to go
in front, so I went in front instead and set the pace, and if I
went off the path we all went off the path until it came to
Mesna's turn and he woke up from his reveries and shouted at

us. This was effective unless Mesna was some way behind. The name of one of the donkey-men was Mohammed. He wore a yellow vest and had two front teeth missing. He was unendingly smiling and spoke Swahili after a fashion. The other man's name I did not know. He had a markedly round forehead surmounted by a round dirty linen cap and he rarely laughed. The donkey-men made a lunch of coffee and dates in the plantation and passed the hubble-bubble pipe round among themselves. They carry the pipe dismantled in a little goatskin, and bring it out at the least provocation. Next to their wives, and a little money, smoking is the greatest of their pleasures, and probably the most abiding of them, for they can indulge it all their lives, being never too old for it, and even in disaster and distress they cannot be deprived of it. But the smoking makes them cough badly, for the tobacco is rough and uncured.

A lean old man came up to us while we rested and asked for medicine. He was quite ill and had a racking cough. He sat down on a stone with his head in his hands and we saw he was feverish and that he had been burned by the *wasm* all round the perimeter of one lung, probably as a treatment for pneumonia. The burns had been rubbed with mud which had dried grey on his wrinkled flesh. He sat there spluttering and mumbling distractedly while Richard tried to get him to take camoquin tablets for his malaria. These tablets are bitter as gall and must be swallowed whole immediately with water. But the old man chewed the first one he was given, vomited the second and refused the third. After the second tablet he went into a coughing fit and sat groaning while we photographed him, an object of anthropological study because of his *wasm* marks. We had to go and I shook his hand and John said to him in English: "Goodbye, old man. I hope you get better."

> "I heard the old, old men say,
>   'Everything alters,
>   And one by one we drop away.'
> They had hands like claws, and their knees
> Were twisted like the old thorn trees
>   by the waters.
> I heard the old, old men say,
>   'All that's beautiful drifts away
>   Like the waters.'"

The old man hardly saw us go, mumbling thank you, thank you, and we left him rather worse than we found him, with nothing more tangible than a little more hope in that hopeless place. We went away and forgot about him soon afterwards. It is difficult for most of us in our own hygienic and well-doctored world to conceive what it must be like to be ill and without hope of recovery but a blind faith in the will of Allah, with no knowledge of the devouring sickness and the only solution a recourse to the red-hot iron on the bare flesh. When I saw the old man I had an insight into the condition of despair and it was like staring through the gates of hell.

We set off at 2 p.m. and Mesna insisted that we keep together with the donkeys because the way henceforward was obscure and we might lose it. So we walked behind the donkeys at a slow and tiring pace through the Ma'abath valley. This is a great water-catchment area, now dry and reddish brown in the sun, covered with shoulder-high leafless bushes, no grass anywhere. We went down the wadi getting tired and cross until we dropped steeply down into the Garrieh Basin. The hamlet of Garrieh was perched on the western edge of the erosion wadi, and all the people of the place came out and perched on the edge of the cliff to watch us as we progressed wearily down the track. The khor is salt and tidal and stretches for some miles inland. As it nears the sea it gets deeper and wider, and though a bar of sand appears almost to close its mouth it is apparently impossible to ford except a mile inland. In the rainy season it must take all the drainage of the Garrieh plain. A decrepit green *sambuq* lay on the eastern bank. We thought it was a rotting wreck, but it turned out later that it was the Sultan's dhow, one of two on the island, which manages to sail to Aden and Zanzibar. Judging from its appearance from a distance, it must have been at sea since the time of the Prophet. We came down to the khor's edge and clambered over some rocks to get to the fordable part, and as I breasted the top of the rocks the wind hit me suddenly with an angry violence and whipped the sunglasses off my face and blew the jungle hat that was jammed on my head into the waters of the khor. I became suddenly immensely angry. If I could have done the wind injury I would have done it, but I could only rant impotently against the impersonal force that had baited me at the end of the day.

We camped that night at the edge of a plantation. The floor

of the plantation was covered in the dead branches of date palms. I slept only half an hour that night because insects crawled all over me. About one in the morning I got up to look for some water and sleeping tablets. The others were awake also and we all drank water and swallowed barbitone but slept not at all and got up before dawn.

We set out after coffee soon after 6 a.m. We went through the miasmatic palm grove, and came out of it near the village of Arrirahun, a collection of rubble huts with a few people living in them. By half-past nine we had reached the oasis of Timareh, a small village by the shore, with a delightful little palm grove through which bubbled a shallow stream of fresh, curiously flat water. There were young women at the head of the stream, where it sprang out of the earth, filling their clay pots with the water. They ran away when we came, gliding over the stony ground like frantic mannequins with the half-full pots on their heads. We drank the water, ate a little, and bathed in the sandy cove that lies in front of Timareh. The impact of cold salt water on hot bodies that have trudged some distance with a mental outlook conditioned by flies, sweat and the sight of endless sharp brown stones and the bandy legs or pigeon toes of the person walking in front, is electric. The cool water lapping round the disgruntled flesh produces an immediate physical and mental reaction, a return to normality, even to sanity, a happy phlegmatic condition. So we bathed in the green sea and felt better and better. We swam beneath the surface and found nothing growing, only black rocks and sand. The wind blew in sudden fierce gusts and drove the sand off the beach so that it cut our backs like tiny stinging flails and made us submerge.

We walked for another hour and a half and came to the village of Sigira. We wanted to go further, but Mesna said the donkeys were tired and that there was no more water to be found for many more miles beyond Sigira, so we reluctantly camped, having travelled only a short distance during the day. The water of the village came from a well and had the familiar taste of camel urine. We treated it with our disinfecting Halazone tablets, and mixed the flavours of urine and chlorine with lemonade powder to produce a remarkable drink.

We camped that night in the lee of a stone wall that surrounded a grove of date palms, amongst fleshy, bean-like shrubs.

A small girl-child visited us, looking like a pixie with hair close-cropped except for a fringe of longer hair round the top of her head. She had beads of coloured amber round her neck and watched us shyly. She was a sweet little kid and it seemed strange to think that she would grow up and die in this lonely, arid place, knowing no more of Socotra, let alone the world, than that crude village of a score of stone huts on a barren shore. We gave her a barley sugar and she came back with her father. He carried in his arms a baby girl who clutched a bare knife with which she prodded him from time to time.

Another old man came for Richard's attention, covered with scabs. Richard suspected smallpox and on enquiry found that over twenty people had recently died of it in that neighbourhood.

Sigira lies between the sea and the sheer scarp of the limestone plateau which occupies the whole of the eastern end of the island. The edge of the plateau, grey and rotted and fallen away, ran parallel with the narrow strip of coast along which our track led. At this point it was over 500 feet above us and we wondered who or what was on top of it. There seemed to be no way of getting up there.

We slept peacefully in the lee of the wall, while the wind came furiously in the night and shook the palms and stirred up the dust around us.

The next morning very early we set off on the last leg of our trek. The path led a little way inland from Sigira and we climbed round a hill in confused country which got wilder and wilder the further we went. The boulders became larger, the track less distinct. Massive slabs of granite, like slices of cheese standing on end, littered the path. Some of them were the size of a large house and must have been tossed by some gigantic force during hectic days. For a while there were metayne trees growing, then nothing but a few camel thorns and clumps of low useless plants between the stones. And then nothing at all. The path led back to the edge of the sea, and we stumbled over the rubble and the black lava rock and the sand dunes, going straight on when we could no longer detect the track, or following the sporadic footprints of someone who had preceded us, his large toe clearly imprinted in the sand, like a dog's foot in wet cement. When his footprints disappeared on the indelible rock it was interesting to speculate how his appreciation of the line of least topographical resistance compared with ours. Sometimes, when the next stretch of sand appeared, we could find no trace of his feet, and imagined that he had suddenly become airborne in the wind or died abruptly on the last patch of rock. Or perhaps he was just sitting behind a rock cocking a snoot at us and saying "Ya, find your own way, you beggars."

The wind became very strong as we approached the end of the island, lashing a slaty blue sea into paroxysms of white spray and scattering the tops of the waves into a blizzard-like film that swept across the surface of the sea and veered with the eddyings of the wind. The rocks were black and lifeless. Clouds covered the place and we felt spots of rain. Above us towered the eaten-away, drab and formidable cliff of the plateau, 1,500 feet high and pock-marked with deep caves.

We passed the hamlet of Gobhill and its satellite Yobhill. The former was deserted because its wells had dried up. Each dry stone hut had its own courtyard, with the worn branches of trees still in their place where the women attached their querns to grind the maize. One of the houses had a minute wooden door three feet high, fastened with a wooden lock. When we passed the next hamlet a man came out of a house, having seen us from a distance, and bawled continually at us until he reached us.

"Where is water?" we asked him.

"Water! Water!" he shouted. "Water!"

He was an astonishingly exuberant little man in clothes incongruously bright for the depressing place he lived in. He shouted continuously at the top of his voice, his agile beard-fringed mouth a foot away from our ears. He passed the time of day with Peter who muttered commonplaces to him and received raucous replies which were utterly incomprehensible to him. At last he directed us:

"Go to below the broken rocks beyond the farthest white. Water! Farewell!"

He disappeared back to his lonely hamlet and we went on towards where the cliff was broken-topped beyond the farthest of two enormous sand dunes that had been blown up against the escarpment to the height of many hundreds of feet. We crossed the red and black and old and deserted and unfriendly narrow strip of shore and came to the sand dunes. The going was hard in the soft sand and we were nearing the end of our tether and very thirsty when, coming round a green desert bush, we almost fell into a spring of clear water. We had passed the farthest white and were indeed below the broken rocks.

Fikar Springs was the name of this place and to reach it we had marched four hours without stopping. The spring bubbled out of the sand and made its way a hundred yards to the sea through a narrow bed of fine white sand. Little fishes were trying to make their way upstream driven by some elemental urge which served only to make life difficult for them. Their maximum strength just equalled the force of the stream so that they remained suspended in mid-stream, waggling their ends violently till they tired and were swept towards the sea again. I would like to have told them that if they reached the end of the stream they would only succeed in disappearing into the bowels of the earth. Perhaps this was the idea, a sort of Freudian urge to return to the womb of Mother Earth, like mystics and worms and pot-holers. They were very young fish. We drank handfuls of the water, the best of the whole journey, and paddled in the stream, nibbled by the frustrated fishes.

The donkeys arrived an hour and a half later, very tired. John had disappeared to climb up into a cavernous hole half way up the cliff-side. The cave looked only twenty minutes away and when John had been gone over an hour and not yet appeared on the cliff face we became worried and scoured the place with our binoculars. We at last found him, crawling on his hands and knees along a narrow ledge, the size of a fly. By comparison with him the entrance to the cave was enormous. We were amazed at our underestimate of both the size and the distance of the cliff. Throughout the expedition we continually underestimated this country and the time and effort required to traverse it. John eventually appeared looking very hot, stumbling and falling down the sand dune.

After a brief lunch we set off again at 1.15, leaving the donkeys and the donkey-men behind, with the object of reaching Ras Momi itself and looking for the charnel-houses for which we had ostensibly come. The clouds were very gloomy and the wind occasionally gusted and blew sand in our faces, which stung so much that we had to cover them with our arms, crouching with our backs to the wind.

The plateau began to dwindle. We came out into hilly, yellow country, devoid of any vegetation, the plateau stuttering down to the sea in a series of ever-diminishing hills. We could see the end of the island, a narrow projection of sand, and the Southern Plain, and a village of small stone houses where three men lived and nobody and nothing else. We went down to see them and they were neither sorry nor glad nor surprised to see us, but sat like inanimate brown things half-wrapped in cloths. Just as we arrived a surprisingly plump young man (plumpness in this country is most unusual, and I cannot recall anybody else who had so much flesh on him) was being greeted according to the complicated ritual of kissing and handshaking that prevails on Socotra. He had a new white cloth on and had obviously returned from a journey. I suspected him of being the man whose big toes I had followed all day. These people lived on nothing but fish and shellfish. All around their houses were the remains of their meals—the backbones of fish of all sizes, and the shells of crustacea and turtles. Some of the huts were roofed with turtle shell. I remember wondering at the time why these people chose to go on living in such a place, because it was the loneliest and barest I had ever seen in my life. No doubt the pull of birth-place and home, friends and relations, the familiar and customary, is as strong here as anywhere, and no doubt they would be unhappy if they were moved to where there was grass and water and fruit and goats.

We went down a slope between two yellow hills, past the tracks of perambulating hermit crabs, to the beach of the Southern Plain. The water here was rougher, and westwards the clouds glowered darkly over the plain and the even steeper escarpment of the plateau. This country was impossible for animals, as Mesna had said. A fine salt spray blew overland from the sea and we sat on the pebbles and smoked a cigarette and watched the sea pounding on the rocks. As far as we could see southward the ocean, which if you went far enough would take you to the Antarctic, was covered in low, grey, driving cloud.

We returned the way we had come, leaning against the frenzied wind, and reached the springs exhausted to find the donkey-boys brewing coffee for us and full of praise for our long journey. They gave us dates and we gave them biscuits and then cooked Porage on their fire, while Mohammed examined the Scotsman on the Porage tin who is dressed in a rather short *futah* and eternally about to throw a cannon-ball.

That evening we went down to the beach and I again had that impression, so strong to me and peculiar to this island, of standing at the beginning of the world. The mountains to me had seemed elemental. So elemental that life had not been created and the mountains waited with an austere and brooding patience for life to crawl out of the scum. And here at Fikar life was coming. The whole shore was alive and creeping with crabs, crabs crawling out of the sea, small white crabs scuttling with a terrifying premeditated sideways shuffle up the beach, up the bank of the spring, to a large bush. As each wave lapped gently on to the sand more and more crabs stepped out of the water, flocking like an incredibly sinister football crowd to whatever attraction lay under the bush. We had a torch with us and held it down at ground level and shone it along the beach. The result was horrible and repulsive. Each crab had developed an enormous long shadow and it seemed that each crab was a creeping monster. The beach for as far as we could see crawled with pre-Cambrian crustacea. It *was* the beginning of the world.

The next morning John spent some time photographing a narrow track in the sand that disappeared under a little stone. He said it fascinated him as he believed it had been made by a small man on a very small bicycle. I was not the only one, it seemed, who was losing touch with reality on this extraordinary island. . . .

Ras Momi is a dangerous place. The current runs very strong by the end of the island and all passing ships, sailing by from Suez to India, are warned to give the island a wide berth. The combination of wind and current can drag a ship on to the rocky coast. In addition, this part of the island is invariably covered in cloud and mist, and there are dangerous hidden rocks, extending seaward from the Cape. Many ships have struck these rocks and sunk with loss of life. Two of the worst shipwrecks occurred at the end of the last century.

In 1887 the North German Lloyd liner *Oder* struck Ras Momi in the middle of the night. There was a tiger on board, being carried to the Berlin Zoo, and when the survivors of the wreck were rescued the tiger was released from its cage. Arabs on the land, waiting to loot the ship, watched the tiger for over a week pacing up and down the deserted deck, becoming thinner and thinner, and howling. When the looters eventually came on board they found the tiger a neat pile of skin and bones on the deck. I sometimes wonder what would have happened if the tiger had managed to reach land.

A much worse disaster occurred at the same place ten years later. The P. & O. First-Class mail boat *Aden*, a steel screw steamer of 3,925 tons, carrying 138 passengers and crew and a valuable cargo of 2,500 tons of brick tea, tin, silk and mails, left Colombo at the beginning of June at the height of a particularly severe south-west monsoon. The vessel became 27 days overdue, and on the 28th and 29th the Press printed reports that two ships had seen "an unknown steamer in a dangerous position on the east end of Socotra, apparently abandoned". The next day, in the middle of Queen Victoria's Jubilee Celebrations, the news was confirmed. The *Aden* was wrecked, with great loss of life. For the first and only time since the island had risen above the waves in Permian times Socotra was the centre of national publicity. The Jubilee Celebrations were effectively dampened. Questions were asked in the House. Why was there no lighthouse on Socotra, in view of its menace to Far Eastern shipping and the many wrecks that had occurred there? An angry old man wrote to the *Pall Mall Gazette*: the cause of the wreck was indisputably the malicious practice of employing lascar seamen who, Goddam it, didn't know one end of an oar from the other. The Queen sent a message of sympathy.

The *Aden* had struck Ras Momi at 2.50 a.m. on June 9th, having been unable to take sights for two days and nights due to the fog. The only order from the bridge had been "Stop". The water rose quickly and put the fires out. Enormous waves pounded the ship which was firmly stuck on the reef. By 4 p.m. all the front woodwork, bridge, chart-room, captain's cabin and funnel had been washed away. All the boats had been lost. Three lascars had launched one and it had drifted away. The Chief Officer dived into the sea and swam after the boat. He was not seen again. A second boat was launched to retrieve the first, and this also disappeared. The passengers were forced to take refuge in the bar and live on 10 lb. nuts, some baby food and 6 dozen bottles of soda water. The next morning the last boat was launched and boarded by twenty passengers with the object of reaching the shore. The boat drifted out to sea, and was never seen again, although the seamen continued rowing in vain against the wind and current. For the next seventeen days the survivors huddled on the disintegrating wreck, officers and passengers picked off one by one by the waves. The Captain, stupefied by events, refused to take shelter and was hit by two waves. The first broke his leg and he said, "There! My leg has gone." The second wave knocked him overboard. Children were dragged out of their mothers' arms and the Fourth Engineer was knocked into a coma for six days as he crawled about the hulk looking for food.

The survivors were eventually rescued at 8 a.m. on June 26th —9 passengers out of 34, 3 officers and 33 lascars. 93 people had lost their lives. Shortly afterwards the ship's back broke and the sides burst open. The subsequent looting of the ship by the Socotrans caused estranged relations between the British Government and the Sultan, and until quite recently one aged inhabitant of Hadibo wore the jacket of a ship's steward.

CHAPTER TEN

OVER THE PASSES

THE next morning we divided. Peter and myself, and the donkeys and donkey-men, returned to Sigira the way we had come. Richard and John set off in the opposite direction with the object of ascending to the *jol* or plateau. They would walk along the *jol*, descend to the coast by a track just behind Sigira and rejoin the rest of us.

Peter and I reached Sigira and waited for them. A man brought us water in a clay pot that had previously contained fish. Bits of it were floating in the water. A little of this water seemed just as satisfying as a long draught of good water. Normally we polluted our drinking water with chlorinating tablets, making it rather less palatable than the fish-water we were offered at Sigira. We also carried a Spanish wineskin containing water which we occasionally squirted into our mouths. This water tasted strongly of tar and a little was quite enough. Thirst in such a country is an important consideration. One cannot avoid thirst, but experience diminishes it or enables one to endure it more easily. When we first arrived on the island we were continually thirsty and no matter how much we drank we remained thirsty, but some weeks later we were able to go for long periods without drinking. There are two schools of thought about drinking in thirsty places. The first, the medical school, believes that you should drink whenever you feel thirsty, as it is physiologically bad for you to deny liquid to a body that has lost many pints through sweating and dehydration generally. The other, the school of experienced desert travellers, believes that you should drink only in the morning and evening, filling your guts tight full of liquid like a goatskin. Only the smallest of sips should be taken during the main part of the day. No doubt both schools of thought are right from their various points of view.

Peter and I rested in the shade of the palm trees, shifting with the shifting shadow, and at three there was still no sign of the others. So we went on to Timareh, where we had arranged to

Ascending the mountains. A spring of welcome sweet water on the way up to Kishin.

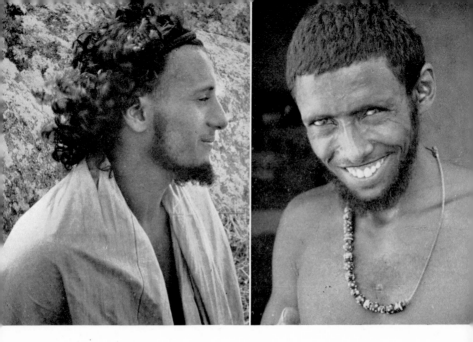

Abdulla Hadhrami, looking like a Biblical prophet.

A bedouin blood donor, wearing a necklace of medicine beads.

Little Ali, son of Salim of Kishin.

Unknown bedouin boy.

spend the night. The light began to fail and we began to give up hope of seeing the others that day. We made a fire and started mixing some soup, and Mesna cooked some fish that he had bought for us. We had just cooked the soup when an excited man appeared and shouted to us:

"They are coming! They are coming! A *woman* has seen them! A *woman* has seen them on the *road*!"

John and Richard appeared just as night was falling, looking remarkably fresh, though they had travelled the best part of ten hours over rough, waterless, unmapped and depopulated country, lost for most of the time. The route up on to the *jol* marked on the map could not be found and they had to round the island and find their way up a difficult and precipitous path from the south. They crossed over flat, gently undulating country devoid of all vegetation and water, but the earth a rich red and capable of being cultivated, given the water and the inclination. They had not brought a compass and to keep their bearings they set their map, its contours useless and place names erroneous, against the blue horizon of the *jol*, keeping the wind to their left cheeks. They had a drink at the most primitive village they had yet seen, just a wall built against a rock face, a windbreak without a roof. There were a few goats and sheep about, and three women, one of them making butter in a goat-skin massock, two children, some sick people, and many fleas. They drank some water out of aluminium bowls which tasted of excreta, and went on with foul-tasting mouths and empty stomachs, for they had not eaten all day. In the fullness of time they regained the coastal strip, a little west of Sigira, where they were informed that the procession of donkeys and Englishmen had gone west earlier in the afternoon. And so they found us.

I decided that we should try and reach Kishin from Timareh the next day. I believed that if we went to the seaward side of the Batageber, the 2,000-foot hill that lay between Garrieh and Suk, we would cut several hours off what was normally a two-day journey. Normally one had to detour the hill, as the track along the seaward side of the hill was impassable for donkeys. The distance to Kishin along the seaward route was nearly 30 miles. John and I had already travelled almost this distance in one day and I believed we could do it again. But I had not taken into account the idiosyncrasies of the Batageber track, which was of course unknown to me.

K

We set off at a tremendous pace for Garrieh. The track was good and we reached Garrieh at 8.30, very confident of reaching Kishin in the evening and looking forward to it. We waited for the donkeys, relieved them of the sleeping-bags and a little food, which we were to carry ourselves, and left them to make their journey round the Ma'abath wadi and join us in Kishin two days later.

Our first disappointment was when we had to walk two miles inland in order to reach a fordable part of the *khor*. Our second disappointment was when we saw just what sort of track crossed the Batageber to seaward. It was an incredible track and Mesna barely knew the way. We made him go on ahead, but he was reluctant to do so and sometimes he dithered on the cliff face uncertain whether to go up or down, for there was no obvious route. "He doesn't know," we whispered, and averted our eyes politely while he made up his mind where to go. The path led up high over the sea, and we had to edge warily along narrow ledges of loose stones with the cliff face dropping sheer several hundred feet into the clear green sea. We could see the black rocky bottom and bright motionless fish in the translucent water far beneath us. This was not walking but rock-climbing and had to be done carefully and slowly, and the hours slipped by as we made our painful way westwards. We had left Garrieh at 10 a.m. and at 1 p.m. we were still high up on the face of the Batageber, clinging to the rocks when the wind suddenly gusted. The way, clearly impossible for any animal, was not ideal for men.

We passed the Batageber at half-past one. Miles away we could see the sand-hill of Jebel Hawari and our hearts sank when we realised how much farther we had to go. We had already been seven hours on the march, and there were at least three or four more hours marching before we could reach Suk, let alone Kishin. We traversed some sand dunes and walked in the sea. A group of fishermen invited us into a stone hut, the roof supported by stone pillars and wooden branches, and with great gaps between the stones of the walls where the wind came rushing in. We asked for water and they sent a boy off to get some, while we and they sat round the walls inside the hut and watched each other without talking much, because we were too tired. The water took over half an hour to come and we grumbled at the delay, our tiredness getting the better of our manners, though we said nothing to the people themselves, remembering (just) that we were their guests and that they had gone to the trouble of going on a long journey for water for our benefit. The water arrived with its familiar flavour, and we sipped a little from a rusty Lipton's coffee-tin provided for the purpose.

Then we went on again and the road seemed endless, and when we came to Deleisha we found that we had indeed shot our bolt and that we could not reach Kishin that night and would need all our strength to reach Suk. The endless brown, undulating, gravel plain stretched ahead of us. We came to the sand dunes which lead eventually to the beach that runs to Suk, and here in the soft sand Peter began to show signs of overstrain. He began to feel dizzy and had a pain in his side. John carried his sleeping-bag, and the rapid pace which we had somehow managed to maintain throughout the day, where the country allowed it, slowed to a dawdle to allow Peter a chance to recover. We were all very tired and thirsty. We came out to the beach and Richard stayed with Peter who walked in the sea and drank some of the salt water. John and I went on at an angry pace, with Mesna pad-padding on dumpy legs behind us. He was a good tough old bird, and no doubt his reputation among his countrymen has been enhanced to glory because of his walk from Timareh that day in August with the sahibs. We reached the palm grove by the beach at Suk and threw ourselves on to the ground and lay there for a quarter of an hour. It was like coming home. Mesna brought us dates and water and at five Peter and Richard arrived.

The locals were amazed and appalled that we had marched from Timareh. They thought we were magnificent but nuts. We had been marching for eleven hours and could not have gone a step farther.

We bathed in the sea watched by the men and children of Suk and then we ate the last of the food (our first meal in twenty hours)—some bully, some biscuits, some hot thin soup made from the scrapings of the Marmite tin. Richard and I cut the remaining cigarette in half and smoked the halves slowly. We picked the fleas out of ourselves and our clothes and held the clothes over the fire to fumigate them for good measure.

I slept that night on the pebbly ground in a cotton sheet jammed between a fallen palm tree and the wood fire, having

left my blankets on one of the donkeys. We did not sleep too
well because of the roughness of the ground and our own over-
tiredness.

We left at 5.45 the next morning, the last day of August and
the eighth of our short trek. We were more tired than we knew
and went only slowly up the wadi to Kishin, Mesna stronger
than all of us, leaving us behind as he sprang up the mountain-
side. On the way up we passed two bedouin squatting on a flat
rock amid the anatomical segments of a slaughtered cow. The
stone was red with blood and Salim was there, his feet and hands
blood-stained. The guts of the cow were hanging up on a bush
to dry. An old woman who lived in a cave near Kishin had at
last died and so all the bedouin could eat a cow. They only eat
cows when people die, and possibly when they are married and
circumcised: when it appears certain that a person is going to
die they select the cow and eat it immediately after the awaited
death. We had met the funeral cortège on the plain, six bedouin
bearing the body of the old lady on a rude litter, their faces
suitably lugubrious but their minds, I imagined, fixed on the
cow which even now was being prepared for them in the hills.
When the bedouin on the flat rock saw us they screamed at us,
demanding matches to light the fire to cook the meat.

"Shinnig, Shinnig! *Kiberit! Kiberit!*" they shouted.

"Oh, shut up!" Peter said. "*Mafi kiberit,* I haven't got any
matches. Anyone would think I *had* some matches!"

We took a few more steps up the hill and then suddenly and
unanimously burst into howls of laughter. Of course Peter had
matches, we all had matches. Having decided that we couldn't
spare them any matches we had actually *believed* that we hadn't
got any.

"These trogs are bloody hopeless," Peter said finally, and
we howled again as we went on up the mountain.

So we reached Kishin and breakfasted hugely off the best
that Abdullahi could offer, which was the best by any standards.
We consumed hamburgers and sausages, baked beans, Porage,
chupatees, Cornish wafers and coffee. Then a bathe in the
pool and DDT for the fleas and a change of clothes.

We had not found the charnel-houses but we had seen some
of the country and a few of the people.

During our absence at Ras Momi the Little Sultan had paid

a visit to the camp with his retinue. Neil and Mike returned one evening and found a flat football and a bright chrome pump on the table. "Eh, the Little Sultan, a little boy, a very little beggar, he wanty his football mended," Abdullahi told them. The heir-apparent was spending the night in Salim's cave and would come down the following morning to collect his ball. So Mike and Neil, with a due sense of responsibility, examined the royal plaything and discovered a hole an inch long in the bladder. They repaired it with some shoe-repair adhesive Mike had bought in Oxford and with a rubber insulating cap they found in the lid of a tin can. They pumped the football up and left it overnight. The next morning it was flat. The Little Sultan came down from the cave and while Mike and Neil again repaired the ball he amused himself with the Very pistol. He pointed it down the valley, wavered, giggled and finally fired. The negroes in his retinue were round-eyed with admiration and one of them began beating a drum. Eventually the ball was mended and Neil began to lace it with a bandage and a pair of forceps. There was a hissing sound, the ball slowly deflated, the Little Sultan's face fell and the drummer stopped drumming, his hand poised in mid-air over his drum. "It's just one of the many holes given way," Neil explained. After considerable time and effort the football was mended a third time, and it was safely laced and given to the Little Sultan with the injunction that it was not to be kicked until the next day. The jubilant prince and his retinue disappeared down the track and vanished behind a dragon's blood tree and down the hill. Neil and Mike waited. They heard the thump they had rather expected and shortly a hot-and-bothered negro came running back up the track, holding in his hand a flat football. To this day, as far as we know, the football of the youth who is to rule Socotra and Mahra is as flat as a bus ticket and he has nothing to play with.

Four days later another trek was arranged, this time to the Southern or Nawgeed* Plain, where Peter hoped to find traces of Portuguese forts at Feragey, in the Southern Haggier, and at Ras Qatanahan, at the western end of the Nawgeed Plain. On the way Mike would make collections of plant and animal specimens. John accompanied them because he was interested

*Also spelt variously Nogood, Nankad and Nugget.

in the country and because he rejoiced in pure physical effort. The rest of us had business in the mountains.

Their first attempt at a start proved abortive. The Poor Relation offered to guide them as far as Feragey. In spite of some misgivings the party decided to accept his offer and set out in a line behind his diminutive and slightly pathetic figure. He led them up the by now well-known path to Adho Dimellus and then stopped and waved airily southwards towards a topographical tangle of hills and twisting wadis. "That's your road to Feragey," he said, "I'm going no further." Peter argued with him and abused him and told him that he could expect no pay for such meagre services. The donkey-men were angry. "*Kelb wa ibn el kelb!* Dog and son of a dog!" they shouted. "*Wad el haram!* Bastard!" But the Poor Relation merely grinned. Then he said he had fever. There was nothing for it but to let him go, with a note from Peter addressed to me saying "Give this man nothing but a kick in the pants." The party attempted to press on without him, found themselves lost in dense cloud on top of a hill, and decided to return, rather disgruntled, to Kishin.

The next morning they set off again, "this time with a far more reliable looking guide," Peter wrote in his diary, "who stalked in front of us holding Mike's alcohol jar for insects and reptiles in a Biblical manner on the palm of his hand. We turned off the Adho Dimellus path to the left, up a fantastic rock face where the donkeys had to be unloaded, the baggage carried up and the donkeys themselves lifted, with difficulty, over the worst bits. It was clear that we had two good donkey-men— Guman, the head-man, small and brown; and Mohammed, largely negroid. We also had Salem, nicknamed 'Rubberlips' from his extraordinary rubber face and thick lips, who was a complete idiot with almost no control over his animal and whose load always required retying; the others nearly always loaded for him, while he stood and looked on amiably but hopelessly. He comes from Mukalla, was shipwrecked here a year before and has been unable to get away.

"We passed over the grassy slopes of Adhein, 'The Passes', in thick cloud and heavy rain and descended into the wooded country lower down the valley which was to take us south—a steep descent over rocks and past bushes which caused the donkeys much trouble, the rocks tripping their feet and the bushes on either side of the path—often no more than a goat track—catching the baggage."

In the afternoon they entered the fertile Feragey valley and camped under one of the enormous acacia trees that abounded there. John and Peter went to look for the fort but were chased away by an irate bedu who thought they were after his wife.

The next morning they found the fort at a point where the valley narrowed. It was built on a natural outcrop of rock and was roughly triangular-shaped. Two towers were joined by a massive wall (12-15 feet high) of large red granite boulders. An artificially deepened pool ran beneath the wall and might well have served as a moat: the wadi, when in spate, would flow into the pool. There was a third tower in the other corner of the ruin, and there were the remains of small rooms and an earth courtyard containing what was left of a well. A Portuguese fortress, a previous traveller had said: the most Peter could say was that it was no more Portuguese than the Kremlin, though from its design and commanding position it was almost certainly a fortress of some kind. Probably invading Mahri Arabs had used it as a blockhouse during their conquest of the island in the 15th and 16th centuries. It completely dominated the major route across the island from north to south and lay right in the heart of "enemy" bedouin country—an ideal position for a base for conquering or punitive raids.*

During the rest of the day the party marched south. The floor of the wadi was covered with palms and the air was hot and still. Soon the wadi began to descend and narrow; its sides, covered with the pallid, grey, bloated adeniums, rose to 1,000 feet and were topped with a rotting grey limestone cap, 300 feet thick.

"We camped in a narrow and grim part of the wadi," Peter noted, "where the only life was lizards in the rocks and vultures wheeling overhead. The cliffs were very eroded, red and packed with adeniums—very sinister. In the dusk the bats came out and during the night it rained. . . ."

---

*Bent also saw the fort in 1897 and reported that near by were the ruins of an ancient town, earlier in date than the fort. He saw walls of heavy boulders 100 feet long, 5 feet high and 8-10 feet thick, which must have been constructed when the inhabitants knew how to lift great weights. Obviously Feragey was a place of great importance and activity in the past, and may have been the centre of ancient gum cultivation and incense collecting.

The next morning they set off on the last leg of their outward trek :

"The day started with a minor tragedy, as Ali told us a tin of condensed milk had upset in the night and all the contents poured away. Then the donkeys were found to have strayed and it took over an hour to get them. We didn't start until 8 o'clock and in an hour came out on the plain of Nawgeed. This is a flat lava plain with very low scrub of camel-thorn growing in holes in the rock—seen under a low grey sky it was a scene of remarkable desolation and dreariness. We travelled west along it until we came to the village of Haif, a small group of stone huts with a poverty-stricken population and extremely salty water in its wells, owing to their proximity to the sea. We sent a man to fetch a 'goat skin of water from far away'. The huts of Haif were interesting and very reminiscent of those Stone Age houses excavated at Skara Brae, in the Orkneys. They were extremely primitive, merely rough dry stones piled on top of each other, with a roof of stone blocks supported on beams. Some were rectangular, some circular; the circular ones had a central pillar to support the beams. Between Haif and the sea is a range of sand dunes, and in the afternoon we crossed them to bathe on a sad-looking pebble beach beneath leaden skies. It was the most miserable, gloomy and isolated place I have ever been in. We bought a miserable, skinny sheep for 15 shillings to feed the men. Ali ate the sheep in Somali fashion, consuming the two front legs and two chops only. 'The other men,' he said, 'eat everything inside out. Such food is for women only.' I was offered some but the smell was so strong I couldn't face it."

The following day, owing to the extreme paucity of water on the Nawgeed Plain and their own lack of rations, they decided to turn back rather than push on to Ras Qatanahan where another fort had previously been reported.

During the return journey to Kishin they stopped again at Feragey fort. Here they met a bedu who said he could show them another fort at Dikoily. They all set off, very interested at the prospect of discovering a second fort. But they were soon joined by a second bedu who was much less friendly and seemed to tell his companion that he shouldn't be giving information. "I then asked about the Dikoily fort," Peter wrote, "to be met with a complete change of front. A conversation like this ensued:

Peter Shinnie: 'Now we want to see the fort at Dikoily.'

Socotran: 'What's at Dikoily?'

P.S.: 'The ancient fort.'

S.: 'What fort?'

P.S.: 'You told me that at Dikoily there was a fort like the one I saw at Feragey.'

S.: 'What's at Feragey?'

P.S.: 'The fort we saw not far from here.'

S.: 'There isn't one.'

P.S.: 'Yes there is.'

S.: 'No there isn't. What *is* a fort?'

P.S.: 'Like the thing you said was at Dikoily.'

S.: 'There isn't one.'

"So I gave up!"

On the morning of the seventh day of their trek they arrived back at Kishin, having seen a rarely visited part of the country, collected a large number of plants and animals and examined a strange and enigmatic archaeological ruin.

CHAPTER ELEVEN

THE TERRACES OF INCENSE

THE highest peaks of the Haggier Mountains are among the oldest land surfaces in the world. They have never been submerged during the constant ebb and flow of great oceans in primeval times and have formed an ark of refuge for many species of plant and animal life. At one time, so many million years ago that it makes no difference to you or me, Socotra was joined to the land masses of Asia and Africa. Plants and animals in these regions flew, crawled and seeded, not barred by the seas that have divided islands from mainlands and parcelled continents and nations in subsequent aeons. Then came one of those catastrophic and unimaginable changes in the shape of the world and the distribution of land and sea. India became an island and the ocean lapped at the foot of the Himalayas. Most of Socotra was submerged, all except the highest peaks where many species of plants and animals contrived to carry on as usual while half the world lay drowning in an enormous all-embracing flood. Then the sea receded and for a time Socotra was joined to Somaliland and Arabia. The flora and fauna spread to Socotra, the sea rose again and finally severed the island for ever from the mainlands. But the plants and animals remained, species of varying ages, originating from Africa and Asia, Madagascar, Polynesia and South America. Such species are mostly unspectacular, but many of them are unique to this island and are of considerable scientific interest because of their age and their far-flung relationships.

The mountains, where most of these old and unusual plants and animals are to be found, were Mike's hunting-ground. Since he was the first to make a biological collection during the Socotran winter there was a fair chance that he might find one or two species unknown to science, and so he collected anything and everything indiscriminately, hoping that something new would find its way into his large collection. He also aimed to carry out an ecological survey of the vegetation of the island, which, in short, constitutes a study of plants in their environment, their inter-relatedness to each other and to the soil and climate in which they grow. The vegetation of Socotra varies from the scrubby desert plants of the coastal plains to the dense European-type plants of the mountains. The vegetation also differs in different parts of the mountains themselves. Thus on the red sandstone foothills and in the lower reaches of the wadis grow scrub and cucumber trees. Up the first 3,000 feet grow aloes, *adenium obesum*, dragon's blood trees, oranges, acacias and hibiscus. Then comes the first of the water-parting plateaux of green fields and, perhaps a thousand feet higher, the second of these plateaux where crocuses, gentians, thyme and mushrooms grow. Then, rising to 5,000 feet, are the granite peaks covered with a scab of lichen where alpine flowers peep between stones and crevices in the rock. It is among the highest peaks that the most interesting plants grow, though there is nothing particularly unusual in their appearance.

At nights a civet cat used to visit our camp at Kishin, looking for scraps of food. It caused Ali and Abdullahi several sleepless nights by jumping around inside the kitchen, upsetting tins and pots with a great clatter. They wanted to shoot it with the .22 rifle because it annoyed them intensely, but Mike wanted to capture it alive and take it to England for the London Zoo. It took to visiting the verandah of the tent where we slept and Mike used to spotlight it with his torch as it sat on the top of our table sniffing the wild oranges in the clay bowl. Mike made a trap from a large Huntley and Palmer's biscuit crate. He inverted the crate and propped up one end with a tent peg. He tied a length of string to the tent peg and put some condensed milk inside the inverted crate as a bait. The first time the cat went under the box to get the milk Mike pulled the string and the box dropped in a fraction of a second—just long enough for the cat to turn right round and make its escape. It came back two nights later and entered the box again. Mike pulled the string, the cat was successfully trapped, and Mike went to sleep very happy. When he went to look at the cat the next morning he found that it had again escaped. This was remarkable since the gaps between the slats of the biscuit crate were only an inch wide, while the civet cat was about the size of a weasel-shaped domestic cat. Mike covered the gaps in the crate and the next night finally caught the cat. It remained in the box till it reached the R.S.P.C.A. in Aden, a handsome little beast, spotted and striped black and white, with a ringed tail and black feet, wicked little stoat eyes, all teeth and claws and growl and stink. It was so fierce that it was impossible to handle it, even with leather gauntlets on, and it was fed on meat scraps, rice, milk and water.

The locals catch the civet cats and extract the valuable musk (used as a natural base for many perfumes and cosmetics) from the perineal glands of the female, squeezing it on to a wooden knife. It is evil-smelling stuff.

Apart from a few sorts of mice and rats, there are no other naturally wild animals on Socotra. This is because the island was separated from the mainland by wide seas long before mammals appeared on the face of the earth. There are wild goats (which the bedouin catch in nets and prize highly for the good meat they afford), wild cats and wild asses; but these are all feral versions of ordinary domestic animals imported at some distant time. The wild ass is an attractive grey and white creature with a pure white muzzle and black shoulder stripes, which roams the plains in herds, and is caught by the Arabs and tamed for use as a pack animal. It is thought to be of Nubian origin, imported by ancient Egyptian traders.

More interesting from a scientific point of view were the lesser forms of animal life which, like the plants, were primitive survivors of drowned lands and of countries now divided from the island by oceans. They have developed indigenously in their isolation, with forgotten relatives in Africa, Asia and Polynesia— the orange and purple crabs scuttling in translucent mountain pools, unspectacular snakes and lizards, molluscs, scorpions, butterflies and bats. Mike collected everything—the moths and flies that bounced off the pressure lamp into his soup in the evenings; ticks from the dirt floors of bedouin caves and the hair of their goats; centipedes under rocks and snails under leaves. He despatched bedouin minions to collect whatever they could, in particular the *shigidahan* (owl), and they would come back with little goatskins full of squeaking bats, creatures which inhabited the mountain caves and had never before been caught on Socotra. Salim's son, little Ali, a happy, helpful child, turned over stones at Adho Dimellus looking for the giant centipede that lurked beneath them. This monstrous insect reached ten inches in length and the thickness of a man's thumb, and each of its numerous feet was prickly and poisonous. Salim himself was terrified of it. We showed him a coloured reproduction of it in a book and he jumped back with terror at the sight of it. Then when he saw that it was lifeless he tried to prise it from the printed page, thinking that it had been squashed in the book. He did not like the picture of the spider called *fitameh*, a large and ugly insect with a bite fatal to men and camels: fortunately this was rare. Mike collected a large selection of chameleons and tethered them to the tent pole to catch flies. But they can go weeks without eating anything and never, as far as we know, caught a single fly. They just crawled up and down the tent pole, tangling each other's tethering strings. When they reached the ends of their tethers they dropped off and hung hopelessly, their pop-eyes revolving independently of each other like bagatelle balls, while their scaly sub-human fingers clutched at the thin air. Peter had a chameleon as a pet: he called it the Johnson and took it to Uganda with him: coals to Newcastle—perhaps it will start a new species and puzzle specialists for generations to come. There was a baby chameleon called Arbuthnot: the big ones picked on it and hissed at it, opening wide their dinosaur mouths and throwing back their dragon-ridged green heads. When this happened Arbuthnot lobbed off into space, preferring to dangle by his tail than fight. Mike always kept a bottle of cyanide on the dinner-table labelled with a crimson skull and cross-bones and the words "DEADLY POISON". Into this he popped flies at meal-times and we watched them die as we ate, like Tiberius banqueting in his torture chamber.

We paid for biological specimens with shillings and biscuits and the bedouin brought them in continually, uncomprehending. They did not know why we had come to their island to put bugs in bottles and tie labels round the necks of snakes. Perhaps we ate them, the way they themselves ate certain snails. Perhaps we stewed them into a medicine, a potent charm. Perhaps we were barmy. Whatever they thought, how could they know that in distant England men would come and prod the things with tweezers and give them strange names, double- or triple-barrelled names in an antique language nobody understood, and stick pins through them and consign them to dusty drawers in dusty rooms after writing many words about them? A complicated ritual by men of wisdom: the Nasara's fetish.

There are many birds on Socotra: sparrows indistinguishable

from London ones hopped around our camp looking for
crumbs. No one, in all their lives, had ever given them crumbs
until we came and then their habit of crumb-picking, ingrained
since their evolution but unpractised, came out. Then there
were white Egyptian vultures waiting for carrion and flopping
out of stone's throw reach. And pretty little pigeons, delicate
and pastel coloured, flitted among the trees on the hillsides.
Once, on the occasion of Peter's wedding anniversary, Richard
and I went pigeon shooting. The unusual bangs of our shotguns
echoed down the valleys and reached the ears of those remaining
in camp. But when we returned all we had was one tiny pigeon
which I had shot unawares. Abdi cooked it and it turned up
on a plate the size of a shrivelled sparrow. Peter gave it to
Richard and me to share and we gnawed minute particles of
flesh from fragile bones. There was another common bird like
a large blackbird with orange wings, and many others we never
attempted to catch because we had not the time or the facilities
to skin them. On the plain and the sea-shore there were different
types of birds, wheatears and waders and oyster-catchers and
gulls, but no birds living on Socotra today are so remarkable as
those amazing birds of days gone by, the rukh and the phoenix.
The rukh was an enormous eagle which darkened the sky when
it flew and terrified all who were unfortunate enough to be
within its range. It carried off elephants in its talons and laid
eggs the size of temples. Sindbad encountered this remarkable
bird and many think that this meeting took place on Socotra.
The phoenix was no less remarkable:

". . . that famous bird of Arabia is the size of an eagle and
has a brilliant plumage around the neck, while the rest of the
body is of a purple colour—except the tail which is azure,
with long feathers intermingled of a roseate hue. The throat is
adorned with a crest and the head with a tuft of feathers. It is
sacred to the sun and when old it builds a nest of cinnamon and
sprigs of incense which it fills with perfumes and then lays its
body upon them to die. From its bones and marrow springs a
small worm which changes into a little bird. The first thing it
does is to perform the obsequies of its predecessor and to
carry its nest to the City of the Sun near Panchaia (Socotra).
There it deposits it on the altar of that divinity. The revolution
of the great year is completed with the life of this bird and a
new cycle comes round again with the same characteristics as

the former one, in the seasons and the appearance of the stars."*

These birds are now, alas, extinct. We found no eggs like temples, no cinnamon-lined nests, no phoenix-larvae on the point of turning, like radiant dragon-flies, into eagles sacred to the sun. They would, no doubt, have interested Mike immensely.

Undoubtedly the most spectacular and characteristic forms of life on Socotra are the trees which give the mountains the appearance of a strangely fertile moon-scape. Toad-like cucumber trees crowd the lower hill slopes, their grey trunks distended with milky sap like elephantiatic limbs, surmounted with a brief fringe of stiff crinkly leaves. These trees produce a small yellow flower and a small useless fruit—a cucumber, I suppose. The adenium trees are similar and more abundant higher up the mountain, and they are even more bloated and grotesque. Often two or three fat squashy trunks will spring from the same base, each with a crest of stiff, formal leaves which begin to fall when the red blossom comes. Then there are the euphorbia trees, equally full of a thick white sap, with branches that curve upwards like the arms of a candelabrum. But most spectacular of all are the ubiquitous dragon's blood trees, with an appearance as strange as their name. They are dotted along every sky-line, project quaintly from every crag, like umbrellas blown inside out.

The Socotrans refer to the cinnebar-like resin that exudes from these trees as the Blood of the Two Brothers, a reference that recalls an old Indian legend from which the Socotrans themselves probably derived it. According to this legend dragons were always fighting elephants. They had a passion for elephant's blood. They used to twine themselves round the elephant's trunk and bite behind the elephant's ear. Then they drank all the blood in one gulp. But on one auspicious occasion the dying elephant, falling to the ground, crushed the dragon beneath it. The matter exuding from the dragon together with a mixture of the blood of the two animals was called cinnebar and the name was applied to the rich red earth where the red sulphide of mercury occurred, and later to the gum of the dragon's blood tree. This legend accounts for the English popular name given to the resin of the tree—dragon's blood—and for the Socotran name—Blood of the Two Brothers.

*Pliny: *Natural History.*

According to the Hindu religious tradition the elephant and
the dragon were closely related: the members of the Brahman
triad were Brahma (the Creator, in the shape of an elephant),
Vishnu (the Preserver) and Siva (the Destroyer, usually in the
shape of a cobra, equivalent to a dragon). The combat between
the elephant and the dragon, between the Creator and the
Destroyer, the forces of life and death, was eternal. The fact
that a reference to this Hindu concept occurs in Socotran
mythology establishes that Indian contacts with Socotra must
have been much closer in the past than they are now, an
hypothesis for which there is plenty of other evidence.*

Of all the unusual trees that grow on Socotra none has such
exotic associations or has had such an importance in the past as
the frankincense tree and the myrrh tree. In parts of the mountains and in particular in the valley which leads down to the
town of Qalansiya, these trees grow in abundance. In the
summer they blossom and fill the entire valley with a magnificent scent.

The myrrh tree (of which there are six species on Socotra)
is like a low spreading cedar. The frankincense tree (of which
there are three or four species on the island) looks like a de-
composing animal. It has stiff low branches. The leaves are
scanty, curly and indented. A thick bark (which the local
bedouin sometimes make into buckets) and a tiny whitish peel
cling closely round the trunk of a peculiarly blotchy colour.
The woody fibre of the tree, distended with sap, looks like
rotting animal flesh, and the clear yellowish-white resin oozes
from incisions with a strong aroma. The fruit is a berry the size
of a marble and the flowers are few, red and geranium-like on
the end of short spikes.

The trees are not now cultivated and only a little incense is
collected, for local purposes, not for export. During the summer
the bedouin make 10-12 deep oblique slashes 2-3 inches long
and with a wrench of the knife tear the lower end of the incision
open. Into this pocket the gum collects. At the end of a month
the partially hardened resin is ripped out and more incisions
are made. Mike once saw two bedouin climbing an incense tree
to collect the gum and he once met the Poor Relation carrying a

*Indians lived on the island 2,000 years ago. A Gujerati inscription, discovered
on Socotra during the war, is now in the Aden Museum. As late as the 17th century
Gujerat sailors were contracting temporary "marriages" with Socotran bedouin
women. Indian dhow sailors still call at the island, though none stay there.

Dr. Neil Orr sprinkling DDT dust to kill the fleas in Salim's cave at Kishin. Salim is on the left, and with him is the Poor Relation and Salim's daughter.

Outside Salim's cave at Kishin. The entrance is walled up with stones as additional protection against the weather.

Salim's small daughters in the entrance of their cave-home.

sack full of incense twigs. He asked him what he was going to do with them and the Poor Relation replied that he was going to lay his head on them when he slept. This is one of my pleasanter memories of Socotra—the idea that the Poor Relation, a poor and simple troglodyte, should each night lay his weary funny head on a sack of sweet-smelling frankincense twigs in his dirty little hovel.

For several thousand years before the birth of Christ, incense was the most valuable product of Arabia and made the men that collected it and the merchants that traded it as rich as their successors whose revenue is the oil that gushes from the once-fertile deserts. Vast quantities were purchased by the ancient world: yearly, Chaldean priests burnt 10,000 talents'-worth of incense before the altar of Baal; the Babylonians used it as a purification after sexual intercourse, and in Jerusalem gigantic garners were constructed to contain this gift to God. All over Greece incense was burnt to honour Zeus, and later a regular cargo-boat service carried incense to Rome. The three wise men who followed the star to Bethlehem brought each a present for the baby Christ—gold, which according to the Persian legend signified the kingship; frankincense, which signified the divinity; and myrrh, which signified the healing powers of the child.

Probably the greatest consumers of incense were the ancient Egyptians. Round about the year 1200 B.C. 2,189 jars and 304,093 bushels of incense were delivered to the Temple of Amon at Thebes alone, at a price so prodigious that it cannot be estimated in modern terms. The Egyptians used it as a medicine and embalming agent and in the religious rituals concerned with the regeneration of the spirits of the dead. They believed that a corpse was not physically resurrected but that if it was embalmed and properly protected by magic ritual it had the power to generate a spiritual counterpart which, by the ceremony called the "Opening of the Mouth", was liberated and journeyed to heaven to enjoy life everlasting. The spells that released these spirits were known collectively as the Book of the Dead, and the priests who performed them had to protect themselves from injury by purification with the fumes of burning incense. Thus, without the incense they could not protect themselves, the spirits could not be released and the dead could not go to heaven. It is obvious that the Egyptians would go

L

to any lengths to obtain the one item necessary for obtaining eternal life.

In his mercantile specifications of 1200 B.C. Rameses III laid down that the colour of incense may vary from a cloudy amber-yellow to a jade-green as pale as moonlight, but that anything else was worthless. Such perfect incense was produced by the frankincense and myrrh trees alone, and for many hundreds of years it was brought overland from the region of Dhufar and the Hadhramaut in Southern Arabia, where these trees grow. Heavily-guarded camel caravans, loaded with the precious resin, made their way westwards through South Arabia to the Yemen where they turned north and progressed slowly along the Red Sea coast till the incense route divided and one branch led west to Egypt and another east to Babylon and Syria. Each camel-load cost £100 and bore a 500% profit by the time it reached its destination. It is therefore not surprising that the enterprising Egyptians should have attempted to reduce expenditure by cutting out the middlemen in the incense business. They decided to go and collect the incense themselves and, if possible, bring back the saplings of the incense trees for transplantation in Egyptian soil.

The first known Egyptian expedition to the incense-bearing countries, which the Egyptians called the "Land of Punt" or the Land of God, set out in approximately the year 3000 B.C. Little is known about this expedition, except that it brought back 80,000 measures of myrrh and 2,600 pieces of costly woods. From time to time during the subsequent hundreds of years other expeditions sailed down the Red Sea to bring back from Punt the priceless incense. The last and greatest of these expeditions set sail in 1493 B.C. at the express command of the great Queen Hatshepsut. The fleet consisted of five large galleys, each with thirty rowers, and was away for an unknown period. Preserved on the walls of the temple at Dehr-el-Bahri are lengthy inscriptions and drawings of the homecoming of the expedition.

"The ships," the inscription reads, "were laden with the costly products of the land of Punt and with its many valuable woods, with very much sweet-smelling incense resin and fresh frankincense, with quantities of ebony and ivory, set in pure gold from the land of Aamu, sweet-smelling resin, ahem incense, holy resin, painted with dog-headed apes as a delight to the eye, with long-tailed apes and greyhounds, furthermore leopard skins and natives of the country and their children. . . ."

The artist has drawn pictures on the temple wall depicting the ships of the fleet, with potted myrrh saplings, boxes and sacks of incense, apes and dogs and little humpless cows.

The Egyptians never revealed the exact location of Punt and the question is a matter of controversy to the present day. Frankincense and myrrh grow in only three parts of the world—in Somaliland, in Dhufar and in Socotra. Undoubtedly the Land of Punt was in the region of these three neighbouring countries and modern opinion places it in Dhufar. But wherever it was, it seems impossible that the Egyptian sailors should not have visited Socotra, for the island lies right on the route both to Somaliland and Dhufar and itself produces more different species of frankincense and myrrh than any other part of the world, besides other aromatic gums with useful properties, like aloes and dragon's blood.

The ancient Egyptians knew of Socotra and knew that it produced incense-bearing trees. There has been preserved down to us a little fairy-tale which proves as conclusively as anything can prove at this distance in time that Egyptians had been there and knew of its characteristics.

This story (now about 4,000 years old) relates how an Egyptian nobleman is shipwrecked on a strange and very fertile island, abounding with figs and vines, "all sorts of magnificent Aaqt plants, Kau fruits, Nequt fruits, melons of all sorts, fish and birds." The nobleman is surprised by the approach of a large and resplendent serpent, its coils encrusted with gold, who takes him into his charge and assures him that shortly an Egyptian vessel will call for him and return him to his country. The serpent is the ruler of this island and king of the Land of Punt, the Frankincense Country. The name of the island, he says, is Pa-anch, the Isle of the Genii, and it is inhabited by seventy-five other serpents and one young girl.* The nobleman is greatly relieved by the assurance of his safety and promises to reward the serpent with treasures brought from the Pharaoh in

---

*In Arabia it was believed that each frankincense tree was protected by a serpent—hence the serpents living on this incense-island and the name given to it, the Isle of the Genii, the genii of the incense tree.

Incidentally, this Egyptian story crops up again in Homer's *Odyssey*, when Ulysses is shipwrecked in similar circumstances on the fertile island of the Phaeaceans, the prototype of which seems to have been Pa-anch. The chief serpent becomes King Alcinous and the young girl becomes Nausicaa in Homer's version

Egypt. But the serpent, smiling, replies: "You are not rich in myrrh, for all you have is simple incense, but I, the prince of the Land of Punt, have myrrh of my very own. As for the Hecken incense which you said would be brought to me, why, that is the chief produce of the island."

Then the serpent gave the nobleman many valuable presents, including a great freight of myrrh and other incense, and the sailor went down to the shore and called to the sailors in the ship that was anchored there. "On the beach I gave thanks to the prince of this island and to all those who lived there."

It is a simple story but interesting in many ways. I believe an actual incident at an actual place has been fictionalized and curiously transmuted down the generations. No doubt Egyptian galleys were wrecked on their voyages to Punt, just as the ship was wrecked in this story. No doubt some sailors survived and were eventually picked up. It seems almost certain that the original prototype of this island of Pa-anch was Socotra. What other island in the world produces myrrh, the best incense and unobtainable in Egypt? We are told that the ruler of Pa-anch is the prince of the Land of Punt, the Frankincense Country, a region probably corresponding with Mahra and Dhufar today. We know that in historical times Socotra was subject to the King of the Frankincense Country and at the present day the Sultan of Socotra is also ruler of the Mahra territory in the "Frankincense Country". In short, it would seem that this island of Pa-anch, made fairy by the needs of successive story-tellers, was based on the experiences of ancient Egyptian sailors on the actual Socotra.

Depicted in the Dehr-el-Bahri inscriptions are cattle without humps, one of the numerous items brought back from the Land of Punt. Now one of the unexplained mysteries of Socotra is the presence of cattle which are quite unlike those of neighbouring coastlands in Africa, Arabia and India. Indeed, they resemble only the cattle of the Jersey islands, though it is impossible that they came from there. Not only are the Socotran cattle minute (the result of unusually conditioned breeding) but they have *no humps*. In the rest of this region all the cattle are humped. This is not sure evidence that Queen Hatshepsut's expedition to Punt called at Socotra and collected some of the cattle, as it is possible that a breed resembling the Socotran cattle also lived in Southern Arabia and has since died out and been replaced by a humped breed. But it does surely establish that the ancient Egyptians did call at Arabia and it is difficult to see how they could miss Socotra, as I have already said.

That is the evidence for Egyptian contacts with Socotra in ancient times. It is built on deduction and hypothesis drawn from a fairy-story 4,000 years old and drawings and inscriptions on a temple wall at Dehr-el-Bahri and common sense and probability. Whatever specialists may think, I like to imagine that Egyptian sailors landed on Socotra, rowing their galleys up the creeks at Qalansiya or Suk with their square sails lowered, anxious for land after long days at sea. Then, when the ship was securely anchored, they

"Tumbled out of their ships on to the sands they craved so,
And laid their limbs crusted with brine upon the shore."

I have said already that our camp was sited on an ancient man-made terrace, like a terrace for grape-vines in Southern Europe. Could this have been a work of these nameless Egyptians of so long ago, a construction to shore up the rich earth against erosion, where the incense trees could be planted and tended? The ancient inscriptions mention a place which they call "The Terraces of Incense". There are a number of these terraces on Socotra, their origin and purpose unknown to the locals. Perhaps Egyptian eyes had stared down this same valley to the plain and the creek at Suk where they could have beached their boats, huddling in scant clothes as the drizzle and chill came at night, talking much as we talked, of home and the things we had done and seen here and on the way here. And so sailing on to Punt, away from the aromatic mountains of the Island of the Genii, the island of the terraces of incense, the Happy Isles—away to Punt, the destination of their long voyage, where a "heavenly and indescribable fragrance seems to strike and still the senses of everyone. For even far out from land as you sail past you do not miss a share of this enjoyment. For in the spring whenever a wind arises from the land it happens that the fragrant odours blowing from the myrrh bushes and others of the kind reach the neighbouring parts of the sea."*

If, as seems highly probable, Socotra took part in the ancient incense trade, either directly with visiting Egyptian expeditions

*Agatharcides.

on their way to Punt or later via Arab middlemen settled on the coast for purposes of trade, in much the same way that foreign Arabs are settled there now, it is difficult to believe that the island did not become prosperous, just as the city states on the Arabian mainland became prosperous until the incense trade declined. In Arabia many of these once rich and thriving cities are buried beneath sand and are only now being discovered and, in a few cases, partially excavated. On Socotra we saw no signs of such former opulence, but we worked under adverse conditions, with limited time and inadequate facilities. And in any case such ancient remains would doubtless be buried deep beneath the debris of many succeeding centuries. Even the fort at Suk, which was only 450 years old, was barely visible at a cursory investigation.

There is some evidence, admittedly slight, that suggests that Socotra was at one time engaged in the incense trade and waxed prosperous for a while. This evidence is contained in the geographical work of a man called Diodorus the Sicilian, who lived during the first century B.C. He says that there are to the south of Arabia three islands—Socotra, Abd-el-Kuri (a barren islet to the west) and an island called Hiera (or Panchaia). Now Panchaia is the Roman version of Pa-anch, the island I have already mentioned as the location of the ancient Egyptian fairy-story. Pa-anch is the prototype of the actual Socotra and it appears that the Romans confused the semi-legendary Panchaia with the actual Socotra and in time came to write of the two as if they were equally distinct and authentic places. The result is that Diodorus the Sicilian mixed together legends he had heard about Panchaia and descriptions brought back by sailors who had actually been to Socotra, so that he is unable to distinguish between the real island and the semi-mythical one and mixes fact and fiction indiscriminately. It is easier, and probably wiser, to treat the two places as though they are one.

The island, Diodorus wrote, produced sufficient frankincense to supply the whole world, together with myrrh and other aromatic plants. The inhabitants sold the incense to Arabs on the mainland, who conveyed it northwards to Egypt and Syria and distributed it throughout the whole of the inhabited world. The island produced little else. There were four different sorts of people living on the island—the aboriginals, the Greeks, the Indians and the Arabs, who worked variously as herdsmen, farmers, soldiers, artisans and priests. Presumably there were also traders, since much incense was exported. There is every reason for believing that these details are based largely on fact and describe Socotra as it was round about the first century B.C.

If the Socotrans did indeed take part in the great incense trade, as Diodorus suggests, it is difficult to believe that they did not become rich as a result of it. Are there no traces of such ancient opulence on Socotra? We found none during the course of our expedition. That does not necessarily prove that there are none. And here I come to the most interesting and remarkable of the details provided by Diodorus the Sicilian.

He says that outside the capital town of Panara (which bears a remarkable superficial resemblance to Tamara, as Hadibo was sometimes called before the 19th century) there was a flat plain, backed by a range of mountains. On the plain was an eminence, near by which ran a river on which boats could sail. On top of this eminence, dominating the plain, was a magnificent ancient temple. Now it so happens that at the present day there is outside Hadibo, on the flat Hadibo Plain (backed by the Haggier Mountains), a remarkable symmetrical hill called Hasun. Near by runs the wadi Hanefu which, as it approaches the sea, widens into a lagoon. Before it silted up, like most of the creeks on the north coast of Socotra, this river undoubtedly debouched in the sea and was almost certainly deep enough for small boats to sail on. On top of Hasun is the ruin of an Arab fort. The situation of this fort is identical with the situation of the ancient temple which Diodorus describes. If this is a coincidence, then it is a remarkable one, for the number of corroborating details is considerable.

I have always been suspicious of the hill Hasun. Whenever I passed it I was always struck by its remarkable symmetry and artificial appearance, for it rises like a conical pyramid out of an otherwise perfectly flat plain. I was so suspicious that I once asked Peter whether he thought it was the result of natural forces or whether it may have concealed a rather large ruin. Peter assured me that it was a natural hill and I have no doubt at all that he was right. But it is several hundred feet high and completely commands the plain beneath it. It is a perfect acropolis, an ideal situation for a building of importance, whether a fort or a temple or a ruler's palace. Could it be that under the ruins of the Arab fort and the débris of several millennia lies the remains of the great temple that Diodorus described in such careful detail? Could this temple, which was "specially admired for its antiquity, the costliness of its construction and its favourable situation", with its "thick columns, ingenious designs, massive fine statues" and doorways worked in gold and silver and ivory and citrus wood, actually lie concealed beneath the rubble on Hasun, just as many magnificent ancient buildings, likewise the product of an incense civilisation, have remained buried until recent archaeological discovery beneath the sands of the Arabian desert? We shall never know until someone cares to dig into that hill.

So much for the legend of Panchaia, this semi-Socotra, this demi-Eden of the ancient world. The legend died with the Romans, when sailors revisited the island, 2,000 years after the Egyptian who had started it all, and found that the island was not the Abode of Bliss it was made out to be, but was as it is now, obscure, barren and poor, the fabulous incense no more useful than dandelion juice and only the little flowers and the bugs and lizards of interest to the occasional biologist. And yet it has not always been like this.

CHAPTER TWELVE

THE CAVEMEN

SALIM BIN ABDULLA was a Sheikh. We never referred to him as Sheikh Salim and only mentioned the word in our diaries, in apostrophes, to shore up our romantic illusions. He had nothing in common with Rudolph Valentino and the Sheikhs of Araby, the tall scimitar-faced princes of the picture books and the *Seven Pillars of Wisdom*, the Oriental Juans of the movies, galloping in flying robes across the desert to rescue the Sultan's daughter. He lived in a cave and complained of the fleas that shared it with him—"*Hakak*," he said, and scratched himself all over to convey his meaning. *Hakak* became a familiar word. All the caves had *hakak*. All the bedouin, the goat-skins and the goats, had *hakak*. Certain lonely deserted valleys had *hakak*. They just skulked in the ground waiting for the occasional visitor like hungry lions. They must breed in these places for years and years, obtaining sustenance from the few infrequent travellers. When they come the fleas swarm out, over their legs, up into the middle regions, biting. We had DDT dusting powder and it became reputed among the bedouin as a killer of *hakak*. Neil used to go around with tins of it, dusting the caves, the goat-skins, the bedouin, the women's hair, himself. "Whatever you do," he told the bedouin, "don't let your goats back into the cave. They bring in the fleas." But the custom of a thousand years is not so easily broken. The goats went back into the caves, the fleas went back with them, the bedouin came down the mountain side again. "*Hakak, hakak*," they said, scratching themselves.

Salim's cave was the nearest to our camp at Kishin and was dusted more than any other. The fleas were never obliterated, and no doubt Salim is still there scratching himself. His was a typical cave. A cave is a cave and all the bedouin caves were much the same, larger or smaller,* more or less precariously

---

*A cave in the limestone plateau to the west of the island was reported to be 250 feet long, 175 feet wide and 87 feet high. Another one was 120 yards long and divided into compartments by stone walls.

situated on the edge of a steep slope or a precipice, beside a fig
tree. Which came first, we wondered, the fig tree or the cave?
Did the fig tree have now or in the past some special significance
connected with religious ritual, like the holy fig trees facing
Mount Kenya where the Kikuyu held their ceremonies? Or did
they just choose to have fig trees near their homes in order to
have ready access to the raw material of their tobacco pipes?
I watched Salim make a pipe one day. He cut down a slender
branch from a fig tree and stripped it and cut it to the required
length. He beat it with the flat side of his knife to loosen the
bark, clenched one end between his teeth and sloughed the
bark off in one piece, making an obscene gesture in the process.
Everyone laughed, the bedouin, the Arabs, ourselves, standing
round chuckling at the obscene joke. In that unanimous and
spontaneous laughter a gap was bridged between us all. The
dissimilarities of colour, race, outlook, were annulled. We were
like a music-hall audience, suddenly solidified, howling at a
man with a custard pie in his face. We all understood the
obscenity, the coarse vulgarisation of a natural function, and
we understood why Salim had done this and why the others
were laughing. Is this the way to international understanding?
(In the National Assembly the Soviet delegate stoops towards
the microphone: "Have you heard this one . . .? The delegates
of the United States, the United Kingdom, Egypt and Israel,
sit forward straining to catch every word, earphones pressed to
ears. The Russian makes his joke, obscenity of obscenities, and
the Assembly is in uproar. White and black slap each other's
backs, the American is speaking, "I can cap that one. . . ."
There is peace in the world.) Salim put a container of bone
in the end of the hollow fig bark, filled it with tobacco, placed
a red-hot brand on top of it and sucked deeply. Smoke seeped
out of his mouth. There was so much smoke it looked as though
it was coming out of his ears.

Once you have seen one cave you have seen them all, but you
can never get used to people living in them. It seems always a
game, like a week-end country outing, eating watercress sand-
wiches in a hole in the cliff. But the caves would be quite
comfortable if it weren't for the fleas. They are supremely
weather-proof, no rain could seep through the towering granite
roofs. The entrance to the caves are walled up with stones as
additional protection against the wind and rain. There is

usually an inner recess for the female members of the family, and mud ledges may be built up round the sides of the cave on which the occupants can sleep. A baby may be suspended in a cloth bundle from the roof, out of reach of centipedes and rats and spiders. There may be some round clay pots to cook in, a battered, blackened saucepan or two (Salim had some, but he was a Sheikh, they hadn't all got saucepans), a spoon perhaps, a wooden box, goat-skins on the floor, to sleep on, piles of grey scab-like flakes of lichen chiselled off the rock (they take them down to Hadibo to sell to the merchants there who export them to Muscat where they are used for some obscure purpose —the bedouin sniffed the backs of their hands to demonstrate the use of lichen, could it be for snuff or for scent?), a goat-skin to churn milk into butter, and that is all. Bare, dark, dirty caves, full of *hakak* and a musty unmistakable smell, with goats going in and out. Mike one day stood on top of a rock gazing at the lonely crags and smelt the musty odour of bedouin. But he couldn't see a bedouin anywhere around. Then he discovered that he was standing on the roof of a bedouin homestead. Their caves certainly merged with the landscape, gaps beneath massive granite boulders, the only sign of habitation, if you are close enough, the smell and the piles of dry stones walling up the entrance.

Saad, the Poor Relation, was a nephew of Salim, very destitute as bedouin go. He was a small, naïve, child-like man; I don't think he had any wives. He smiled unendingly and came at nights and stole things from us. It was impossible to take him seriously. If ever we said anything to him he said, "Uh?" and we had to repeat ourselves two or three times and even then it was touch and go whether he had understood us. He and Salim were always around the camp, talking to Abdullahi, eyeing everything, with a view, we thought suspiciously, to stealing things in the night.

On the other side of a valley beyond Salim's cave lived Salim bin Seid, a relation of Salim, in a small cave which you only reached by a climb up steep slippery rock. He had curly hair and a bright look. He was an independent sort, he didn't clamour for shillings or steal things. I have a picture of Seid before me now, his eyes startled by the flash-bulb, crouching between the projections of rock in his low circumscribed cave, everybody's idea of a Stone Age man. Seid also had a poor relation, a small man with a huge tummy and squashy toes, who loved flowers. Beyond these lived other bedouin in other caves, high up among the mountain peaks overlooking the Hadibo Plain.

High up on the other side of the Kishin valley, at a place called Molse, lived a young man of 21 called Ali, an unusually vigorous, intelligent, independent-minded bedouin. His cave overlooked the Hadibo Plain and was situated at the edge of a precipice, a wall of stones separating his home from a sheer drop of 700 feet. He lived here with his second wife and five children, three by his first wife and two by his second. His first wife lived in the very distant village of Etzumah, in the Southern Haggier, and from time to time he paid her visits—an arrangement which was, apparently, perfectly amicable. Ali also had a poor relation, a terribly emaciated young man called Abdulla, stricken with chronic malaria and pneumonia, his face long and haggard, his ribs protruding. He made a remarkable recovery after two injections of penicillin. In neighbouring caves lived an ill-assorted collection of sisters, cousins and aunts.

These were the bedouin who lived near by, who came to our camp with their children, collecting empty tins and wearing the rubber caps from our film cans round their necks as ornaments. We met other bedouin but mostly we had to look for them.

They didn't all live in caves. They came up the mountain-side to where the caves are, over 2,000 feet, when the water dried up in their low-lying villages and the pasturage for their cattle withered away. They moved up to their traditional high-altitude property (you couldn't just come and occupy a cave—it had to belong to your family by long-established right), their wives carrying their worldly possessions in large bundles on their backs, driving their goats and cows before them.

I saw some of their villages. There wasn't much to choose between their houses and their caves, they were both equally primitive, crude shelters built out of what raw material lay around—stones, the limbs of acacia trees, earth. Neil, Richard and myself went to Alleyhan one day. We passed over Adhein in mist and rain, through the squelching grass, past the scented shrubs, down, down past a hillside of dragon's blood trees, grey sheer walls of rock, a lonely orange tree, its fruit like bright orange lamps shining out of the dark greenery and the mist, down the red, tumbled, difficult path till we came to a track that ran southwards along the ridge of a hill. There, at the bottom of a hill, in a valley surrounded entirely on all sides by hillsides and peaks of red granite, lay a village of low, square stone houses. It was a long way down and I could see people moving and smoke from fires but not a sound came up from the village but the cawing of birds. It was a well-sited village, the best I ever saw: a stream ran beside it, date palms grew along its bank—they could pick their own dates without bothering to trade in Hadibo for them—there were little garden plots where women, black meandering figures, stooping and unstooping, watered the ground. They grew millet there and a few vegetables. The gardens were walled with stones, the area determined by the amount of ground one woman could dampen with one pot of water. The people had seen us, we could see them looking at us but no sound carried up. It was eerie; peering down into the village in the bowl of the hills was like watching water-bugs at the bottom of a clear pond, everything distant and quite detached; the life down there meant nothing to you. It struck me then very forcibly that only people driven by fear, by the oppression of invaders, would choose to live in places like these— in the caves high up the crags, in villages so shut in by mountains. This village was like the Country of the Blind of the H. G. Wells story, a world cut off from the rest of humanity for countless centuries, hemmed in, absurdly remote and unreal, living out its own strange and incommunicable life.

We went on down the path. It reminded me of walking through a pine wood at home, the ground muffled with fallen leaves from the trees that overhung the track. We came out into a still, stony red valley. Adenium trees grew in the valley and on the hillsides, their silver-grey trunks swollen obscenely like toads. The trunks were squashy and oozed a thick white sap, and they were surmounted by a fringe of leaves, primeval, surrealist shapes. There were several deserted villages in the valley and on the slopes of the hills around, and long walls of stone, marking off the grazing grounds. Here the whole world seemed empty, life had withdrawn and except for the buzz of large blue hornets and the whistle of small birds and the whirr of my movie camera it was a silent world. The air was still. The monsoon wind did not penetrate the valley and the atmosphere was fetid and clammy. All around were the peaks of the lower Haggier and out of the ground came the fleas, crawling over our socks, up our legs. We sprayed DDT from an orange Flit-gun down our trousers and moved out of this unpleasant place. There was a small village here called Dikoily, each house with a courtyard wall, the entrance topped with a lintel, the floor of the yard paved with stones. Outside the yard were little stone cairns where the goats were kept at night. The village was not derelict but simply abandoned. The whole region gave me the impression of a place overcome by plague, only the fleas and the birds and hornets left.

We turned right and went up a hill. At the top of the hill we came across two bedouin with heavy sacks on their backs, full of dates. They were tall, wide-shouldered, straggly limbed, light-brown men with large protruding teeth. They looked like twins. They made fire with a fire-making apparatus they carried around with them the way we carry cigarette lighters. This apparatus consisted of a small piece of soft wood with two or three holes in it. A peg of hard wood fitted into one of the holes and by twisting the hard wood between their hands, drilling into the soft wood held between their feet, they collected a small pile of smouldering sawdust on the blade of the knife on which the operation took place. The smouldering sawdust was placed on the dry porous core of a dragon's blood branch which smouldered and then flamed in the wind. Then they lit their pipes, two-foot-long, flexible, fig-bark pipes plugged with a bowl of horn, while Richard smoked his Dr. Plumb. I was suitably impressed—they really were primitive, this was the final proof, I could tell people back home they made fire by rubbing two sticks together, it placed them categorically. I wondered how I would set about getting a light if my matches ran out.

We went down the hill and came to Alleyhan. A cluster of stone huts stood on a flat piece of ground at the foot of a low hill. It was a bare, scrubby, stony, silent area. The air was still fetid and there were fleas in the dirty courtyards of the huts. The huts were dark, dirty, square and small, the height of a man and about 12 feet long and 8 feet wide, with a small entrance to stoop through. They were roofed with stones and earth on which grass was growing, supported by acacia branches supported in turn by pillars of stones piled on top of each other. No mortar was used to cement the dry stone walls. There was an old man there who had been scratching himself for two years with scabies. Neil had been here before and given the man some insect powder. This time the man squatted naked on a stone while a boy tipped pots of water over him and washed him with soap. Soap was what he needed most. There was another fellow who looked like death, bony and anaemic and apathetic, his shoulders hunched over a concave chest. Neil treated him with medicine for conjunctivitis. Some small boys had malaria, everyone was ill-looking, nobody cared about anything, our arrival provoked no interest, they were like dead people in that dead place, indifferent to anything, poverty-stricken and dirty. They didn't seem to have any occupation, nothing grew around, there was no sign of goats and cattle. It was completely depressing and we stayed an hour and a half, dispensing aspirin and insect-killer. My camera developed a serious fault and Neil's simple blood groups didn't come out right—we were glad to leave. Was it worth it, we wondered? It had taken us almost five hours to get here and what good did we do? Our medicines could do little in such a short visit, only the scabies man had shown any signs of improvement and probably he, too, would lapse and start scratching himself, for the rest of his life. There were only two hopes in that hopeless place—one a small boy of ten, with a bright, cheerful face and intelligent eyes, who smiled shyly and hid his face when I wanted to photograph him, and a man who brought his small daughter for treatment, a "character", who talked loudly and jovially, alive and authoritative, with a dominating sort of personality. The rest of them were dead to the world and we were glad to leave.

On the way back Salim Rubberlips, the shipwrecked Arab sailor who worked as a donkey-man trying to earn the £10 that was necessary to buy a passage on an outgoing dhow to return to Mukalla (he hadn't been able to earn the money and had been stranded on the island for a year), dropped farther and farther behind. He hadn't enjoyed himself at all that day, and had sat down at Alleyhan with his head in his hands and his grotesque rubbery mouth sullen and woeful. Now he was calling out to us from way behind, hidden among the trees. He said he wasn't going on, he was going to stay the night here, he was tired and his load (my film equipment) was too heavy. We told him to come on and he came on a little way and then sat down on the top of a hill with a definite resignation. He wasn't going to come a step farther. We all howled. We shouted back at him *"Mafish felus!* No money, no money!" and went on chortling to ourselves. He really had got a heavy load to carry and we felt heartlessly gay in abandoning him with it. I was only worried that he might dump the equipment and come on without it. We went on without him, tripping nimbly over the rocks, Neil leading the procession carrying a bag of flowers, Richard following holding an Elastoplast tin full of mosquito larvae, myself bringing up the rear with the orange Flit-gun. It was unfair, undemocratic, it was oppression of the blacks, and we screamed with laughter all the way up the rocky track. Thani bin Ali screamed as well, carrying the medical bag. Salim was a huge joke, no one—Arabs, bedouin, ourselves—could take him seriously and he came in later that evening, sulky.

On another day later Neil, Richard and myself went on another trek, to the village of Mifsuel, three valleys away to the east. Neil and Mike had already been this way during the absence of the rest of us at Ras Momi. They had reached the most easterly slopes of the Haggier and descended towards the main wadi system south of Deleisha, overlooking the route along which the others were toiling to Ras Momi. During this trek they were continually beset by what they called "The Pestilences of the Three H's"—*hakak* (fleas), which bit them in the caves in which they slept, *hagal* (smoke), which choked them in the confined stone huts in which they cooked, and *humera* (donkeys), which jumped on them if, retreating from the onslaught of fleas and smoke, they attempted to camp in the open. But they had seen many interesting things and observed many of the customs of the people, and it was worth following their route again.

Seiyid Ali bin Mohammed was to be our guide and donkey-man, and Abdulla, a bedu, was to be our porter. Seiyid Ali was a brother of the Little Sultan by a different father. He was a religious leader on the island (a Seiyid claims direct descent from Ali, the brother of Mohammed the Prophet) and an utter rogue. He was extortionate and dishonest and we called him Spiv Ali. He had thick, slightly sinister lips and a thin black beard fringed his jaw. He had three *futahs*—one chequered mauve and yellow which he wrapped round his legs, another red with black swastikas all over it which he wore as a shawl or turban, and a white one which he slept in. He also slept in a green blanket, labelled "Kuweit Trading Store". (On the second morning of the first camel journey from Hadibo to Kishin, Mike had pulled this blanket off the dormant Ali because he and his men refused to get out of bed, and Ali had threatened to throw Mike off the mountain.) He also wore a dirty white shirt, stained red from the dye that had run out of his *futah*, a round white skull-cap, and a green money-belt in which he kept his wrist-watch, the face of which was covered with a little green felt pad. He was cocky, unreliable, conspiratorial, friendly and inimical by turns. We hit him hard and he always bounced back and twisted us. He was just tiresome and it was impossible to be really angry with him. Wherever he went he was treated as the aristocrat he was, and goats were slaughtered in his honour (the bedouin did not eat their animals often but were, as I have said, grateful for any excuse—a visiting distinguished guest, somebody's death, a wedding, a circumcision) and in the course of a day Ali was able to eat several goats. He enjoyed his treks with us immensely. I wish we could say the same.

The morning of our departure he came to us at 5.45 and said it was raining and too cold for the donkeys. He went back to Salim's cave to eat a goat. After breakfast Richard began to write his diary and I began to sort out films and recording tapes and clean my cameras. Neil struggled with his bed legs, which had jammed. Ali came back and said there would be no more rain, everything would be *tamaam*. Abdullahi came and asked for eight shillings for his share of a goat. Richard still wrote his diary, I still cleaned my cameras, and Salim the little gentle-voiced donkey-man came and asked for an advance of eight shillings for *his* share of a goat. Richard began to clean small glass tubes for mosquito larvae. Neil stacked things and shouted to Ali eating goat who shouted back that it was raining and quite unsuitable for the donkeys and in any case Salim the donkey-man couldn't stand the cold. Salim appeared chewing a bone and said that as far as he was concerned it was not raining, whereupon Ali commanded him imperiously to fetch the donkeys. Neil sat and whittled a stick, impatient—it was his trip and everybody was procrastinating, everybody procrastinated if you let them and already it was half-past eight. Salim came back. One of the donkeys was lost, he said. An hour later it was still lost and Richard had found a puddle with

M

mosquito larvae in it on the top of a rock. He crouched over the puddle, his pipe hanging out of his mouth, absorbed with the larvae.

We set out at 9.45. It was a late start and Abdulla the bedu, a replacement for the missing donkey, carried our rucksack upside-down. We came to the stream at the bottom of the black rocks that led up to Adhein and the donkeys were beaten, cajoled, pulled and shoved up the impossible-for-donkeys rock face. We crossed over the grass at Adhein, our feet squelching in the mud and wet grass, while thick mists rolled by in the valley. At Adhein, Abdulla lay down and covered himself with a piece of cloth. We asked him what the hell he thought he was doing and he said he was not well, he had a fever and an ache in his head, behind his eyes, in his shoulder, in his hips, in his knees, he was in a bad way and would we please give him another shilling. We became abusive; no he couldn't have a shilling, he had agreed to come for eight shillings a day and if he didn't like it he could go home. To our surprise and consternation he set off home, miserably, walking painfully because of his imagined aches. We had to call him back. Our bluff had been called and we paid him the extra shilling and he picked up the rucksack upside-down and heaved it on to his shoulders and set off sprightlily. His was the most effective cure any of the doctors had made, a bob's worth of increment.

We crossed Adhein, passed Dehobey and Shehaly in clouds, rounded the Chlohar valley, where a tiny village was perched on the edge of a col overlooking the southern mountains, and came down at Maddla'ad on the west side of the Zerich valley. We went up to the end of the wadi and crossed the Aduno pass and in the course of time reached Mifsuel high up on the east side of the wadi. There was a great view down the wadi to the sea. We could see the Batageber and the sea beyond it and the red sides of the valley were divided and shaped by the setting sun. It was magnificent country: the peaks, the clouds rushing over the peaks, the plateaux of short, dripping grass, where the Scotch mists swirled thickly, streaming in the wind and dispersing like cigarette smoke to reveal distant vistas of grey hills and red snaking wadis; the deep gorges, precipitate, 1,000-foot green slashes in the face of the massif, the sheer sides tangled with dense undergrowth; the patterns of sun and shadow.

The villagers came out to welcome us and greeted Seiyid Ali

according to his rank. Socotran greetings are complicated and vary according to the social status of the individuals involved. I never succeeded in properly working out all the various categories of personal greetings. We ourselves were often greeted by the bedouin with a slap of the open hand which was then brought up to the nose or chest, loosely curled. Sometimes a bedu will greet someone of somewhat higher rank by taking his hand and stooping to kiss it. In the case of Seiyid Ali the greetings were much more complicated. Each inhabitant of Mifsuel took Ali's hand and kissed it many times, then kissed his cheek and shoulders many times with a sort of gentle pecking motion, then placed his nose against Ali's with much loud sniffing, and finally stooped down to kiss his knees. Then they stood apart from each other and mumbled a series of compliments which seemed to go on endlessly. I believe the stooping to kiss the knees was the mark of respect for high rank, though children sometimes greet their elders in this way. No doubt there are different forms of greetings between relatives, acquaintances, men and women—I only wish I knew what they were.

We ate rice and bully and fried sardines and I looked for a place out of the wind which swirled round the terrace where we had camped. There was nowhere out of the wind, and in the night it blew the blankets off my bed and exposed me to the rain that began to fall steadily so that I slept hardly at all and was grateful when a grey wet light appeared over the mountains at dawn. A crescent moon had lit the clouds on Adhein till the rain rolled over. It was the only consolation that night.

CHAPTER THIRTEEN

THE BEST ENCHANTERS IN THE WORLD

MIFSUEL is a village. It is not marked on the map—very few bedouin villages are marked on the map and it would be difficult to find them if you were not told that they were there. To reach Mifsuel you climb up the steep side of the wadi till you come to a few caves and a few rubble huts built against the rock face. About a score of bedouin live there under the headmanship of an old, bewildered man in a bit of coarse brown rag, with wrinkled skin and fallen breasts. Among the hangers-on there was a youth with a mop of black curly hair, light skin and broad white teeth, another bald-headed and highly extortionate youth with a grating voice, and a member of the Sultan's household who had appeared mysteriously in red *futah* and green money-belt ("Who is that man?" asked the distinguished scientist when I showed him a photograph of the aristocrat. "Oh, he's a member of the Sultan's household." "Really? I thought he was a sunburned member of your party; he looks very intelligent, doesn't he?") Then there was the witch. She was blind but not so old that she hadn't still got all her teeth. She just sat in the mouth of her cave like a preserved mummy in a museum show-case, motionless except when she brushed away the flies with a skinny claw. The other bedouin went past her on tiptoe, putting their finger to their mouth: be quiet so the old witch doesn't hear you. "She's a *Kubwa*," Spiv Ali told me, explaining in broken, barely comprehensible Swahili. *Kubwa* means big, important, a boss, a person of authority. What this old witch did to earn her reputation I couldn't imagine, except that she looked like a witch. Richard gave her some life-boat biscuits. "She's a nice old dear, really," he said. She listened, trying to make out the noises, the whirr of the ciné camera, the rattle of shoes on the stones, the European voices and the strange language. I filmed her, incredibly decrepit; she had to be fed by the bedouin, and went in and out of her cave like the people in the weather gauges, out when she could feel the sun she couldn't see, in when the air became cold, wrapped in tattered brown rags.

Perhaps one day there would be a witch hunt and she would be accused of sorcery, of making women sterile, or holding back the rain. On Socotra they still believed in witches and anyone could lay a complaint that so-and-so had done witchery. The Sultan was bound to intervene and order a trial to see if the accused was in fact a witch or not. Such a thing is most remarkable in a Muslim country like Socotra. It only goes to show its still medieval and idiosyncratic character. Witchcraft is not accepted or recognised in any form in Islam but it is not surprising to find it on Socotra—it is not really surprising to find anything on Socotra. For one thing, its insularity and its jealous resistance to outside interference breeds and then maintains unusual tendencies. And its religious history—the mixture of paganism, Christianity and Islam—has been always confused, neither one thing nor another, so that even now though everyone professes to be Muslim there are peculiarities.

Socotra has always been a source of sorcery. Marco Polo wrote about it in the 13th century.

"And you must know that on this island there are the best enchanters in the world. It is here that their Archbishop forbids the practice to the best of his ability; but 'tis all to no purpose, for they insist that their forefathers followed it, and so must they also. . . . I will give you a sample of their enchantments. Thus if a ship be sailing past with a fair wind and a strong, they will raise a contrary wind and compel her to turn back. In fact they make the wind blow as they list and produce great tempests and disasters; and other such sorceries they perform which it will be better to say nothing about in our book."

Among these "other such sorceries" that Marco Polo hesitates to mention was the ability of women to lure foreigners into their beds in order that they might procure children if their husbands failed them, and the power of turning women into seals by sorcery—the only recognized way a woman can leave Socotra unless she is deported for prostitution or witchcraft. A certain class of woman was believed to waylay people after dark and devour them, and Socotrans also believed in a vampire demon in the guise of a bat or bird which was called *maleiarid*, and a genie that haunted the lagoon at Hadibo during the nights. In Marco Polo's day they practised a form of trial by ordeal—the suspected man was bound and placed on top of an eminence for three days and if rain fell on him or near him during that time he was stoned to death. There was a variation of this, a rainmaking ceremony—if the rains failed they selected a victim by lot, placed him within a circle of rainmakers and addressed prayers to the moon: if no rain fell they cut off both the man's hands. Even to-day they believe in a mythical and terrible fly which I have already mentioned, and the bedouin believe that the Devil in corporate form walks the mountains at dead of night. They still fear a haunted mountain in the southeast of the island, and many stories are current of the translation of people into donkeys, civet cats and vultures, and of deaths and diseases caused by witchcraft. Witches are so feared that once an Army officer was offered four milch cows and six goats if he would put to death a local witch. From time to time witch trials are held; this is how a previous visitor to the island describes one such trial:

"As has always been the case in places where witches are an accepted part of the population, a person may be accused of being a witch in Socotra purely out of spite, in revenge for some action or because they are of an unpleasing aspect, and thus up to some fifteen or twenty persons a year are sent in for trial. Men are believed to practise witchcraft as well as women, but I have heard of no case of a man being brought to trial. Accusations may be laid before tribal chiefs, town elders or the Sultan himself, and all trials take place in Hadibo, the capital of the island.

"On the arrival of the accused under escort in Hadibo the Sultan, or in his absence his deputy, carefully examines the reasons for the accusations, the evidence and the characters of the accuser and accused so far as is known and then, if he considers that the case is strong enough, he appoints a specially selected person to carry out the trial or test.

"This tester (for want of a better name) is selected from about half a dozen men who are accepted experts and who are all of slave origin. As far as I can ascertain this expert knowledge is not necessarily hereditary, although it may be in some cases, but is usually coupled with 'the power to conjure evil spirits out of mad persons'; and these men are in effect also the local doctors. The tester's fee is forty rupees. The tester is first summoned before the Sultan and is made to swear on the Qor'an that (a) he is a true Muslim, (b) that he is not a witch himself, (c) that he will commit no act during the test which may prejudice its efficiency, and (d) that he will carry out the test justly and properly. This oath is certainly contrary to Islamic teaching and gives another indication of the unorthodoxy of the island's faith.

"The accused is then fetched and asked if she pleads guilty or not guilty to being a witch. Actually at any time during the trial she may make this admission and therefore stand self-condemned and be exempted from the test. Presuming that she does not plead guilty she is then handed over to the tester, who takes her off to prepare her for the test which takes place at dawn on the following day in the presence of the whole town and any persons visiting from the interior. During the night the tester and his assistants bind the accused hand and foot with strong ropes, and two bags, each containing five pounds of stones are attached by further ropes, one across her chest and one in the small of her back. Finally, one end of a long rope is tied round her waist and the preparations are complete.

"At dawn the accused is placed on a board and carried down to a point on the beach about a mile east of Hadibo, where she is loaded into a dug-out canoe. This is paddled out to sea by the tester and two assistants until they reach a point where the depth of the water is three local fathoms, about fifteen feet. The sea-bed slopes fairly slowly at this point, so they would probably be about half a mile out.

"Now begins the test proper and the accused is lifted out of the canoe and dropped into the sea, the long rope attached to her waist being paid out. If she sinks straight down to the sea-bed she is immediately hauled back into the canoe and examined to see if there are any particles of sand from the bottom adhering to her. If so, the operation is repeated twice, and if on every occasion she sinks to the bottom, she has survived the test and is proclaimed not guilty. If, on the other hand, she is actually a witch, she floats to the surface of the sea in an upright position with her head and shoulders clear of the water and moves slowly shorewards until she reaches the shallows.

"If the test finds her guilty she is taken once again before the Sultan to be sentenced. In the old days the sentence used always to be death by being hurled from a cliff (Ras Qur), to the west of Hadibo; but to-day the sentence is always banishment. She is therefore escorted immediately to the town of Qalansiya (a port in the west of the island at which dhows call fairly frequently) and deported on the first dhow leaving, irrespective of the vessel's destination. Her fare is paid either by her relatives or from her property, and she is allowed to take with her any movable belongings. Her children, if any, remain on the island.

"The trial which took place in November, 1955, was of three women. One of these—a crone of about seventy years of age—admitted on the shore to being a witch, at the last minute before being subjected to the test, and was thus held to be self-condemned and exempted from the test. The other two women both floated to the shore and were therefore proved guilty.

"As far as I can ascertain there is no action taken against accusers who are proved false by the test, and the reason for this is that they are not in effect 'accusers', but 'reporters of suspicious actions'. As regards the actual test, since the preparations are carried out *in camera*, it is very difficult to say whether the tester could insert any form of float under the rather scanty clothing of the accused. It is quite possible that a form of float may be used if the tester is personally convinced that the woman is guilty.

"However, whatever the truth may be, this practice is still carried on and I really believe that the wretched women who are proved guilty, though sorry for themselves, are actually convinced that they are witches and therefore justly punished.

"A somewhat embarrassing situation can be conceived where a banished Socotran witch might be repatriated by a conscientious Consulate official, to the great chagrin of the Sultan who would have no international power to prevent it!"*

The witch at Mifsuel was a harmless old bird. I hope no one decides to have her thrown overboard.

We had a goat specially slaughtered at Mifsuel. We bought it for eighteen shillings, a tough old goat, and the bedouin slaughtered it ceremonially for the benefit of my movie camera and tape-recorder. The bald-headed youth demanded one shilling for intoning the ritual chant and they all sat round him chanting (after I had re-arranged them so that the light fell on their faces). He held the goat's horns with his left hand, stroked its spine with his right hand and intoned the solo part, while the

*Colonel I. E. Snell, O.B.E., *Witch Trials in Socotra—November*, 1955. Typescript. Residency, Mukalla.

others, their hands covering their mouths, their *futahs* wrapped tightly round their knees to support them as they sat, replied in chorus *"el hamdu lillah!"* (Praise be to God). Neil had seen it all before, watched them unseen as they performed the ritual properly, by firelight that glowered sinisterly on their faces in the blackness of the mountains, the wind bellowing in the gorges, the chanting getting faster and faster, rising to a frenzied crescendo and then stopping suddenly when they all rushed forward and seized the goat and cut its throat. Now there was no sinister firelight, only the bright sunshine of midday, and they were self-conscious because of the cameras focussed on them and the microphone stretched out at them. They giggled, the chanting broke down in whimpers and grins and speeded up sporadically and then stopped. "I want another shilling," the bald-headed youth said, "to cut the goat's throat." It was a carefully-timed demand. I had used just enough film and tape on the whole business to make it necessary to continue the ceremony to its logical conclusion unless the material so far was to be pointless and wasted. So I paid another shilling and they stroked the goat a little more and chanted again and then stopped and nattered while the bald youth demanded more money. "I want another shilling to pay another man to hold the goat's legs while I cut its throat," he said. "Oh, Lord," said Neil. "Good God," I said, but we paid the shilling, there was nothing else to do, and they chanted a little longer, embarrassed and disinterested now that they had got the money:

> "Look down on us,
> Look at the sick ones,
> *EL HAMDU LILLAH!*
> Look down on the Sultan,
> Protect our Sultan.
> You brought him safely back from his pilgrimage
> And we slaughtered fifteen goats to celebrate his arrival
> And we thank you God.
> *EL HAMDU LILLAH!*
> O God, you brought these Christians here,
> Keep them here
> Because they bring us work
> And we are poor people.
> *EL HAMDU LILLAH!*"

They stopped, the bald youth got his knife, another man held the goat's legs and they bent the neck back and cut the throat unceremoniously. They skinned it and boned it and emptied the stomach and chopped it up and put it in a clay pot of boiling water and in 20 minutes they had eaten it. They had the meat, an unexpected windfall, and a few shillings, and I had some motion pictures and tape-recordings of some value. Later they explained that they usually performed this ceremony in circumstances of misfortune. For example, if someone is sick the local bedu "doctor" will offer a goat as a sacrifice to God in front of a gathering of the people after nightfall. While stroking the goat's back he will incant a supplication to God to heal the sick person, and after the animal has been duly sacrificed the people will eat it, their stomachs getting the better of their souls. This rather pagan ritual is another example of the religious unorthodoxy of the Socotrans, and is not confined to the bedouin alone since Seiyid Ali, a religious leader, took part in a number of these ceremonies.

There are numerous other peculiar practices among the people of this island which seem to derive directly from their pagan pre-Christian pre-Muslim ancestors. Cupping, for example, is carried out in a way which smacks of the *mundu-mugu* of Kenya. The doctor will make several slashes on the top of a sick person's head and suck the blood through a horn, but the operation will be interspersed with magical rites— blowing in different directions, waving the hands as if to mes- merise the patient, mumbling charms and spitting in the patient's eyes. Another unusual and inexplicable custom is that of transferring new-born children to another family. Many children in Hadibo have been brought up by a bedouin foster- family until about the age of six, and many families in Hadibo have fixed and long-standing connections with certain bedouin families whose women undertake to suckle the children of Hadibo. The decision to transfer a new-born child in this way is made during pregnancy and must have the consent of the mother. At one time the bedouin also transferred babies to other bedouin families (and probably they still do). A fire at the entrance of the cave signified that the decision had been made and the baby was transferred as soon as it was born. All through their lives such children were called "Children of Smoke". Circumcision among the coastal Arabs takes place at the age of five or six, in accordance with the usual Muslim practice, and newly circumcised boys will sometimes wear their foreskins round their necks, wrapped in a piece of raffia. Among the bedouin, however, circumcision is much more of a pagan initiation ceremony and takes place at puberty. Until quite recently the operation took place at certain special places where there were stone seats on which the boys were placed. It is an occasion of feasting and celebration. It appears that fathers are responsible for the circumcision of their sons and each bedu carries a sheath of three knives and a skewer: the skewer is for sewing and spearing meat, the rear two knives are for killing goats, eating and general purposes, but the front knife, more ornamental than the others, is reserved specially for circumcision and the shaving of head and body hair.

That evening we basted the legs of a goat in the hot embers of our fire. It was an experiment, and the trogs nudged each other and watched us bury the meat in the grey ashes and tittered quietly among themselves, wondering what the Christians thought they were doing with the meat. The Christians themselves were not sure and when the meat was taken out of the fire it was covered in cinders and quite uneatable and the bedouin perched like owls on the tops of rocks went away amused. We had kept the livers and boiled them and ate them with relish.

As we were preparing this supper we saw a boat anchor off Ras Haulaf, in the bay to the east of Suk. We became quite excited. It was so far away that we could not make out what sort of boat it was, but this reminder of another world made us think of cold drinks, fresh vegetables, a warm bath. Could we have a hot bath on a British destroyer? Ali came along. "It is a European boat," he said, "four *ferangis* have landed and gone to Hadibo. They are *Inglizi*." We doubted it but thought long about it. I tried to flash at them with the bright lid of a tin, but they could not see us, we were so far away and how could they know that their fellow-countrymen were lurking in the bare hills beyond the bare shore where they had anchored? At night a bright lamp shone from the boat and we watched it with a kind of nostalgia. I had not realised how closely Socotra resembled a prison till I saw that boat anchored mysteriously off the Cape. But it was not Englishmen that had anchored there. No one in Hadibo knew much about the boat—they thought it was a dhow.

I slept better that night, on a slope beside a wall of rock partially out of the wind. The next morning Spiv Ali came and said that at Kuberigo, at the other side of the watershed of the Aduno Pass, there would be a great ceremony, a marriage feast. Bedouin would come in from all around, 300 of them, killing cows and goats, singing and dancing, the occasion of the season, one would have thought. I decided to go and film and record this ceremony, but we hadn't enough film and tapes left, and only a few biscuits and the remains of a tin of condensed milk upset in the bottom of the rucksack. Neil decided to go back to Kishin to get supplies, and Richard decided he would go down to Hadibo to try and get the refrigerator going. I was left with Spiv Ali and the cameras and recording machine. I went down to Achile on the lower slopes of the other side of the valley, a small village of tiny stone huts, with rich grass growing all around, the whole village built under the branches of one enormous tree, a spreading fig tree with a colossal trunk that had become overlarge and now lay along the ground extending its branches upwards, draping creepers and sending up roots. I sat in the lee of an overhanging rock and the bald-headed youth came down and sang songs for me into the microphone—wedding songs, a song in praise of the Sultan ("Don't move the foundations of the Sultan's house," he sang over and over again, never tiring, never changing either the tune or the words), a love song. The love song attracted others, a small boy who had had drops in his eyes yesterday, Seiyid Ali, a whole chorus, and they wailed into the microphone as earnest as a glee club at its first audition. They sang about a young man and the pangs of unrequited love, an eternal theme among people of all times and all places. Afterwards the song was translated for me, though they jibbed at certain parts of it on the grounds that they were obscene. This is the gist of the song:

"I am in love with a beautiful woman but she scorns and has left me. If she does not turn back to me I will search for her on my camel.

"I set off on my camel along the road she has taken and come to three branches in the road. O Lord, show me which branch I must take because I have lost my heart in one of the roads.

"I come to a great mountain which stretches before me. My love is on the mountain and I will climb up the track in my search for her.

"But my camel turns to me and says: 'Why are we going on this terrible road. We are going on and on without avail.' And I reply: 'So long as this woman goes on ahead of me I will keep on the road until I obtain some benefit.'

"O Lord, this woman is very beautiful and I will continue after her for ever though she does not turn back."

This melancholy song was sung very melancholily.

I was expecting Neil back later in the afternoon but he didn't arrive, and as dusk came on the bald-headed youth offered to lead me to Kuberigo carrying my equipment, for a small consideration. I passed him the consideration and we climbed back up the wadi, through the thick, scented shrubberies, till we saw smoke wreathing skywards and found Neil under a rotting tree, poking some frothing goat's meat in a round pot, supervised by an old man who apparently owned the pot, the meat and the tree, which was just beginning to catch fire. He seemed relieved to see me, just as I was relieved to see him. He had had a terrible day, he told me. "The cloud was very low and it was pouring with rain: Richard and I felt positively intrepid as we went over Aduno. The wind added to the general effect. We got hopelessly lost in the mist and rain and found ourselves much too low—almost at the bottom of the valley. We climbed as steeply as we could through the scrub and foliage which separates one plain of fields from the other about 1,000 feet above. The bushes were full of all the sweet fragrances that go with the rain—crushed mint; thyme; that little yellow fluffy plant. There was the odd hibiscus and frankincense and the whole mountainside was covered in a cascade of terraces, all very small. The last few hundred feet we climbed almost vertically up a rock face—it seemed the only thing to do to get back to the proper level—but it was very slippery with our damp crepe on the damp rock. We came across one little village—Berk—situated on an outcrop of rock in the most marvellous position overhanging the valley; the clouds lifted for a moment and the view was breathtaking. We wondered if the inhabitants ever leant on the wall of their terrace of an evening and considered themselves lucky—when we looked in one house we saw a woman and child had hidden themselves in a far recess with their clothes over their heads. We padded along asking the way but getting little satisfaction—everywhere seems to be in the opposite direction—until we found ourselves at Chlohar. From here things were not so difficult and I allowed myself a little dream: I was knocking at the door of an English farmhouse—the mud and cow-dung stimulated this—and there was a huge fire and a huger tea, bacon and eggs, fresh scones and home-made butter and great white cups of tea, and so it went on. I reached Kishin at 12 and had some tea and Porage, collected what I had come for and set off back here.

"The clouds were still low and wet but I made a big effort and kept high. I recognised the path occasionally by barley-sugar papers, but at times I felt hopelessly lost. When I heard voices I approached to enquire but it was nearly always women who ran away wildly when I appeared out of the mist, and those I did manage to collar waved their hands hopelessly, in that rather elegant way they have, so that I was no farther on and only more tired and lonely, cursing horribly. Now and again I would slip on the wet rock and mud and there amidst an aroma of crushed mint I would invoke the deity most blasphemously. At about four o'clock when I was wondering what I should do if I found myself wandering about in this when night fell, I found myself at Aduno. The cloud was not more than seven feet above the pass and there below it was the Zerich valley, clear as a bell, and so I came back to Kuberigo."

We sat round the fire at the foot of the old tree and drank coffee and ate bully and dehydrated potatoes (since Salim had stolen most of the rice) and night fell as we shivered in the damp and waited for things to happen. I was greatly disappointed that nothing happened before dark, because I had wanted to film at least the opening ceremonies. At six o'clock sharp as night fell, two rifle shots were fired. I heard the hissing of the bullets as they went eastwards and was most surprised. That these bedouin should have rifles and ammunition had not entered into my calculations and I wondered how on earth they got them and whether anyone knew they had them. (I learnt later that some bedouin—the head-men presumably—have rifles and a small quantity of ammunition on licence from the Sultan for use on special occasions like this. I never saw the rifle that was fired that night but it seems likely that it was a muzzle loader.) Then they started. Shouts and a wild imprecatory kind of halloo from the men in unison, the sort of shout they make to call in their cattle. And then the singing, slowly, gingerly at first, a few women, a few men, singing in the field near by while the sparks from the fire they had built scattered in the still damp darkness. We ate our food, waiting for them to warm up. The voices drifted towards us, sounding lost in the stillness and emptiness of the mountains. They belonged and yet they didn't belong. These wild shouts, the primitive adenoidal wailing, the figures flitting like ghosts in the dark in best and cleanest white *futahs*, the silhouettes of men beside the fire—they belonged to these mountains, they were a complement to the unageing, aged, ageless peaks and torn crags and the wind and the rain and the solitude. They were sending up their voices just as their ancestors had done, the same words probably, the same excuse of a tune, celebrating a marriage, and yet they didn't seem to belong here either—no human seemed to belong.

We went to the edge of the field, concealing ourselves behind a large rock so as not to deter the bedouin—though probably Ali had told them it would be all right—I hadn't seen him all day but doubtless he was here somewhere—and I set up the tape-recorder and laid the microphone on top of the rock directed at the group standing together round the fire. A lamb was bleating ceaselessly near the microphone but I let it stay there; it provided atmosphere, it added interest to the chaos of noise in that field. The women started singing in a group all by themselves and then the men began singing again and the groups sang different songs, the high-pitched wail of the leader of the women making the needle of the level-meter of the recording machine kick right over. The song was in two parts, a conversation between a man and woman: "O Lord, when I was young I was active and I could do most things, run and climb the mountains; but now I am old and can do none of these things. My heart is like the sea, sometimes it is stormy, sometimes it is calm." We sat for five and a half hours behind the rock, hoping that a new tune would emerge, but it was the same two tunes all the time and nobody did anything, no bride appeared, no bridegroom, there was nothing happening but two groups standing in a field beside a great bonfire.

Perhaps they were waiting for us to go. I had another moment
of complete unreality. What was I doing here, in the drizzle
that now began to fall, in the middle of these mountains
watching these people in a field? What was I doing sitting
cross-legged in the middle of a circle of men, scented, their eyes
ringed with kohl, chanting into the microphone I extended
towards them? I had not only a feeling of unreality but of
remoteness, of detachment, of not belonging to one world or
the other, of feeling lost in a fog. There was nothing to restore my
balance, to establish my own niche—my wrist-watch, it
registered meaningless time, time meant nothing here, only
growing old, dying, being born, growing old, being buried
like one's ancestors in a grave with stones above and an aloe
plant and a bitter foul-smelling weed, the sun rising, setting,
the rain coming, the wind changing directions . . . the hour,
the minute, no longer mattered; the tape-recorder, the shilling in
my pocket, my memories, my aspirations, my everything, were
out of place.

We decided to go. It was raining and there was no moon.
We had nothing to sleep in and we had to get back to Achile,
to the overhanging ledge of rock where our beds were. Ali was
nowhere to be seen—the brother of the heir to the Sultanate
was obviously enjoying himself in the field, waiting for the three
cows and the thirty goats that he said would be slaughtered.
An old man and two young sons offered to take us over the
mountain pass to Achile in the darkness for four shillings. It was
the best earned money we had ever paid. He slung everything,
including the tape-recorder and the cameras, into his spare *futah*
and slung it over his shoulder and we set out to follow him. He
held a torch we had given him to show the way, more for our
benefit than his, and we climbed up the rocky, indiscernible
track in the blackness and driving wind and rain. Our guide's
small boys laughed as we stumbled—poor, blind, hopeless,
tender-footed Christians, blind as bats, not seeing anything
unless the old bedu flashed the torch in front of us and showed
the path, sodden in rain, the ruts full of water. We clambered
around in the darkness for two hours and it seemed only like
half an hour. It was all so bad that one ceased to fight against it
and I began to enjoy it all immensely, rejoicing in the misery
and entrusting myself implicitly to the bedu who watched over
us and warned us off rocks and sudden descents, while his

children laughed when we stumbled and cursed. What a game, the Christians blind as bats . . . "*Karib, karib,*" the old man said; Achile was near, quite near, and we went on for another half-hour. Half-way over the pass the torch began to give out. I fiddled with the tape-recorder in the pouring wetness and extracted the batteries and put them in the torch. The light was much brighter and we clambered down into the Zerich valley and came at last to the overhanging ledge where the beds were. I had set them up in the daytime and now pools of water lay over the canvas and there was an old man unravelling himself out of a cocoon of blankets (Neil's and mine), grunting and surprised by the dazzle of the torchlight. He was *shaib*, so old that he couldn't remember his name, so that everyone called him *shaib*, old man. Ali had set him here "to keep watch". Dear old *shaib*, with wrinkled bags under his eyes, and a large blobby nose, trying to make conversation: "*Haboob,*" he said, "the south wind." "Yes," we replied, "the south wind." *Haboob, haboob*, it whistled down the wadi, swirling the rain, and we were grateful for the shelter of the rock and the protection of our sodden clothes. "*Barid,*" *shaib* said. Dear old *shaib*, yes it was cold, we were too tired to make conversation, we just agreed with whatever he said—it pleased him immensely and he went on saying things while we wrapped the blankets round us and curled up uncomfortably in the lee of the rock, shivering uncontrollably. We asked our considerate guide for a fire and he brought one and set it down in front of us, and we paid him a shilling, and then we asked him for water and he brought a *burma* full and we paid him another shilling. He earned his money. Then we made the discovery that we had been robbed at Kuberigo. A tin with thirty shillings in it had disappeared, and a tin of sardines and a tin of condensed milk. All that was left was some Porage and Nescafé. We couldn't care about the money or the sardines but the loss of the condensed milk shattered us. We made some unsweetened Porage and Nescafé and tried to sleep. I could hear Neil's teeth chattering above the wind and the hissing of the rain. Then we had one of those bursts of hysterics which so often give relief to misery and bad feeling. As an awareness of the ludicrousness of our situation suddenly dawned on us we started howling with uncontrollable laughter. Here we were, two fairly rational human beings, wrapped up in blankets, crouching haggard and forlorn round a

N

bubbling cauldron and a crackling fire, in the lee of a large rock in the middle of a black night on a desolate mountain-side, sheltering from the driving wind and rain, our teeth chattering like the rattle of bones, nattering to an aged Stone Age man in a language we did not understand. We were like witches.

"When shall we three meet again
In thunder, lightning or in rain?"

It was all too much and we took a long time to subside back into our sodden wretchedness.

I can't remember whether *shaib* slept in the lee of the rock with us that night but he was there in the morning—I remember playing some of my tape-recordings to him. He listened to them, incredulous, and patted me on the shoulder. "*Tamaam*," he said, and his eyes were round with admiration at the *ferangi's* superlative magic. Ali had joined us then, at the first wet blur of dawn, leaping over the rocks shivering and soaked. We sang to them and they sat around listening, very interested and clapping and dancing whenever the rhythm permitted. We sang "Lloyd George Knows my Father", "The Yellow Rose of Texas", "Praise my Soul, the King of Heaven", "In Mobile", "Jealousy", "The Good Ship Venus", "Davy Crockett". The songs were well received, especially by *shaib*—they quite made his day. Our guide of the previous night made up the fire and brought us two pints of fresh warm milk in a metal bowl for a shilling. It was the most delicious stuff we had ever been offered on the island and it kept us going for the next eight hours, till we reached Hadibo. Everything got better. The rain eased off, we got packed, driving the numbness out of our bodies, looking down the valley to where the sun began and anxious to get there and dry out, and Neil found his first blood group B. He had been taking pricks of blood from the ears of the bedouin and grouping them simply into A, B, O. He had found no B group and thought there was something wrong with his technique until he pricked the ear of our aged guide and discovered, on processing, a group B.

Neil went on ahead to treat an epileptic boy who had fallen into the fire, and I meandered down the valley with Abdulla, a fine-looking Hadhrami type with long milked hair that fell over his shoulders and was bound with a fillet round his brow. Wrapped in his shawl he looked like everybody's idea of a

young Biblical prophet. We came down into the sun and felt
the wet drying out of our clothes. The grass and the grey rocks
ended, scrub appeared and the ground became dry and hot and
red shale. We went down and down through the scrub, seeming
always to be going the wrong way, away from Hadibo, till we
came down to the plain, behind the eastern hills that ring the
Hadibo Plain. We left Ali and Abdulla to pray at midday and
went on to Hadibo in the dry heat. We reached Hadibo at
noon. For me it was like coming home, but Neil left for Kishin
after an hour.

I went back to Kishin the next day. The plain was beautiful
in the orange late-afternoon light. I liked the plains because
they were flat and still and uncrowded, and because one felt
free and could see everything. I felt very serene, slowly crossing
the hot plain towards the mountains. I sat on a donkey, on a
sack thrown across the donkey's back. There was another
donkey on the track in front of me, and Salim, the quiet little
donkey-man, walked behind it making the encouraging-to-
donkeys rasping sound. I had a stick and now and then I hit
my donkey's rump with it, but so gently and ineffectually that
the donkey hardly felt a thing and made no effort to increase
its slow plodding walk over the sharp stones. At the rate we
were going we would not reach our camp in the mountains
until after dark, and at that moment I couldn't have cared less.
I wanted the donkey to go at whatever pace it chose, carrying
me wherever it wanted to go. I didn't mind. But Salim was
much more sensible and occasionally he darted round behind
my donkey and walloped it so that it trotted for a few yards.
I sat on the donkey and carried my stick as though it was a
rifle. The plain was hot and deserted, and on my right hand
were the mountains, with two peaks sticking up their obscene
fingers and a bit of mountain broken off and fallen and lodged
between the two peaks; and on my left hand was the blue strip
of empty sea.

Seiyid Ali had been causing trouble at Kishin. Neil found
one of his medical boxes was missing, all the medicines having
been tipped out on to the floor of the laboratory tent, and Mike
could not find his mosquito net. Abdullahi came and told us
that Ali had "given permission" to Salim and all the bedouin
to steal as much as they liked from us. I had a furious row with
him and told him that unless the stolen articles were back by

nine the next morning he would receive no pay from us. He came back later that night, his eyes gleaming with conspiracy, hands on chest in a profession of guiltlessness, to say that he was going to see all the local bedouin and tell them that unless all the articles were returned by the next sunset he would take them all down to the Sultan. Then he went away—probably to retrieve the loot from under the bush where he had hidden it. The next morning the medical box, the mosquito net and a clay pot (a peace offering) were found lying on the camp terrace.

I paid him off but before he went he discovered that his set of knives were missing. We suggested that the bedouin had stolen them from him, and he went away very disgruntled. After he went I found my pullover was missing.

CHAPTER FOURTEEN

NIGHTS ON THE BARE MOUNTAIN

NEIL liked the mountains and spent most of his time on the island wandering among the villages of the interior. He was usually accompanied only by Ali, the young man from Molse, who proved an admirable guide and a congenial companion. He rarely took any money with him, expecting the bedouin to offer him hospitality in return for the medicines he distributed freely among them. The ultimate purpose of his journeys was to establish close contact with the bedouin and break down their natural shyness and suspicions so that he could take blood samples from them during the last few weeks of the expedition.

One or two of his treks are best recounted in his own words.

"*Saturday, September* 15*th*. Ali has moved into a new cave at Molse. It isn't quite up to his old cave but it has a magnificent view. It is higher, right at the top of a valley, nearly on a level with Adhein and under the sheer grey rocks of Shehaly. His little baby, aged eleven months, had a cough, fever and stomach pains. I noticed that previously it had had the *na'ar* (branding) round the navel, so it must be something it has had before. I could see no sign of malaria and as it lay on my knee, howling and gurgling by turns, it let out a little fart and sploshed yellow diarrhoea just six inches from my knee. Ali whipped the child away and cleaned it up with the chatty of drinking water. I managed to get two blood samples here.

"We left Molse at 10 and set out for Rachen, where I hoped to obtain some more blood samples. We reached Rachen at 11 and found the inhabitants preparing for a funeral. I asked if I might see it but Ali said 'No! No Christians allowed.' I found myself a flat rock from which I could get a distant but clear view of the proceedings, and lay down to sun myself. After an hour Ali brought me some dates and said that I might come and look at the grave. Two men were inside the five-feet-deep grave, loosening the earth with crowbars and passing it up in grass mats and opened goat-skins. I went back to my rock and dreamed, while three more men came and went carrying great flat stones on their shoulders.

"After another hour Ali came and asked if I would like some meat. The funeral breakfast was obviously getting under way. He brought me the liver, a tangled grey mass of muscle and gristle, and an interesting piece of gut which I couldn't place. I ate what I could and buried the rest and then I went off to pick some oranges from a tree that grew through the foliage of an expansive coolibah tree on the hill. The oranges were firm and pale and looked very beautiful, while lemon-breasted pigeons flew among the branches.

"After a while men began to carry skins of water to the grave and mix up a great grey mud-heap. Soon afterwards Ali returned to say that I could watch the funeral from a distance: I had hoped he might if I was patient.

"I sat about 50 yards from the grave under some bushes, where a party had killed a goat for lunch and the children were breaking the bones and sucking the marrows. It was 4 o'clock before the body appeared and the Egyptian vultures hopped around expectantly. The body of an old woman was brought down, rather casually, in a rush mat. As far as I could see it was wrapped entirely in clean white cloth, brought no doubt from some deep recess of a cave. It was dumped unceremoniously near the grave and the men then lined up in front of it, roughly facing Mecca. One old man stood in front and intoned, while the men (there were no women present) fidgeted and looked to see if I was watching. It made a good scene for a photograph, the group of men on the edge of the plateau, the sea beyond and one white sail. As soon as the intoning had finished they made a dash for their tobes and then lowered the body into the grave. They all clambered in after it—I imagine to arrange the old girl so that she could sit up and face Mecca on judgment day; though considering the number of stones which they began to pile on top of her I think she would have a job. After they had passed all the stones down into the grave they poured in the mud, so that the old lady must have been firmly fixed. Then they clambered out again and using hands, feet and sticks they shovelled the earth back until there was an appreciable mound which they patted and shaped, then squatted round and intoned some more. It all seemed a little impersonal. I don't know who was the next-of-kin—one man did a little praying on his own during the ceremony—but I imagine she was soon forgotten.

"*Monday, September 17th.* A most exciting day. I set off this morning with Ali for a 3 or 4 day trip round the Western Haggier. We got no further than Etzumah, but up and down so many mountains and seeing so many patients. . . .

"First thing this morning I settled down to arguing terms and routes with Ali. Once we had fixed that he would get 9/- a day (for carrying my bedding roll and medical bag, and for seeing that I had wood, water and food if necessary) and that I would be taking no money at all, everything went extremely well and I couldn't have asked for a better guide. He went at a decent speed, collected innumerable patients, took their names and addresses, packed my medical bag at times, even laid out my sleeping-bag and held it open while I climbed in, and came down the mountain laden with firewood like a Christmas tree.

"We set out over Adho with a herd of goats and Mohamet, a local clown with a mobile face who appears in camp from time to time with bats or skulls or promises of even greater rarities such as huge owls or deadly spiders. He seemed to pop up all over the place, asking for shillings for something or other. I sent him home with a giant centipede and a bough of japonica for Mike.

"We went south through Azagal and over Adho Dimme-galahesh. Spring has come to Has Hus and that red and rather barren valley is green in parts, with grass where there used to be only red sand and shingle, and all sorts of trees in flower. There are great cascades of white jasmine—waxy and very fragrant; those yellow flowers, somewhere between a chestnut and a laburnum upside-down; and those blue-grey succulents with the rust-velvet flowers.

"At Buz (an appropriate name for this fly-infested village beneath the gaunt red cliffs of the valley) there was an accumulation of the sick and suffering. There was a man almost delirious with pneumonia and very difficult to examine. There was a baby hung up in a tree in a cloth—I suppose not uncomfortable. Then there were the usual numerous malarial and chest cases and hypochondriacs. By the time I had finished I was in a very bad temper and the flies were driving me up the wall. They are an unsmiling lot in that village.

"We made our way to Etzumah, where we were enthusiastically welcomed by Abdulla, a silly man with a little beard like a goat. He showed me to a place under some bushes which was obviously used by travellers, and here a fire was lit and water brought. I had a splendid wash in the stream and made myself soup and Porage, while the sun went down and the crickets sang.

"The men came back after supper and brought their pipes. We drank Nescafé from my tin mug and were very convivial. After much amusing back-chat and realistic mime I realised they wanted an aphrodisiac which I refused to give despite the enormous price they offered.

"We all lay down to sleep on the sandy floor of the same grove.

"*Tuesday, September* 18*th*. The men were up by five, sitting round a little fire and waiting for me to make a move. Everything I did was watched with the utmost interest and I made a pint of Porage under the careful supervision of six pairs of eyes.

"We set off south towards the Nawgeed Plain, down the wadi with its broad winding river—I could do with some of that water now—and its flat floor of round reddish stones. Walking along here is like constantly crossing stepping-stones. The walls rise steeply on either side of the wadi: half-way up red scree and cucumber trees; then a cliff of grey rock, topped with dragon's blood trees.

"We went on for a couple of hours, left the wadi and climbed up amongst the cucumbers and those pink flowering trees whose name we don't know, and came out on to one of those flat limestone plateaux that one can see all over the South and West. The change in the rock was most noticeable. Instead of the red and lichened sandstone I have become used to, there was a mixture of limestone and sandstone and the path ran over yellowish rock and sand with little flowers very bright in the cracks. Most of them I hadn't seen before: mostly blue, purple, yellow or white, very small, very bright, and I imagine very short-lived. There were aubretias, tiny cornflowers, something like lavender, little yellow buttercup things on creepers, and spikes like larkspur. They were very many and very varied. The pink adeniums were also in flower and I saw a dragon's blood tree with pale green blossoms—what a pity they don't produce something huge and red and exotic.

"We walked for more than two hours over this flat plateau,

travelling westwards around the southern slopes of the Haggier. It was very flat and very bare, except for a few dragon's blood trees and very small figs: just stones and some grass and a few flowers. It was divided into huge fields by tumbled lichened walls, quite unlike the tiny green fields of the Haggier. The lichen here is orange as well as grey.

"The walking was pleasant and easy with a cooling breeze and no ups and downs. We came in the evening to some sort of shallow valley made up of the most fantastic layers of limestone laid one upon the other in terraces and caves, sometimes quite flat, sometimes broken into a giant crazy paving, and sometimes pot-holed like a great Gruyère cheese, with bright red succulents and tomato plants growing in the holes. Some of the holes form very splendid caves and some form great pools, the sole source of water of these people. It is a crazy land.

"We reached the village of Zerich, a collection of caves in the limestone walls of a narrow defile. There was very little vegetation around and the only water was what was left in the natural pools—by now thick, green and alive. Ali suggested that we stay here the night and in the morning he would arrange for all the local sick to rally round and we would set off again in the afternoon. So we found a cave—just two rocks leaning together, open at both ends, but shelter from the rain. The worst of the goat droppings was removed and a little very disgusting water was brought, full of mosquito larvae and little things of all sorts. A fire was made, someone brought a goat-skin and the place was quite like home. I gave it a good going over with DDT when no one was looking and tipped enough down my shirt and up my trouser legs to frighten the most intrepid flea.

"Ali wouldn't so much as let me blow the fire and wouldn't go until he had seen that I had everything I wanted. Someone brought me sour goat's milk in a wooden bowl. I thought it would be better boiled. Of course it curdled and even with plenty of Nescafé was more than I could cope with. The local lads gathered round and talked. Finally I had to ask them to let me sleep. They were sitting all over my sleeping-bag spreading sputum and fleas and tobacco smoke in a most convivial way. They even offered me a woman. . . .

"*Wednesday, September* 19*th.* No sooner had I disentangled myself from my cocoon in the morning than Ali came and blew up my fire and a little boy took away my mug and brought it back frothing over with warm goat's milk—a great improvement on last night's sour milk—and I drank it with such obvious relish that they brought me more.

"As soon as I had breakfasted and Ali had gone away to bring in the sick and suffering I started on my medical work. I started at 7 o'clock and didn't finish until after midday. There was an epidemic of measles as well as some interesting cases. One man had gross osteomyelitis from a wound six months ago. His leg was grossly deformed and all the joints seemed to be cockeyed. It was swollen to about three times its normal size, shiny and hot and covered with the marks of the fire and a paste made from aloes. The poor fellow was very wasted and in great pain. I am surprised he had lasted so long.

"My whole day in Zerich has given me a good idea of the life of these people. One arrives very much a stranger and slightly irritated by all the shouting that goes on across the valley, none of which I can understand. Then, with a small gathering, we set out to find a place for the night. I always refuse a house and prefer the hazard of rain under a rock or tree to the certainty of fleas in a cave. Then a stone is brought on which I sit while a fire is lighted and skins and water fetched. A few smiles and a few handshakes and the people, who initially made me quail with their loud voices and impudent laughs, become friends. The men gather round my fire and talk together, occasionally bringing me in when we get more familiar. The atmosphere is relaxed and I am content. At sundown Ali asks leave to go and eat and I am left alone for an hour while darkness falls. I make myself a pint of soup, followed by a pint of Porage, followed by a pint of coffee all in the same mug—and could wish myself nowhere better in the world.

"The men come back and sit around the fire after their meal of *meqaderih*, as they call their sweet corn. They bring their pipes, and sit in the firelight with their tobes wrapped in a variety of ways or just thrown across their shoulders, the folds heavy and impressive in the firelight. Their faces are all good-featured, with well-shaped noses and fine eyes. They play continually with the fire, arranging the wood, blowing the flames, tossing stray embers back into the fire with their hands. There must have been fire taken from place to place in the island for thousands of years without ever going out. One rarely sees them make a fresh fire but often meets them carrying a smouldering stick over the mountains. The wood is strangely fragrant and these nights by the fire I shall remember as some of the most pleasant on the island.

"The people seem to get along on remarkably little food. I think our Western bellies must be geared to a higher intake and a greater wastage. I would never say that any of them looked undernourished and yet their diet seems to consist of dates and milk during the day and *meqaderih* at night. Occasionally a goat is slaughtered, but only for the chosen few.

"The men are nearly all well built, though small. They shave their heads at intervals so that their hair is always short. They never shave their beards but I think they shave their pubes. The few who keep their hair long may be another caste or tribe—I have never found out for certain. They wear two pieces of cloth, one round their waists, and one over their shoulders or heads, in a variety of guises—as a turban; or a rucksack; or a hood over their heads, long and sleek, like an owl. Anything they want to carry they tie in a corner of their tobe, and they wear long plaited goat-skin belts round their tums, with their leather sheath of three knives and a needle. Their hands are well formed and well kept, and their teeth are usually good.

"The women have broad faces and often protuberant teeth, with fine eyes and flashing smiles. When young they can be very beautiful and when old very ugly indeed. They don't give themselves a chance in their sack-like black dresses with tarnished silver braid. Their hair, incredibly dirty, is usually done in long rope-like plaits with the elf-locks tied in little braids and all hidden under a dirty, coarse, black veil. Their jewellery consists of crude silver ear-rings, up to twelve in each ear, and locally made bracelets. They are usually much dirtier than the men and suffer a lot from conjunctivitis—I imagine from blowing fires all day. I managed to get a blood sample from one, who also ate with us, and another wanted to be examined for infertility. At one cave I received flashing smiles and obtained a photograph of a two-year-old child at the breast. I got nits from one lady's hair and made her wash it out and comb it with the comb I lent her. Her hair came down to her waist and was very lovely and glossy with milk. She was not at all pleased when I rubbed DDT into it.

"We stayed at Zerich until 3 o'clock and before we left I was surprised by an outburst of British Army orders: 'Left, right, left, right!' 'Stand at ease!' 'Attenshun!' The orders came from a group of young and most uncouth troglodytes. I nearly had a fit. They told me they had learnt the words from the R.A.F. at the airstrip. They must have been very young at the time.

"We set off, northwards towards the peaks, over the clanging limestone. It looked here as though black metal had suddenly cooled in the act of boiling, leaving a surface bubbling and pock-marked. The hard limestone surfaces are worn almost imperceptibly into definite paths by generations of bare feet.

"A lad of 15 joined us and carried the medical bag. We hadn't gone more than half an hour when he decided it was time for a halt. We stopped by some water-holes while Ali relieved himself—very much in view—and Seid, the boy, washed and said his prayers. While one prayed and the other defaecated they talked to each other.

"Another half-hour and we met some women. Much shouting across open spaces. This is what irritates me more than anything else: this habit of starting a conversation half a mile away and finishing it long after they have passed on their separate ways. I think it is the fact that I cannot understand and join in which annoys me.

"That evening we found a pleasant place on soft, apparently dry sand, under a dragon's blood tree. Soon the sick had gathered round and I managed to get one or two bloods—two from women—before it got too dark. Then the fire was built up. We talked that night of women—one of the men had a barren wife and wanted me to make an examination—and of ages. They seem much older than they really are. Ali for instance, with his two wives and umpteen children, is only 21.

"Ali and Seid bedded down by the fire, and I lay looking up through the branches of the tree to a cloud lightened by a near full moon. . . .

"*Thursday, September 20th.* There had been quite a lot of rain in the night and Ali and Seid had retired to a near-by cave. My *shamlah* had kept the worst off me, and a goat-skin makes a fine groundsheet.

"The men brought me a young kid and offered it to me

buckshee. So it was killed there and then and eaten within half an hour. As soon as it was skinned the head and hooves were put on the fire while the limbs were put in the pot. They were given about ten minutes to boil and were then spread on a flat stone to be shared out, while the less choice bits of meat and the liver were put on to boil. I was given first choice and had the two fore limbs and the kidneys, all deliciously sweet and tender. I drew the line at gnawing the gristle off the bone and I think they looked askance at my bones—they gnawed theirs like dogs—but no one set out to finish them for me and they were thrown on to a near-by rock. I got the liver from the next brew. Ali ate half the head, skin and all. I threw in my hand at the final brew, now a thick cream soup of entrails of all sorts.

"We set off almost immediately after breakfast at about 7.30. We walked north-east for an hour across the plateau, all in cloud, and then began to climb almost imperceptibly with the Haggier. The grass became lusher, the rock was granite and the walls of the tiny fields were grey-white with lichen. The flowers were once again familiar: crocuses, those little things like violets, and white meadow flowers that covered our wet shoes and feet with their petals.

"Quite soon we stopped and ate dates from Ali's skin. He is always very good about giving food. We played hop-skip-and-jumping games and ran races down the hills. I feared a sprained ankle but was glad to see that I could beat the two of them.

"We met an old shepherd emerging from his house, with a cloud of smoke and his goats. He had sore eyes—I'm not surprised—and I managed to get blood from the poor old boy.

"By this time, having found that there was a good path from here to Kishin, I gave up the idea of going down to the plain, but I went with Seid to see whether the clouds would lift enough for us to see the airstrip and the valley marked on the map as Wadi Vera. We walked for about half an hour and then sat and whittled sticks with each other's knives. Seid suddenly said "*Shuf!*" and the cloud had rolled away to show the red and the blue of the plains far below and the wadi 1,000 feet sheer beneath us, winding its way to the little hills where I used to wander during those first days on the airstrip. It was one of those glimpses that make clouds in the mountains so very worth while. The cloud rolled back and we raced each other back across the meadows.

"We found Ali stirring *meqaderih* in a huge pot in a goat pen under a cave perched high in the rocks. They make it like Porage in a huge blackened *burma*, stirred with the wide end of a palm frond. They put in coarse brown salt from a piece of sacking, and I thought of the Scots in their little stone houses with their peat fires and staple diet of Porage. These people live not much differently but the Scots have that pride and clan consciousness which made them progress instead of remaining static or regressing. I don't think these trogs have an ounce of fight in them. When the *meqaderih* was cooked Ali—I don't know why the guest always does this—selected a large flat stone from the goat-pen wall, wiped the worst of the goat droppings from it and poured a layer of *meqaderih* all over. As soon as this set he scooped the middle away and built up the sides and poured on some more. This went on until a huge pancake three inches thick covered the stone and was in danger of cascading over the edges. A further hole was scooped in the middle and some sour milk poured in. Then Ali, Seid, and the old shepherd who had followed us up, settled themselves round the stone and rolled themselves neat little mouthfuls which they dropped in the sour milk, while the host took what was left (not much) into his cave for his wives and children, and then into the cave next door. I accepted some but had it in my mug. When I pronounced it excellent my mug was removed and filled until the *meqaderih* (like thick, coarse, unsweetened Porage) stood an inch over the rim. I preferred it without the sour milk and it was one of the most delicious things I have ever tasted.

"As soon as they had finished they turned the stone over and we left with the briefest adieus. Seid left us, and Ali and I climbed higher into the Haggier. We clambered along the precipitous side of the Wadi Debithaggier whose walls were grey cliffs 1,000 feet high. The ever-present and industrious *zamaan*, the men of old, had piled rocks and stones to make some sort of path, but it was still nerve-racking hanging over the deep defile. We suddenly descended almost straight down to the valley and up the other side, then across more damp meadows between the cloud and upper peaks till we came to the head of Has Hus valley and descended 1,000 feet. The path— if there was one—went almost vertically down an echoing chimney. Ali kept turning round and saying '*Shooey, shooey! Tariq jebal mushtamaam!* Careful, careful! The mountain

track's no good!' while I said '*Mashi* bloody *tariq* at all', and
sent stones echoing down from under my feet. We had a halt
half-way down for dates. I should have been happier on a rope.

"We climbed up to Iberi and down to Leilach and then up
to Adho Dimellus, all covered in hibiscus prickles (they call
it *dirfa*, the itch, with good reason), and from Adho we ran to
Kishin in 15 minutes, leaping from rock to rock in one final race."

One day John and I went to Mourut, half-way up the mountain-side immediately behind Hadibo, beneath impressive peaks
which rise sheer like clusters of enormous cathedral spires.
Mourut is a delightful spot, full of the sound of running water
and leaves and branches of the trees in the wind. A clear little
stream winds between the rocks, gathers in pools and falls over
small waterfalls. The wind blows freshly here, the air is cool
and the sun shines constantly. One can look down the wooded
hillside to the ochre-coloured plain a thousand feet below,
where the Hanefu, dotted with dull green palms, threads its
way to Hadibo and the blue sea.

As far as we ever discovered there is only one cave at Mourut,
inhabited by one family. But it is an important place, because
here are made most of the pots that are exported from the
island and most of the pots used locally in Hadibo and its
environs. Here, in the deep shade of an overhanging rock
outside their cave, sit the three wives of a bedu. All around
them lie pots of all shapes and sizes, drying in the bright sun.
The women themselves—one elderly, one middle-aged and the
other an attractive girl in her teens with very large eyes—sit
side by side busily engaged in making the pots, burnishing
them, firing and decorating them.

The day John and I visited Mourut, the husband and the
children were away from home, but the three wives, finding
strength in numbers, did not seem unnerved by our unexpected
presence and, after we had had lunch by the stream that
bubbled past their cave, obligingly demonstrated the processes
of Socotran pot-making from beginning to end.

The oldest wife first led us a hundred yards up the hillside
till we came to a mine, which stretched thirty feet into the
hillside. The woman lay flat on her stomach and wriggled
through the low opening and disappeared into the darkness
of the excavation. While we waited for her to re-appear we

could hear dull thuds as she chipped lumps of dry clay from the side of the mine with her knife. After a few minutes she wriggled out again, carrying with her the lumps of grey and red clay.

Near the cave were two large flat rocks. Here the old woman was joined by the middle-aged wife and the two of them began to grind the lumps of red and grey clay into a fine powder by rolling and crushing them with smooth round stones. They added water to the powder and mixed it into a stiff dough which they beat against the rock to make sure that it was of an even consistency, without any lumps.

Back in the shade of the rock outside their cave the second woman punched the clay dough into the rough shape of a pot's base and trimmed it with her fingers till it was of the right thickness. Then from a second lump of clay she rolled sausages of clay between her hands and laid the sausages neatly round the top of the base of the pot. She continued to add these coils until she had built up most of the wall of the pot, constantly trimming its thickness with finger and thumb and rounding and smoothing the interior of the pot with a sea-shell dipped in water. Then she moulded the rim of the pot with her fingers and the thing was finished. In the space of five minutes she had, with incredible deftness, made a large round pot of perfect symmetry and even thickness. This is the way our ancestors made their pottery before the invention of the potter's wheel. It is a primitive method and yet requires a skill and care beyond the ability of most of us living in our advanced technological world of television and washing machines. I have always been chary of denigrating the primitive crafts of backward people. I could not have made pots like these bedouin women, I could not easily have made fire if my matches had run out. On the other hand, I could make a wireless set and a motion-picture film. But who is to say, when we come down to essentials, that wireless is more important than fire?

The finished pots are left to dry in the sun. They make different sorts of pots. The largest are about eighteen inches in diameter, as round as cannon balls. These are designed to hold water or to cook in. Others are smaller, bowl-shaped, of general purpose, and in some cases fitted with wing handles. Yet others are deep dishes and some jugs with ordinary handles and spouts. After the pots have dried the youngest wife burnishes them with a sea-shell and they are then ready for

A hillside of dragon's blood trees in the mountains. In the left foreground is a frankincense tree.

Peter Shinnie and some grotesque adenium trees.

Michael Gwynne and a myrrh tree.

firing. The pots are laid on top of a small wood fire and completely covered with burning brands. They are left in the fire for about fifteen minutes and then removed. The temperature of the fire is insufficient to fire the pots properly. In order to produce that unexplained physical metamorphosis which takes place when clay is exposed to great heat, the temperature of the fire must reach 450°F. Socotrans are unable to obtain such a temperature with the result that only the outer surfaces of the clay walls are hardened—inside the clay is unfired and is grey and crumbly. The Socotran pots are thus thick-walled and fragile. They are easily broken and for this reason there is a constant local demand.

After firing, the pots are decorated. Small pots are incised with patterns like the tattoo marks of certain African tribes. Large pots are decorated with dragon's blood dye. Dried or crystallised dragon's blood resin is ground in a pestle, water is added and the mixture is heated. The result is a thick red dye which the woman applies to the pot. She may cover the entire rim with the dye and paint the top half of the pot with simple patterns, circles joined together, dots and lines. These patterns are pretty basic and have not changed for hundreds of years. At Suk we dug up portions of locally made pottery still bearing similar patterns made with the indelible dragon's blood dye.

The pots, once decorated, are ready for use. As one woman can make a medium-sized pot in five minutes we estimated that three women can turn out nearly 300 pots in a day and about 2,000 in a week. The many smooth, round, beautifully symmetrical, ochre-coloured pots of all shapes and sizes that we saw lying outside the cave drying in the sun, had all been made during the morning of the day John and I paid our visit.

Pottery represents the bedouin's greatest single skill, but only a few families throughout the island make these pots, and the industry constitutes an insignificant part of the bedouin economy. Not so long ago pottery was not exported but was used as currency. The barter scale was worked out in this way:

2 pots = 1 cake of Jowari meal, pure or mixed with dates
25 pots = 1 Maria Theresa dollar
500 pots = 250 cakes = 10 sheep = 5 goats = 1 cow = 15
   fraselas (about 48 lb.) of dragon's blood = 20
   Maria Theresa dollars

Nowadays the bedouin economy is founded on the production of *samn* or ghi, a thick, whitish, opaque fluid, made by gently heating ordinary butter until the water has evaporated. Ghi is rancid to a European taste, but it has the remarkable quality of lasting without deterioration for an almost indefinite period. Some of the best ghi in the world is made by the bedouin of Socotra.

They have little else to offer. They collect the musk from the civet cat and a small quantity of dragon's blood, which is used in the processes of printing and as an impervious varnish and dye, although modern synthetic substitutes are now generally employed instead. They still collect a little of the bitter, amber-coloured juice of the aloe, a fleshy-leaved plant which resembles the Red-hot Poker familiar in English gardens and grows in abundance in the earth-filled circular holes on the limestone plateaux. They cut the old leaves of the aloe and lay them in a circle on a skin in a hollow of the ground. More leaves are laid on top of them and the weight of the leaves themselves is the only pressure used to drain the juice. The extracted juice is put into goat-skin massocks, dried and exported abroad, where it is used as a purgative. The Socotran aloe was once the most famous and highly prized in the world; it was renowned among the Greeks and Romans before the birth of Christ, and in the time of Ptolemy, Greek merchants from Alexandria settled on the island to exploit this product; the trade still flourished in the nineteenth century, but modern laxatives, more palatable and less explosive, have now replaced it and it is little used except, possibly, as an application to the finger-nails of schoolchildren, to prevent them biting them.

Obviously the collection and preparation of these products does not take up an inordinate part of the average bedu's time, and it is difficult to see what he does with himself most days. He smokes a little at nightfall; he enjoys his meals but has no coffee or tea round which he can build a little ritual of enter-tainment; he has no musical instrument and rarely sings; he plays nothing that can be recognised as a game; he never dances; he cannot draw, paint, carve or make anything beautiful; his womenfolk cannot weave. Culturally he is still in the Stone Age—he has no knowledge of metal-making, agriculture, navigation or the potter's wheel. On some days he may stir him-self sufficiently to milk a goat or herd a cow or two. Often towards sunset in the mountains you will hear the lonely echoing halloo of a cowherd calling to his cattle. The high alpine call bounces between the peaks and is answered by a similar call from another part of the mountains. "Wooerp! Wooerp! Wooeeeerp! Wooerp!" The normally shy little cows come flocking to the call and are led home for the night.

It is a strange, poor, primitive life they live up there in the mountains. But they are as happy a people as I have ever met, and far more peaceable than any others.

CHAPTER FIFTEEN

A QUESTION OF HEREDITY

SALIM sat one morning on top of a black rock at Kishin. He had shaved his head and all the previously hidden bumps and curves of his cranium were apparent and the bristles of what was left of his hair formed a smooth black patch on the top of his shiny brown head. But he had left his beard and it hung down from his jaw, a thick fringe. I wanted to carry out an amateur anthropological investigation with his assistance and with cook Abdi to translate for me. The moment was not propitious. Salim had stolen the cooks' ration of rice and sugar, 75 lb. of food, and Abdi was not well disposed towards Salim, who suspected this and was quiet and whining and submissive and child-like, more than usual. I wanted to know about the social organisation of the bedouin:

"Ask him, Abdi, what the tribes of the bedouin are."

Abdi translated.

"*Bass*," Salim said, waving his hands and looking up at the sky, his voice apologetic and high-pitched, "there are no tribes, we are all one, the people in Hadibo and ourselves, we are one." Then he added after a pause: "I myself am of the bedouin tribe called Abdulla, because my father's name was Abdulla. We are all the Abdulla tribe round here."

This was confusing, and though I asked Salim to elucidate his statement he was unable to do so. There were no tribes. He was of the Abdulla tribe. There were other tribes. There were no tribes. I had come to expect this sort of thing and imagined that somehow, somewhere, we had failed to agree over the meaning of the word tribe. There *were* tribes, as I found out later. But no bedouin seemed very much bothered about it, and going around the mountains one would not have noticed much difference between the people of one tribal territory and the next. The line of stones along the watershed of the mountains at Adho Dimellus was explained by one bedu as "marking off their territory from ours" and there were other long lines of stones stretching from nowhere to nowhere which served the same purpose. Perhaps also the four main political territories of the island corresponded with the tribes of the island. But who these tribes were, what they were called, how they differed and how they were related to each other, we never found out. We could not find out things like this in only two months, not knowing the language.

I tried to find out something about the past of Salim's people. I asked him where his people had come from long ago. Had they come over the sea? Did he know any legends about his ancestors?

"*Bass*, we have always been here. Ever since the sun came out. We have not come from anywhere."

He had always been here, he would always be here, he knew of no other world, he was interested in no other world. The dirty homes under the rocks, the two bits of cloth wrapped round him, the children growing up amongst the rocks like goats, the rain and lack of rain, the maize and milk diet, growing old quickly, fearing strangers, fearing the Sultan, fearing witches and demons, knowing nothing, not wanting to know anything, not even thinking of knowing anything—this was Salim's world, he knew no other.

I had read that the bedouin at one time had worshipped the moon. I wondered if there was any trace of moon-worship among the bedouin of the present day. Although they were Muslims by name at least, it seemed to me that they were not very enthusiastic or well-informed Muslims.

"Ask him what he thinks of the moon."

Abdi asked him what he thought of the moon. Salim gave this question more thought.

He stared down the valley, his brows knit.

"The moon's all right," he said, after a long silence.

I asked him what he thought of the sun and he said, after considerable deliberation, that he thought the sun was all right too.

"Tell him," he said to Abdi, "that at nights the Devil comes up the wadi and walks across the mountains with a noise like thunder."

With that he rose from the rock and bounded up the hillside and merged with the rocks and was gone.

Even if he hadn't much idea about Allah he knew about the Devil. Perhaps the Devil slept in his cave, like the Little Sultan; everybody slept in Salim's cave when they came up the mountains. Perhaps even now the Devil was eating our rice and sugar. Perhaps he had even stolen the rice and sugar. Perhaps Salim was the Devil. He looked like it.

I wonder what Salim and his fellow-bedouin really believed, if they believed anything at all. They were indifferent Muslims and they had been indifferent Christians. Cut off in their mountain fastnesses, herding goats all day, simple, limited intelligences, believing in witches and devils, perhaps they were really pagans at heart, practising a primitive form of animism.* They have no mosques and are ignorant of even the most elementary of Muslim practices, such as prayer. Once in the hills an extraordinarily vivacious bedu, who had tried to sell us an enormous toadstool for our dinner, said: "Wait a minute while I pray." It was nearly dusk and already cold and damp on the mountain. He crossed over a stream and stood facing me. Then he started praying. He jerked up and down, kneeling, looking up in the direction of Allah, clasping and unclasping his hands, all the time talking pure gibberish. Meaningless syllables issued from his mouth at a rapid rate and the only pause was a pause for breath, a quick, gasping inhalation, and then he was off again, gibbering. I knew it was not Arabic and I had heard sufficient Socotri to know that he wasn't speaking Socotri, strange as this language does sound. He didn't know the right words and so he gibbered to impress me. When he had finished he washed his hands in the stream and set off again with a broad grin on his face. He obviously thought that his prestige, if not his soul, had been considerably bettered in my eyes by his histrionic performance. The only thing was that all through his performance he had his back to Mecca. As any true Muslim knows, one must pray *facing* Mecca.

I suppose one might call their religion "pago-Islam". Though the bedouin are well aware that their ancestors were Christian there is no indication of Christian practices at the present day. According to tradition the Socotrans were converted to Christianity by St. Thomas who was wrecked on the island during his voyage to India. From the wood of his battered boat he built the first Socotran church. By the year 530 there were "a multitude of Christians" living on Socotra. Marco Polo, writing in the thirteenth century, states that all the inhabitants

---

*Major Spencer Cooke, who spent over a year on Socotra during World War II, noticed that the bedouin still practised litholatory (the worship of stones).

of the island were Christian and that they had their own Archbishop who owed no allegiance to the Pope at Rome but was supervised by the Archbishop at Baghdad. In succeeding centuries other travellers were surprised to find on this outpost of the Arab world a race of people impervious to the great tide of Islam, who had retained some remnants of the Christian faith for nearly a thousand years after the birth of Mohamet. But such remnants had been strangely corrupted. As one Portuguese ship's writer noted in the sixteenth century: "The Socotrans call themselves Christians but lack instruction and baptism, so that they have nothing but the name of Christians. . . ." At this time the Socotrans still revered the cross, placing it on their altars and hanging it round their necks. Every village had a minister who repeated prayers antiphonetically in a forgotten tongue, scattering incense. Words like "Alleluia" often occurred and instead of ringing bells they shook wooden rattles. A century later a Carmelite friar, P. Vincenzo, observed the last vestiges of Christianity on Socotra. The people, though they still professed Christianity, had no real knowledge and practised a strange jumble of rites—they sacrificed to the moon,* abominated wine and pork, circumcised, regarded the Cross with ignorant reverence and carried it before them in processions. They assembled in their low, dark, dirty churches three times a day and three times a night. They burned incense, and daily anointed their altars with butter, placing a Cross and candle on top of them. Witchcraft was practised, and the people often committed suicide in old age. Each family had a cave in which it buried its dead. They were all strictly monogamous.

In 1800 the fanatical and puritanical South Arabian tribe, the Wahabees, attacked Socotra, destroyed tombs, churches, and graveyards on the coast round Hadibo, and terrified the bedouin into formally accepting the Mohammedan faith. They are now Muslims, but in name only, and they seem as

---

*As late as the 19th century the bedouin remembered clearly and in detail the rites of their ancestors' moon-worship. At the beginning of Lent and in times of drought and affliction they worshipped and petitioned the moon in their temples and burial-caves. Sacrifice and the burning of incense were included among the various ceremonies performed at the rising and setting of the moon. Among their prayers was one that the moon should prevent foreigners from ever interbreeding with them. They went annually in processions round their temples, preceded by a Cross ; the priest signified that the moon was tired of their worship by cutting off the fingers of the man who carried the Cross, who was thereafter revered as a martyr.

ignorant of the true doctrines of this faith as their ancestors were of the true doctrines of the Christian faith.

We found traces of this past Christianity on the island. Not in the beliefs and traditions of the people but in the enigmatic stone remains dotted all over the island. During his travels round the mountains Neil came across a number of desolate stone buildings, some of them in ruins, some in quite good preservation. On the green plateau at the foot of Jebel Shehaly he discovered an old village, consisting of small stone dwelling-houses built into the wall of a small walled field. Four pillars of roughly mortared stones supported a system of radiating beams of acacia or dragon's blood branches, which in turn supported a roof of stones, earth and sand three feet thick. In some instances these houses (which local bedouin described as being *zamaan*, of long ago) had a more elaborate roofing system, with six-foot lengths of flat stones overlapping each other, supported on pillars of stone; the house walls sloped in to meet the roofing slabs in a primitive attempt at vaulting. Near by were the remains of much larger buildings, one of them sixty feet long and twelve feet wide, divided into almost square rooms, the other built of double-thickness walls of dressed stone into which had been built a wide chimney and a well-constructed fireplace of large and most unbedouin dimensions. There was nothing about these buildings which indicated that they were specifically Christian; but they were much larger and more elaborate than the houses of the present-day bedouin, and it seemed reasonable to suppose that they were the work of a more energetic and technically advanced people—in fact, the Christian ancestors of the cave-dwellers of to-day.

On the limestone plateau near Zerich in the southern foot-hills was a construction about fifty feet long which Ali from Molse described to Neil as being Christian. "I tried to turn it into a monastery," Neil said, "but it was probably just a humble farmhouse." It was floored entirely by the natural limestone; the walls were sturdily built of dressed stone and in places were of double thickness. There was a large rectangular courtyard with three roofless rooms at one end of it. One of the rooms was divided into two, with one half mysteriously filled in with earth and covered with grass. Beyond the rooms were two more courtyards at different levels. One of the yards had a number of upright stones in it.

At Mahadum there was a similar ruin, one among several, with a paved courtyard, walls of dressed stone, and a round room at one end of the courtyard with an upright stone in the middle of it; farther on there was a semi-circle of two levels of stones like the seats of an amphitheatre.*

Certainly the ancestors of the present bedouin built these houses. But when and for what purpose we will never know. All the stone remains we found on the island were anonymous and enigmatic. They told you nothing. They were built of stones of the sort you might pick up anywhere around. And one stone piled on top of another might last a thousand years, though there would be nothing to distinguish it from a stone laid on top of another one only the day before. Probably the small round houses built into the walls of fields were simple bedouin dwelling-houses of years, or centuries, gone by. But the long-houses, the buildings of large dimensions, with dressed stone, double-thickness walls and paved courtyards, they were something special. Churches? We know the bedouin worshipped in churches—the upright stones (particularly the one in the middle of the round room at Mahadum) and the amphitheatre of stone seats suggest that these were the places of worship of the ancient bedouin. Here they sat chanting in choir alternately the uncomprehended rites in the uncomprehended language, repeating three times a day the strange warped vestiges of the faith that their ancestors had been taught by St. Thomas. This upright stone, did it once bear a Cross and a candle, and did they anoint it daily with butter? Or were these the ruins of moot-houses, places of assembly, the residences of rich men, head-men, fortresses against a surprise attack from the warlike Arabs of the coast? We shall never know. I leave it on record that these buildings are there, slowly falling, a stone dislodged in one generation, a roof collapsed in another.

There were other indications of a past community which showed far greater industry and technical progress than their descendants of the present day. Near Feragey, Neil discovered traces of an ancient road, and on the ridge behind Salim's cave Mike discovered similar traces, segments of a stone-paved track which led down towards the Hadibo Plain and which

---

*Major Spencer Cooke told me that he discovered at the western end of the island "a temple like a little Stonehenge, with an amphitheatre worn by the feet and bottoms of many people". This sounds like an arrangement of pews at a primitive Christian chapel, though the temple may be pre-Christian.

was overgrown now with shrubbery, disused and forgotten. Our camp at Kishin was situated on an elaborate terrace, the face of which was carefully constructed of large boulders; there were many similar terraces in other parts of the mountains, all of them of considerable antiquity. We received reports that in the west of the island were large artificial reservoirs, megaliths, temples, and caves containing rock-paintings and glassware fused with dragon's blood, while we read the accounts of Theodore Bent who described among other things the ruins of an ancient town on the plateau above Ras Momi, where there was a building with walls over a hundred feet long and six feet thick. Items of archaeological evidence like these naturally led us to pose the difficult, but exciting, question: who were these comparatively advanced people? Were they the ancestors of the present-day bedouin, or were they a different race altogether? From whom are the present bedouin descended?

Until now the bedouin of Socotra have been among the most isolated and least known people in the world. For countless centuries they have remained cut off from all contact with the outside world, preserving in their mountain fastness peculiarities of race, language and way of life that distinguish them from any other community elsewhere. From many points of view this unique and homogeneous community can be considered a "lost" tribe. One of the main objects of our expedition was to try and find out something about their racial origins and history.

Certain facts are now known. In the first place, although they all share the same language and culture, it is obvious that they were drawn originally from differing racial stocks. Some of them are short, and sturdily built, with dark skins, curly hair and little beard; some are taller, with big limbs, light skin, straight hair, fine, regular, "European" features, smallish straight noses and thin lips; others have large aquiline noses, like Jews, with thick lips, straight hair and lean limbs. This suggests that the original settlers on the island, who had sailed across from the Arabian mainland several thousand years ago, were succeeded in later centuries by other waves of settlers of rather different racial stock. These different waves interbred in time and adopted the same language, merging into the homogeneous community that we now find in the mountains of Socotra.

We also found that the bedouin were predominantly round-headed. This is an interesting fact and needs some explanation. Most people can be roughly divided into two groups: one, the long-headed people, who have a head width less than 80 per cent of the length; two, the round-headed people, who have a head width greater than 80 per cent of the length. Most Arabs are long-headed, but certain small, submerged communities along the Arabian shore of the Indian Ocean are distinctly round-headed. Other characteristics set these minority communities apart: their dark skins, curly hair, short stature and often almost beardless faces; their peculiar, un-Arabic languages; their different ways of life. These round-headed South Arabians comprise the inhabitants of the Sultan of Socotra's mainland territory of Mahra, and the Qara and Shahara tribes of neighbouring Dhufar, opposite Socotra. The fact that the bedouin of Socotra also have round heads suggests that there is a very strong racial connection between the inhabitants of these neighbouring territories, and there are other good reasons for believing this.

For one thing, Dhufar—which in many ways resembles Socotra, with its tall, craggy mountains and incense-bearing trees—is inhabited by bedouin who live in caves, herd cattle and goats, live mainly on dates and *ghi* (their principal export), dress like the Socotran bedouin, greet each other in the same strange and complicated way, are equally indifferent Muslims and in appearance and other ways of life closely resemble the Socotrans.

For another thing, the people of Mahra and Dhufar speak dialects similar to Socotri, dialects peculiar to these territories and known nowhere else outside them. Socotri is the oldest of these related languages. Although no European has ever learnt to speak it, a little study has been made of it and it seems that it is probably a daughter tongue of the languages of the ancient South Arabian city states, of Minaean and Sabaean, the language of the Queen of Sheba. Many of the ownership marks branded on Socotran camels appear to be partial reproductions of the Sabaean alphabet, retained down the ages by Oriental conservatism, and Theodore Bent reported finding Sabaean inscriptions on a rock near Qalansiya. Clearly Socotri is a language of considerable antiquity, and since it has retained a remarkable purity and been little adulterated with modern

Arabic it is reasonable to suppose that the people who speak it are also of considerable antiquity and have kept some measure of distinction from the rest of the races of mankind for many centuries.

It is an extraordinary language to listen to. "In subtlety of sound Socotri is painfully rich. They corkscrew their tongues, gurgle in their throats and bring sounds from alarming depths, but luckily they do not click."* The end vowel of each word is always attenuated and slightly nasal; this is probably due to the bedouins' habit of calling to each other and their flocks over long distances in the mountains. One particularly difficult sound is "Ll", pronounced rather as in Llanelly, in Welsh. Many Arabs are unable to pronounce this sound and use "SH" instead, as in ship. Sometimes these two sounds are combined, producing a remarkable and inimitable noise: the combination is spoken with the mouth twisted, as in a broad American drawl, and spat out as though with a hair lip. The Socotri word for milk, *shkhllaf*, caused us considerable amusement and mystification. Some of the words of this antique language are beautiful, like music: many of the names they give to flowers are delightful; many of their villages of flea-ridden caves rejoice in names as lovely as their views—like Dinkidonkin and Debrahihon. A few words of Arabic are now creeping into the language—there are no Socotri words for numbers beyond three, or for things that do not exist on the island, like dogs, lions and motorcars—but Arabic seems to be making little headway, since the average bedouin knows only a few words and even the coastal Socotrans only use Arabic in converse with foreigners. The remarkable thing is that although the island is of small dimensions the Socotrans claim that each of the four main tribes of the island speak a dialect incomprehensible to the others and that the only man who can understand them all is the Sultan.

One of the objects of the expedition was to make tape-recordings of Socotri for the benefit of the School of Oriental and African Studies, in London. The idea was that Peter, who was the only one amongst us who spoke Arabic, should translate into Arabic little stories I had written in English specially for the purpose. These stories would then be given to a Socotran who would translate them into Socotri. The Arabic and Socotri versions would thus be recorded side by side on tape and might

*Bent.

possibly afford some clues to the idiosyncrasies of the Socotri tongue. Peter first tried to get Mesna to collaborate in this work. But Mesna was frightened. He evaded the issue. When given an Arabic word he would say that there was no Socotri equivalent. He was too afraid of what the Sultan might do if he caught him giving away secrets about his mother tongue. Thani bin Ali, however, had no such inhibitions. He was in a privileged position as the only employee of the British Government on the island, and he was well in with the Sultan. He became very interested in the work and amused by the stories. One of the stories went:

"Ya-Hoo!" said the camel to the little bird as he went along the road.

"Ya-Hoo!" replied the little bird.

"There has been much rain," said the camel. "The rain is good because it makes the thorn trees green and good to eat. How is it with you?"

"Not bad," replied the little bird, who was suffering from a pain in the stomach and was sad because the doctor had gone back to Aden. "Not bad, but I fear Allah is angry with me. He has made me unwell. I think I shall fly to Aden to-morrow."

"Allah is mighty," said the camel and continued on his way.

He walked all the morning across the dry plain, until the sun was high and hot, but not one thorn tree did he see, although heaven had rained heavily the previous night. So he lay under a large rock and dreamed of she-camels and thorn trees.

When the day became cool the camel set off again. He walked for an hour until he saw a solitary thorn tree in the middle of a wide desert. But when he reached the tree he saw that the little bird had built its home in the branches.

"Ya-Hoo!" said the bird, "you cannot eat this tree."

"I am hungry," said the camel, "and there are no trees within a hundred miles."

"Five shillings," said the little bird.

So the camel bought the tree and ate it.

And with the money the bird was able to sail to Aden in a large and lovely boat, which saved him all the trouble of flying there.

He was a clever little old bird, because the tree belonged to his cousin who was far away in Muscat.

MORAL: Never take a thing at face value or pay the first

price you are asked—the result of the wisdom accrued during two months on Socotra.

From data gathered by ourselves and previous travellers we are now able, for the first time, to give a fairly clear and reasonably sure account of the racial origins and history of the bedouin of Socotra. Many thousands of years ago Arabia was inhabited by tribes of small, dark, curly-haired, round-headed people who spoke dialects quite different from those spoken in most parts of Arabia to-day, and who herded small humpless cattle unlike the large humped species found there now. These people were the first, the real Arabs, closely related to the ancient Egyptians in the north, the Ethiopians in the west and certain inhabitants of Oman, India and Ceylon to the east. At some unspecified point in pre-historical time these round-headed tribesmen were invaded from the north by an altogether different race of people, by long-headed Semites, tall, bearded men, with clean-cut, hawk-like faces. These later Semitic invaders now form the bulk of the population of the Arabian peninsula and constitute most people's concept of a typical Arab. Yet they are only Arab by adoption and residence; many of the original inhabitants of Arabia whom they invaded took refuge in the natural asylums at the extreme south of the peninsula—in the mountains of Dhufar and Mahra, and on the island of Socotra. It is the descendants of these refugees, including Salim and the Poor Relation and little Ali and Ali from Molse, sharing their crude cave-homes with the fleas and goats, who are the true and genuine Arabs. Those that sailed across the sea from Ras Fartak to Socotra to found the first human settlements on the island took with them their own language, culture and humpless cattle. Another language, a different culture and a foreign breed of cow superseded them in their homeland.

Once on Socotra the original settlers no doubt lost the art of navigation when they found that there was no wood with which to build ships. Unless they took part in the rich incense trade of Arabia their economy must have been founded on their herds and what they could catch in the sea. They remained cut off on their barren island, detached from events in the outside world. What level of culture they attained, or degenerated from, we shall never know—it is unlikely that any of the ruins we found in the mountains dated from this pre-

Christian period, though the Sabaean inscriptions found near Qalansiya suggests that someone at least knew how to write. Meanwhile Arabs on the mainland had learnt the art of navigation and began to sail the Indian Ocean, trading. It is clear from the first reliable written account we have of the island—the *Periplus of the Erythraean Sea*—that a further settlement had taken place on Socotra by the first century A.D.

"The inhabitants are few and live on the coast towards the North. . . . They are foreigners, a mixture of Arabs, Indians and Greeks who have emigrated to carry on trade there."

In this old Greek shipping guide no mention is made of the aboriginals of the island, of a race apart living in the seclusion of the hills. Then, as now, a mixed population of *émigré* traders lived on the coast. But one may, perhaps, construe that if there were "foreigners" then there must have been "natives" too. It seems likely that even at that early date, 2,000 years ago, the original inhabitants of Socotra were herding their cattle in the hills, unobserved by the occasional Greek and Roman traders who anchored off the coast. This is partly confirmed by the strange account written some years earlier by the historian Diodorus the Sicilian, who says that living beside the foreign trading community were "the people native to the country"— the aboriginal bedouin.

We learn little about the people of Socotra during the next 1,500 years. We are told that in the 10th century there were ten thousand arms-bearing men living on the island. Marco Polo, writing in the 13th century, says that the Socotrans were all Christians who lived on milk, meat and rice and were engaged in fishing, whaling and trading. Many ships called at the island, which was also used as a base by corsairs who sold their plunder to the Christians. Not until the arrival of the Portuguese Navy in 1507 is anything more precise and definite discovered about the island. We then learn that the descendants of the Greek, Arab and Indian merchants had adopted the language and habits of the country; they were no longer foreigners but had become Socotrans, living side by side with the aboriginals. When the Portuguese arrived they found that Mahri Arabs from the mainland—the founders of the present régime of which Sultan Issa is head—were colonising the island, driving the coastal Socotrans up into the hills to join the aboriginal herdsmen who had always been there. After the

Portuguese left, the Mahri colonisation was completed and the population of the island became disposed exactly as it is at the present day. Sir Thomas Roe, of the East India Company, noted in his journal of 1615 that Mahri Arabs and the Sultan of Qishn's slaves lived on the north coast, with their capital at Hadibo (or Tamarida, as it was then called). In the mountains lived two different sorts of people: there were the "bedouins", who had long been domiciled in the country and were quite populous; and there were the aboriginals, "a savage people, poor, lean, naked, with long hair, eating nothing but roots, hiding in bushes, conversing with none, afraid of all, without houses and almost as savage as beasts."

That, briefly told, is as much as we know of the history and origins of the cave-dwellers of Socotra. It isn't much, but it is (I fancy) more than they know themselves. If there is any memory in their tribal consciousness of their ancestors' spacious days in Arabia and their first adventurous crossing to their new island home they have imparted it to no one. The details of many thousands of years have been lost and are not likely ever to be found.

Blood grouping was the responsibility of the doctors and was one of the most important aspects of our work on Socotra. It involved collecting samples of blood in small glass tubes (called Vacunes) from any bedu the doctors could lay their hands on. The blood samples were then immediately despatched to Hadibo, where they were placed in the refrigerator to prevent them deteriorating in the heat. They were kept refrigerated until they reached the Lister Institute in London. Here experts examined them and isolated the various blood groups composing the cells (the best known groups being A, B and O, but there are many others). Blood groups vary from individual to individual, but generally certain combinations of blood groups occur more frequently in one particular race or tribe than in others (though not invariably—we found, for example, that Peter had the same groupings as three Socotran troglodytes). It is thus possible to compare the blood-group frequencies of one racial community with those of another in order to obtain some idea of its racial origins and affinities. This was our intention in taking samples of blood from Socotran bedouin. Although their blood groups have been worked out no definite conclusions

The main wall of the Mahri fort at Feragey. Notice the size of the boulders with which the wall is constructed.

Top right
Stone huts at the village of Haif on the south coast.

Right
Interior of a bedouin hut. The roofing beams of acacia branches radiate from central stone pillars.

Salim bin Seid in his cave near Kishin. All his possessions—pots, goat-skins and a spoon—can be seen stowed among the rocks.

The women of Mourut sit all day making clay pots by hand. Some of the pots are drying in the sun.

have been reached beyond the fact that the groupings indicate a remarkably "pure" Arab community : nothing more can be learned from them until more blood grouping has been done among other communities in Arabia. But it would not surprise many people if, when blood groups have been taken from the inhabitants of Mahra and Dhufar, they were found to correspond quite closely with those of Socotra.

The blood-sucking went into full swing in the last two weeks of our stay on Socotra. Richard had got the frig. working to maximum output of ice. Our relations with the Socotrans were close and friendly enough to enable us to proceed. In Richard's surgery in Hadibo visiting bedouin were invited to proffer a vein without fear of harm. It was hard work. The number of bedouin visiting Hadibo was few. Every bedu who appeared was reported by our collaborators, Thani bin Ali and Musa, accosted, led through the portals of our house and laid on his back on the surgery floor. Before he realised precisely what was happening his arm was bound tightly with a length of red rubber tubing, an antiseptic was applied to his skin and the Vacune needle inserted, while Richard, sweating, strained, his beard unkempt and his hair tousled, bent over the prostrate and mystified bedu with glinting eyes, and Thani bin Ali muttered encouraging words. Before he had been able to make a request for shillings, food, clothes or medicine, the bedu was placed back on his two feet, a pile of lifeboat biscuits were placed in his hand, his back was patted and he found himself outside the door of the house. It didn't always work as smoothly as this. Sometimes no blood would come out of the bedu's veins; more often the Vacune would partially fill and then the flow would cease as if the bedu had no more blood left in him. Sometimes his vein was so tough that Richard was unable to puncture it except on the third or fourth attempt. But as the days passed the billy-cans filled up with glass tubes of port-coloured blood and stood on the middle shelf of the frig., between the fish for the next dinner and the chocolate and the jug of lemonade.

In the mountains Neil tramped around re-visiting the villages he had visited earlier. His work became more difficult when the rains began. The tops were continually in drenching rain and the once dry wadis were becoming torrential. Many of the villages had become mysteriously deserted. Having gone to

P

great pains to locate settlements and establish relations with the inhabitants, he would find that there was not a soul there when he went to collect their blood. It was as though the bedouin, hawk-eyed, had seen from far off the glinting of Vacune needles, and had fled in a spirit of self-preservation. Neil was told that at least there were people at Feragey and Dikoily. So he tramped in the steady rain down the red rocky paths between the dripping incense trees, a bundle of Vacunes in his hand. And when he arrived after many hours he found one old man at Feragey and nobody at all at Dikoily. His last blood-sucking venture in the mountains was typical. "It was a rather depressing day," he said. "Ali and I got to Has Hus in two hours and found nobody there, and no one at neighbouring Buz, and only four people at Etzumah—Abdullah and his clan and one old man with the *nugat* all over his face and his teeth ground as flat as horses'. We went further on to Mahadum and found the place full of the Little Sultan's herds and cow-men from Hadibo and one solitary bedu." But Neil had become used to this sort of thing. En route he would accost everybody. Ali even brought in the women from their millet fields to have their blood extracted. On many nights during the last weeks of our stay the peace of those of us who were living again in Hadibo was shattered by the thunderous knocks of bedouin runners who had brought down from Kishin the blood samples Neil had collected with such difficulty. Often it was Ali of Molse; sometimes it was Abdulla from Kishin, or Hamet of the pendulous tum and squashy toes; whoever it was, he came after a descent of the mountains in the dark, dashed in, tried to sell us his wives' jewellery, refused food, refused to stay the night, dashed out and disappeared in the dark towards Kishin. They all seemed uncomfortable in Hadibo.

It wasn't always easy to persuade the bedouin to volunteer their blood to the odd and fanatic Englishmen who appeared unannounced in their midst out of the rainclouds, or beckoned at them cunningly as they strayed past the surgery door. Often they had to be bribed with shillings and biscuits; Neil offered Ali from Molse a fee of one shilling for every fellow troglodyte he could persuade to give up his blood; Richard guaranteed that the extraction of blood would improve the donor's health, a medieval idea but a comforting one. The arguments were unethical, but time was short.

Not all the people were suitable donors. The *magnun* (madman), for instance, was not at all suitable. I first saw him through the view-finder of my motion-picture camera one day when I was filming from the roof of our house in Hadibo. He was in the bottom left-hand corner of the view-finder and it appeared that he was throwing stones at me. I took my eye away from the camera and had a good look at him. He was a very wild bedu, half-naked, with peculiar sunken rings around his starting eyeballs that made him look like a savage owl. He was throwing quite large stones at me. I thought that the proper reaction to this unprovoked assault should be calm indignation, so I made my face look indignant, calmly. He continued to shy boulders at me, busily rummaging around for suitable ones to add to his armoury. Each time he threw one he shouted at me and he became so excited that his aim got wilder and wilder. He was like a very bad loser at a game of French cricket. Two respectable Arabs came and led him away, grinning up at me sheepishly. They took him as far as the mosque and let him go and he wandered away, swishing his stick as though he was scything nettles.

I met him again the next morning, coming back through the date plantation from the beach. When I saw him coming towards me obscurely among the palm trees I shouted to Richard who was vanishing beachwards: "Here is the lunatic I told you about!" "Ask him to come to the house and I'll take a pint of his blood," Richard shouted back. That was the last thing I wanted to do. We confronted each other on the narrow track, wondering who was going to give way first. The *magnun* took the initiative. He threw a small pot at me. The pot landed at my feet and I saw it contained a filthy ball of squashed dates which were immediately covered with flies. "I am poor!" the man bellowed. I felt like saying "My dear chap", but said nothing. There wasn't much I could say, in the circumstances. He put his beard in his mouth and started sucking it. Then I noticed his eyes. At every third or fourth pulse-beat they seemed to pop out of his head and then sink slowly back again. He had a big, round, squashy face and his mouth was set in the most fantastic leer, very cynical and self-satisfied. He looked as though he had just swindled somebody. I told him, in a reassuring manner, to come to the house for biscuits, and he came an hour or so later and before he knew what had happened he was on his back in the surgery while Richard prepared to insert a Vacune into his arm. But Thani intervened.

"This man is *magnun*," he said. "I shouldn't take his blood. You don't know what he might do when he sees his blood in the tube."

Richard heeded this timely caution. The man was set back on his two flat feet, many biscuits were thrust into his hand and he went out sucking his beard, his eyes popping and his veins intact. He was a beggar and quite mad.

The very old lady wasn't a suitable donor either. She said she had come 40 miles on foot and it had taken her five days to get here. She said she was very poor and she wanted medicines and clothes. She was very old and very wrinkled and she sat in the surgery doorway with her back against the wall and said many things nobody could understand. She talked endlessly and incomprehensively in a high cracked voice, repetitively like a ritual incantation. "*Allah karib! Allah karib!*" she said. "God is near." God was very near to the very old lady.

Richard had an idea.

"Is she a bedu?" he asked, thinking aloud.

"I've no idea," said Peter.

"What's the Arabic for 'Where do you come from?'" Richard asked.

"*Inta min wen*," I suggested.

"*Inta min wen?*" Richard asked.

"*Inta* .. ?" The old lady couldn't understand.

"From Suk? From Ras Momi? From long ago?"

"Ah, from long ago, from long ago." It wasn't the answer Richard really wanted.

"I think she's a bedu," Richard confided. "Shall I take her blood?"

"I don't think she can spare it," said Peter, looking at the frail old woman sitting in the doorway.

So we didn't take her blood because she needed all she'd got, but we gave her some aspirins to take with water in a tin can and she pulled a face when she swallowed the tablets. She was a dear old lady with a wealth of expression in her face and a beauty of gesture to emphasise her chant-like words. I'm glad we didn't take her blood but entertained her for her own sake.

An unusual sideline in our blood-sampling and anthropological work was the business of the bones.

In small caves walled up to the roof with stones Neil discovered human bones. The bedouin told him that they were Christian bones. He excavated some of them. Buried under large flat stones and the accumulation of the dust of centuries (and the dust of the faces and the brown limbs of the people who once had flesh about their now arid bones) he found tibias and femurs and lower parts of jaws and little finger bones and ribs and skulls, all scattered and buried in great disorder. It was as though someone had picked up the rotted skeletons and thrown them all into the cave together with no great reverence; and then the rats had come and nibbled and fought over the marrows of the bones and dragged them to their holes. Undoubtedly these were the family caves in which Padre Vincenzo had said the Christian bedouin of the 16th century buried their dead. Among the bones we found pieces of blue embroidered cloth, a carved and etched ivory khol container, and a wooden jar with a crude wooden stopper. The present bedouin have none of these things, not even embroidered cloth. I spent an afternoon with Neil excavating one of these caves, one of several close together beneath the same huge overhanging boulder near the village of Rachen, overlooking the Hadibo plain. The large stones that covered the dismembered skeletons were thrown out of the cave, causing a cloud of dust to arise and a musty smell, like the odour of a damp dungeon. Then the bones were extricated and the dust of ages was tapped out of the skulls which were arranged eyeless and grinning on top of a rock. Then they were put into the sheet of a sleeping-bag and into a champagne crate and carried back to Kishin. Here jaws were found for the 25 jawless skulls and the bones were sorted out. The bedouin sat around looking at the remains of their forefathers, quite unmoved; but Abdullahi sat for a long time staring at the skulls, lost in thought and very philosophical.

In England these bones will undergo a newly-devised and remarkable test. By an obscure and complicated process these dry old bones will be blood-grouped, and maybe they will shed further light on the racial history of this little-known and isolated community of 3,000 people, the remnants of an ancient and now almost vanished race.

CHAPTER SIXTEEN

THE JUVESCENCE OF THE YEAR

On Friday, September 21st, in the middle of our eighth week on Socotra, I left the mountains for good. Ten camels came up to Kishin to take down my own equipment and whatever camp equipment could be spared. This was the first part of a gradual exodus from the mountains preparatory to our leaving the island. Richard had already moved down to Hadibo to get the refrigerator going and collect bloods from the visiting bedouin. Peter was there also. He had had a disturbing telegram from Aden, informing him that his wife had been ill with pneumonia and asking him to hurry home as soon as possible. Peter became very worried and despondent. He sent a message requesting the R.A.F. to fly him out, and as the days passed and no reply came he became acutely depressed. We did not know what was going on in the outside world: we were as effectively isolated as Robinson Crusoe except for the wireless, and now even this seemed to be breaking down. We received messages requesting replies to messages we had not received, and answers did not come to messages that we sent. Something was going wrong somewhere and, on occasions like this, it unsettled us. Eventually a message did come through for Peter: the R.A.F., not unexpectedly, could not spare a plane.

I recalled what the Kuweiti merchant had said to me: "Socotra is like a prison."

The camels came up to Kishin and as soon as they were loaded I set off down the mountain-side ahead of them. I clambered down the red flinty path, past the dragon's blood tree that stood like a signpost at the edge of the flat buttress of rock beneath the camp, down, down, for the last time. Soon Kishin was obscured by a large uprising of torn red granite. The clouds were streaming over the tops, vanishing mysteriously once they had passed them. The sun shone on the sides of the wadi and the irregular, grey, worn and lumpy face of the mountain-side. The dragon trees lined the horizons: the grass was greener and the once leafless trees were sprouting leaves. Spring was coming to the mountains. "In the juvescence of the year. . . ." The wind blew only gently now, the monsoon was dying. It was very quiet and cool and sunlit. I could hear the camel-men, sharp occasional splinters of voices a long way above me, bringing the camels down. It was very pleasant walking alone down the mountain. The landscape was spectacular, even beautiful, and yet I was glad to be leaving the mountains.

I came to the bottom of the wadi and drank from the cold clear stream. I walked on through the wood of metayne trees and came out on to the flat scrubby plain. Spring had not reached the plain, it was as dry and withered as ever, and I felt the sun and heat bouncing out of the dry, sterile earth and the stones. But it was pleasant walking on a flat surface.

I came to the top of a rise and saw Hadibo in front of me, glistening white through the dark green of the palm trees, with the blue sea beyond, calm now, the horizon severing sea and sky with firmness and precision, giving promise of something beyond it, northwards to Aden, the other, the "outside" world, fresh food, a warm bath, clean sheets, newspapers, books. . . .

I didn't want to leave and yet over the horizon lay an excitement, an enticement, the world—like a meretricious whore, her wrinkles filled in with cosmetics, alluring and repulsive in a dim light, giving promise of a sort of satisfaction? Or like Canaan, the Promised Land, the land of our fathers, flowing with milk and honey, and hot showers and music and life moving somewhere and fresh vegetables? A return to the world. . . . My return to Hadibo seemed an initial stage in the process of leaving, a bitter-sweet business.

Hadibo was hot and almost deserted when I arrived. It was afternoon and the light sprang like knives from the white walls of the houses. A miasmatic stink came from the beach and filled the streets, seaweed rotting, something decaying somewhere near the beach. But I was glad to be here, watching the yellowness of the water-colour sunset behind the minaret and Ras Hebak, the sinking sun like Windsor-and-Newton mixed with egg, very bright and beautiful but fading quickly. Here were the children again (bright and beautiful but fading quickly), laughing and smiling, or shy and retiring, selling us eggs and scorpions and onions and bugs and shellfish as though we needed them all for the same purpose. Here again was the crying from the mosque tower at evening, the braying of the libidinous donkey next door, the twittering of bats, the thumpity-thump of the tambourines, Musa and Ali, happy to be together again, mumbling meaninglessnesses to each other in the smoky kitchen, "*keif halak, keif halak,*" serving the ox-tail soup in the light of the mud-and-kerosene lamp flickering on the table in the courtyard filled with all the sounds of the town lapping over into it, children, women, men, their voices quiet and domestic and confidential at the end of the day. Always it is the end of day that I remember most. The gratitude almost at the absence of flies and of heat and strain to keep going, at the loveliness of the evening, the gentle willed seduction of the senses. Perhaps in Hadibo I was clinging, without ever knowing it then, to the comprehensible, the vaguely familiar, the ever-so-slightly civilised: people here had gramophones, they knew about aeroplanes and taxis, they read the Koran, they wove bright simple blankets, hammered silver ornaments, sailed boats, had been abroad: they were very poor, and yet one felt sometimes an affinity, some point of contact, some moment when East and West, Socotran and Englishmen, with their absolute disparity of background and outlook, reacted the same way to the same thing, could sympathise. ... I remember treating Thani bin Ali to tea on the roof of our house; the pink polythene cups were arranged on top of a drum, with my metal tea-pot blackened from standing in the middle of fires, and a Socotran milk jug; "*Leban?*" I suggested to Thani, passing him the milk jug; he took the jug and made a pouring gesture but nothing came out of the jug and he tipped it right up and tapped it and a fat spider dropped out of it and plopped into his tea; we sat on the roof-top and chortled, he in his blue *futah* and round cap and prominent distinguishing wrist-watch, squatting on the parapet, giggling ... a point of contact.

That evening, coming back from the beach through the unlit streets, I met Ibrahim and Issa squatting in the dust and darkness. I greeted them. It was the first time I had seen them since that rumpus a month ago. They were very affable and polite; Issa with his pointed beard, as apathetic as ever, smiling at the right moments but saying nothing; Ibrahim, courteous to the point of making me feel a peasant, beautifully mannered, interested, intelligent, in complete control of himself, his

family, everybody except the Sultan: his white shirt, unbuttoned
at the neck, was still stained blue from the ink that leaked from
his bulbous fountain pen, and one of the straps of his green
plastic sandals was still torn. They sat, the pair of them, the
Affraria Government, slightly removed from the proletariat,
in the light of a broken hurricane lamp in the warm night air
in the sand and goat-dropping-paved street near the house
with the radio set and the sagging aerial: voices came out of the
radio, metallic and incomprehensible (nothing ever makes me
feel more alien in an alien country than radio programmes I
cannot understand, which make no compromise with my
foreignness and my lack of knowledge of the language or the
music or the funny jokes).

Ibrahim took hold of my arm gently and drew me to sit
down. There was no business to talk about; no question of
money.

"How do you like Socotra?" he asked in Swahili.

"I like it very much," I replied.

"Why? What can anyone find to like in this place? There is
nothing here. What is there to do?"

Poor Ibrahim, poor disillusioned, dissatisfied, demoralised
Ibrahim, Sheikh Ibrahim bin Khaled bin Thkalli, Prime
Minister of Socotra and precisely one-third of the Affraria
Government. He had seen too much of the West: already the
disparity between it and his own country was eating into him.
He had seen the show of wealth and prosperity, the *suqs* full
of goods, other Arabs driving around the streets of Aden in large
Mercédès, the cinema shows, the cafés, the tall large buildings,
paved streets and Coca-Cola vendors. There *was* nothing on
Socotra. No roads, no taxis, no harbours, no natural resources,
no oil, barely enough food to go round, no money. . . . Materially
it was a dead loss: as far as he or I could see it always would be.
His little girl was sick. Always one was faced with disease and
no way to cure it. And primitiveness and poverty. And loneli-
ness. Ibrahim, I felt sure, was a lonely man, feared, respected,
in authority, well off by Socotran standards, but poor by
comparison with overseas, and yet lonely. He seemed in an
isolated position in his dealings with us, distrusted and unliked
by the people he represented, distrusted by ourselves, sitting
on the fence between the two sides negotiating subtly in a self-
interested way. He tried to help both sides, I am sure, but the

sides were rarely compatible and only Ibrahim himself got the best of any bargain.

How could I answer his question? Logically there was no reason why I should like Socotra. He thought I had come here to work, that this two months of exile was part of my job. He didn't know I wasn't getting paid for it and that I was in debt at home in order to come here. How could he understand what attracted me about his country? I murmured disjointed, meaningless replies. I said the bedouin interested me. Ibrahim and Issa laughed.

"Bedui? Bedui?" The idea seemed ridiculous. *"Bedui!"* said Ibrahim with contempt: this place was bad enough, but they were the limit, *barbares*: Hadibo was poor, but the bedouin were poorer, and they could be contemned with equanimity and self-satisfaction.

"Jebal tamaam." I said vaguely. *"Kulu tamaam,* different, interesting," waving my hands to embrace everything. Ibrahim did not understand. How could he?

"My grandfather came from Jidda," he told me. "It is a good place."

I felt sorry for Ibrahim. I felt I liked him for the first time. There was no money question to discuss and he just spoke as he felt. The aloofness, the scheming, the outrageous demands in the courteous, disowning voice, had all gone, and here was just plain Ibrahim, a little sorry for himself, for his country, for his daughter. . . .

That night it rained on us for the first time in Hadibo. About 4.30 in the morning drops came through our mosquito nets on the beds lying in the open courtyard and then a sudden unexpected heavy shower scattered us in confusion to the rooms, dragging our beds clumsily in our sleepiness through the doorways and cursing and wrenching at them as the mosquito net poles stuck. It didn't last long, this shower, but the effect was spontaneous. The season had broken in a moment and the next day there was a coolness in the air that I had not felt before, and low dark puffs of cloud broke away from the mountains and blew low over the plain to the sea and gathered strength during the day so that the sun shone only sporadically and the mountains were almost obliterated in the dark rain. And the wind blew the wrong way, from over the sea. It was the north-east monsoon, just beginning and struggling with the

south-wester. The two met over the mountains and the rain
fell heavily there. At midday it was actually cool. We went
down to the beach and felt the cool wind from the sea on our
faces. Some men of Mouri came in in their canoes. This was
the first time they had been able to put to sea for nearly six
months and they laughed and shouted. They had been released
from prison and they squatted with us on the hard shingle and
talked about it delightedly while Musa stood making string,
suspending a twisting bobbin from his left hand. The boatmen
took on coils of palm rope and some *burmas* and goat-skins
packed with dates and a few *shamlahs*, and they paddled off
back to Mouri tremendously happy.

The whole atmosphere had changed overnight. It was like
spring in England.

"Whan that Aprille with his shoures soote
    The droghte of Marche hath perced to the roote . . ."

Only this wasn't April and it wasn't England, but the spirit,
the rejuvenescence, the sudden gladness was the same. The
men repaired the fences for their gardens, with palm fronds
bound together, enclosing the new now-visible green vegetables
that sprouted vigorously in the damp earth. In the mornings
the women went round the plants giving each a little water
from a *burma*. Tobacco, pumpkins, beans, sweet potatoes,
reared upwards. We reared upwards, the people reared,
sensing strongly the changing of the seasons. Camels came and
went, bearing sacks of anonymous commodities, a carpenter
repaired *huris* under the date palms by the beach and the
climax came on Wednesday. The rotten green hulk that we
had seen lying disconsolate on its side at Garrieh put to sea,
raised its sail, flew a red flag, and sailed through the green sea
along the coast, firing a cannon and beating drums. It anchored
off Hadibo and lay rolling and describing circles round its
anchor-chain while the sailors put ashore in boats low in the
water, rowed with paddles like rifle-target markers, and the
entire juvenile population, girls and all, crowded the shore to
watch. That night the drums beat in Hadibo and the men sang
at the seaward end of the town, a fast repetitive tune appropriate to the occasion.

It was spring all of a sudden. Spring and the completion of
the year's cycle and a release from imprisonment and a promise

of crops and pasturage and *jours de fête* all at the same time. The change of wind, the few drops of rain, and all this. . . . In our urban communities we only rarely experience this sudden quickening of life that spring brings. We don't associate the crocuses which we condescend to notice with the sowing of crops and the breeding of birds. Even the dog feels the spring. . . .

The wet brought out the mosquitoes. They hadn't been bad up to now. But as soon as the sun was down they came out in hundreds. They filled the rooms and the courtyard with their whine, different pitches of whine, suggesting different sorts of mosquito, or perhaps the same mosquitoes at different stages of hate and bad temper. It was a frightening noise and yet they didn't seem to bite very often. I slept under blankets, it was so cool.

It had rained in the mountains. The bathing pool in the wadi was washed away and torrents fell over all the rocks and crags. On the second day of the rain, in the evening after dinner, a small wadi appeared under John's bed as he lay asleep. Neil diverted it round the tent, digging a course for it with a trowel, and in the morning they watched this new insidious waterway splash over the Kishin terrace of incense. Above Molse Ali's house water was pouring in feathery cascades over the black granite cliffs. It came across the fields from Shehaly and poured over the sheer rock in white ribbons which were dispersed into spray long before they reached the bottom, 500 feet below. The paths were all running water and the mud gurgled. A shimmer of green appeared in the red Feragey valley, hardly noticeable except from a distance, and there were the beginnings of foliage on the scrub. The women were busy planting their *bombe* in the little fields and some fields looked strong and healthy with pale green shoots six inches high. The tobacco was thriving, three or four feet high. Over Adho day after day streamed herds and herds of the Little Sultan's goats and sheep and a few cows, seeking fresh pasturages on the other side of the mountain, low down where the new green was coming with the rains. There was a complicated movement of herds all over the island, sheep into Hadibo, goats westwards towards Qalansiya, goats to the Southern Plain. The bedouin were moving, too. The men of Kishin had moved over the ridge behind them. Ali had already moved to a new cave in Molse. The once populated villages of Chlohar, Has Hus, Buz and Etzumah were practically deserted.

Where had they gone to? To the deserted villages on the barren
parts of the island we had seen on the way to Ras Momi and
on the Southern Plain? The whole island was moving, active.
Motivated like the buds of the trees that were pushing out
leaves. The water filled the wadis and came pouring down to
the plains. At the foot of the main Kishin wadi the pools became
deep and almost unfordable for camels. The middle wadi on
the plain was in spate. It had been a bone-dry wadi of sand, and
now a foot-high wall of water was pouring down and had almost
reached the sea. A lot of little silver fish with black stripes were
swimming at the extreme end of the wadi as far as the water
had reached, leaping out of the water and stranding themselves. Then the wadi reached the sea and you had to wade
across.

The last days slipped quietly by. I went round the town
finishing my filming and tape-recording. Peter dug some more
out of the fort at Suk and made a survey of the village. Mesna
helped him with the plane tabling while the rest of the village
stood around in amazement and peered through the telescope
of the alidade. Richard sometimes went with him and collected
mosquito larvae, snails, water-boatmen and fish, helped by the
boy Hamis, who lived with Mesna. In Mesna's house Richard
hunted for bed-bugs while Mesna himself chased hornets
round the rooms armed with a Flit-gun. He got one, two got
away, but he showed tremendous spirit. All the children of the
village were lined up in order that Richard could count the
number of spleens that were enlarged with malaria. Altogether
11 boys, 3 girls and 2 babies formed up under Mesna's orders.
There was only one absent without leave, he said, and he was
in the hills. After the count Richard gave each child a piece of
Kendal mint cake. Richard asked Mesna to find the right
sort of people for blood sampling, and Mesna offered his own
arm first, as an example to the rest. He was a fine man, Mesna,
and a good head-man. But there was only one bedu in Suk, the
Village Idiot, who was bled successfully.

Always there were people demanding medicine. One woman
allowed her breast to be examined. This was a triumph and
showed that the doctors were getting the people's confidence.
Musa came one morning and asked if Richard would like to
go and attend to a man who had been stabbed by a fish. Richard
came back helping along an elderly African. He had been

stabbed on the inside of his right thigh by a swordfish as he was wading ashore from his canoe and the wound caused him great pain. Richard quickly boiled some instruments and injected him with penicillin and morphine. After a quarter of an hour the man became dreamy and comfortable. Richard then applied four tubes of local anaesthetic round the wound. The initial stab gave the patient a lot of pain and bent the needle but soon all pain left him and he sank back with a sigh. Peter passed the instruments while Richard probed the wound. He found no foreign-body and sewed the wound up with cat-gut. The old man was delighted when he felt the pain go out of him and sat against the wall, had a few sucks at his pipe and then fell asleep on the surgery floor, where he remained till nightfall. He made a good recovery, proudly demonstrated how well he could walk after a few days, and was eventually discharged with a tremendous faith in European medicine.

There was never a moment's peace in Hadibo. If it wasn't patients banging at the door it was a host of small boys with squashed and battered insects in a rusty tin full of water, the nearest they could get to formaldehyde. They clamoured for *nana* and *biscot* as remuneration and even brought along a small sparrow, with one foot tied by a piece of thread, which we had to set free. If it wasn't the boys it was Musa with water in the Caltex petrol can, fetched from a well in the street: or somebody to sell fish or onions or a *shamlah* or pearls or silver-ware: or Ali arrived in the dark from Kishin with bloods. Always somebody was hammering at the knocker.

One morning it was Salim bin Abdulla, arrived most unexpectedly from his cave at Kishin. He just drifted into our living-room and said: "Take a piece of paper." So we took a piece of paper.

"Write on it," he said.

"Do what?"

"Write on it." He imitated the motion of writing.

"What shall we write?" we asked.

"Write to the other sahibs on the hill," he said.

So we wrote: "We are all very well and hope you are too. Don't pay this man anything for delivering this letter. Yours . . ."

"Shall I take it to the sahibs?" Salim asked.

"No," we said, in a friendly manner.

"*Tamaam*," he said, and drifted out as nonchalantly as he had come.

We were always having conversations like that.

One day it was Rashid, the diminutive merchant from the Persian Gulf, with the staring round eyes. Rashid had been asked six weeks previously to obtain two *shamlahs* for Richard. He promised to get them from the hills, special bright ones. He showed Richard one black one and Richard said it wasn't what he wanted and so Rashid said he would get a better one. And so one evening he came into the surgery and said he had a *shamlah* to show Richard. Richard was busy with patients but found time to get away to Rashid's house. "After an age of waiting—the best mosquito catching time, too—he produced tea. In desperation I asked him if I could see the *shamlah*. Rashid got it out. It was the same dull old black one that he had shown me weeks ago!"

Very early one morning, as we were starting on our breakfast, there was a thunderous knock on the door and a very agitated Rubberlips was admitted. His elastic mouth was most woebegone. "When are you leaving? When are you leaving?" he asked. We said not for a week or so. He then asked if he could fly back to Aden with us and we said as far as we were concerned he could, but it would depend ultimately on the captain of the aeroplane. "Good," he said, and went out. A few minutes later there were more thunderous knocks at the door. Rubberlips was admitted again, carrying all his belongings wrapped up in a large cloth. He came into the courtyard and sat down against the wall. After we had finished breakfast we again told Rubberlips that we wouldn't be leaving for a week or so. "Yes," he said, "but I want to be sure you don't go without me." As he had been marooned on Socotra for a whole year we could understand his frame of mind.

The days passed. I sent a message to the Royal Air Force asking them to confirm that a plane would be arriving on October 3rd to take us off. A reply came back which was disturbing in the extreme. "Can confirm Valetta will position itself for uplift Socotra end of this week or beginning of next."

I had planned a very tight schedule for the last few weeks on the island, which all depended on our flying out on October 3rd and no earlier. We were going to have allowed ourselves five days for a rapid trek to Qalansiya at the western end of the

island. But the R.A.F. message hit all that on the head. We had
to be ready to move at almost a moment's notice, and it was
likely that we would be sitting on our backsides for an inordinate
length of time waiting for the plane. The move from Hadibo
to the airstrip was a major one. One had to pack and set off
the day before in order to be at the airstrip in time for the plane's
arrival. We did not want to be in Hadibo when the plane
landed at Mouri; it was all needlessly difficult and trying. I sent
off a signal asking for a more exact confirmation of date. But
no reply came and we sat waiting, half the expedition in the
hills, half in Hadibo. At last I gave orders that the bulk of the
equipment should be brought down from the mountains with
John, while Mike stayed as long as he could, and Neil came
down last of all after staying the last few days with Abdi and
an absolute minimum of stores, collecting as many bloods as
he could. John came down to Hadibo with stores loaded on
21 camels. By September 27 there was still no news from the
R.A.F. and I sent word up to Kishin that the camp should be
dismantled and the remainder of the party and equipment
brought down on September 29 in preparation for a rapid move
to the airfield when news did at last come. Mike came down on
Friday, September 28th, and I sent an Operational Immediate
wireless signal asking to be informed when the plane would
be coming.

On the morning of the 29th Neil and Abdi got the camp at
Kishin packed.

"I threw away all the suntan creams which were immediately snapped up by the camel-men amidst great shouts,"
Neil wrote. "They went off down the hill, pulling on their
camels' tails, soon after 8 o'clock, while Molse Ali and I set
off in the opposite direction in search of bloods. . . . By the time
I got back to Kishin I was so hungry that I decided to rake in
the rubbish heap to see if I could find the two packets of
Comprehensive Food I had thrown away this morning. I found
the camp site a litter of tins and paper, everything in the
rubbish heaps having been raked over and scattered. It looked
very desolate and no Abdulla to make me a pot of tea and
bring me new rolls.

"The evening, as I came across the plain, was magical.
Over the sea the light changed from violet on the horizon to
lime-green slashed with salmon-pink clouds and finally through

violet again to deepest blue, silhouetted against it the palm trees of Hadibo. Behind me the mountains rose very still and serene."

The next morning was chaotic. I had informed Sheikh Ibrahim that I would be selling certain items of our equipment and would be interested to know his or anybody else's bids. The items included pressure lamps, Primus stoves, packets of Comprehensive Food, Ovaltine, flour, kitchen equipment of all sorts, boxes, padlocks, everything that we did not need to take with us back to England. In the morning everybody came round, Ibrahim, Issa, Omar Ali (the Swahili-speaking Bahreini), the flat-chested merchant with the bad breath, Thani; they crowded the courtyard inspecting everything, pointing out that the pressure lamp had no glass and that the Primus had no spare parts, that the bed sagged and the chair was broken; I merely stated the price, heard their own bids, settled the price and then sold the same item to two different people, lost in the confusion, the raising of voices, the questioning, fingering, complaining, chaos. I led them into the pantry, and showed them how they could make very agreeable custard with custard powder and Comprehensive Food.

"Has it got vitamins?" Ibrahim asked.

"Yes," I said, "it has every vitamin in the world."

"Will it do me good? Will it do my daughter good?"

I made the custard, but I had mixed the Comprehensive Food with cold water and it came out lumpy. The Affraria Government sampled the custard, and looked at me strangely.

"*Esh hada?* What's this?" asked Issa. It was the first time I could remember him speaking to me directly.

"Custard," I replied in English. They bought it because of the vitamins. It tasted to them like a slightly disagreeable medicine.

Then Ibrahim said he would like to buy the refrigerator. As it would have been impossible to have taken it back to Aden with us I readily agreed and sold it to him for three hundred and fifty shillings, which was much more than I had hoped for.

Richard explained to him how the refrigerator worked, how one filled it with kerosene and kept the burner at such a height and where the ice came and how the back should always be hot. But Ibrahim was not interested. He wasn't listening to what Richard was saying. I doubt if he ever got it working.

Q

I doubt if he ever wanted it working. It is probably standing in his house, warm and redundant, a glorious cupboard, a mark of prestige, like a Cadillac; or else he has sold it.

The buying and selling went on long into the evening and the others packed and waited for dinner. Dinner was postponed until the last of the purchasers had left. The little orphan cried quietly when he saw the preparations for our departure, but he was fed and Musa led him home. We ate Richard's carefully planned and glorious dinner, the last we would have together on the island. We ate it jovially, like schoolboys at end of term, but our excitement was mixed with regret and tiredness at the confusion of the day. Soup, crayfish, omelettes, curried fish and rice, chilled plums and custard, fried sardines on fried bread, washed down with icy lemonade and hot whisky and lemon and coffee and cigarettes afterwards. The last night in Hadibo, I thought, make the best of it. I packed after dinner, fell on to my bed and slept like a pudding till dawn.

The last dawn in Hadibo. We saw it come up in lemons and oranges over Jebel Hawari and photographed it as it lit the white flat houses of the town, the narrow streets, the palms silhouetted like trees in a Florentine painting, the sides of the mountain all cracked and scarred, the puffs of cloud lit at the eastern edges. The muezzin cried out. "Allah is great, Allah is great. . . ."

A hurried breakfast and then the chaos began again as the sun got hotter: Ibrahim still bargaining, the prices accepted last night being rejected this morning; Mubarak wanting beds and chairs free; Thani waiting for a present—we gave him a pair of hair clippers which he shrugged at, so we gave him a mosquito net which pleased him. The camel-men banged at the door, swooped in, handling boxes and cases, trying them for weight to see which were the lightest in their old familiar style. The courtyard seethed. Everybody was doing different things. Noise, shouts, confusion. Omar Ali was bouncing up and down on a camp-bed: "How much, mister? How much this bed? It sags, mister, not worth five shillings." The Little Sultan came and went, carrying bags and boxes, and wheezing through his adenoids. An old man sat passionless in the midst of the chaos in that hot courtyard, clutching a packet of Jeyes Toilet Paper. The auction went on, the orphan was fed. At last the 30 camels were loaded and set off towards the *aqaba*, followed shortly by Neil and John. The rest of us sat watching the bits of paper blow about in the yard, grateful for a moment's silence.

Mike and I set out in the afternoon, holding large round clay pots carefully in our hands to take to England as mementoes. Richard stayed behind to look after the blood grouping. Peter remained with him as interpreter. Two camels and four donkeys were well and truly loaded and set out in front of us. We took a last look back at Hadibo, a long line of white on the plain, the white minaret of the mosque clearly visible and the tall wild palm. We looked back at the mountains. Would we ever see them again in our lives?

It was hot toiling over the *aqaba* again. We reached Kedah at nightfall and found a guide to take us on in the dark. We followed him through the scrub till we saw a light burning in the middle of the plain. It was the hurricane lamp in the dis-used R.A.F. building. Neil and John were just going to bed when we arrived but they gave us some stew which we ate with our fingers, and some cold Nescafé, delicious out of John's *burma* which had been sacrificed on the fire.

We slept that night in the lee of the R.A.F. ruin under the shelter of a tarpaulin stretched between two walls and held down with stones. The wind shook it with a cracking noise, and in the ruin next to ours the camel-men sat in the light of a fire and chattered into the night. Our four donkeys arrived out of the darkness and I slept sporadically till dawn.

CHAPTER SEVENTEEN

THE LAST DAYS

DAWN came early over the Haggier; the great pile of clouds was lemon-coloured and pearl-grey. At five it was still cool and the plain stretched far away to the low hills in the west, covered with rolling clouds as round as pumpkins. On the skyline of the plain were ruined buildings and two donkeys grazing quietly.

The camel-men wanted their money. Ali bin Khaled came up after breakfast and worked out on a scrap of paper what I should pay. He had probably worked it out hours ago in his head. He pretended he was surprised at what the answer was. We couldn't agree over the pay. He wanted money for two days. I refused—the camel-men had done only one day's work. They had taken five hours from Qadhub to the airstrip which was a journey of only an hour and a half. They claimed money for the return journey to Hadibo on the second day, but we had had enough of that. They could have got back to Hadibo yesterday if they had worked honestly, and I refused to pay for the empty return journey. A great shindig arose. They all crowded around. The donkey muqaddem demanded two days' pay for the donkeys.

They stood around demanding money and saying things I could not understand. Mike and I just sat on the wooden boxes. It was difficult to carry on an argument when neither side understood what the other was saying or even cared what the other was saying, firm in the conviction of its own rightness. Then Ali spoke. The gist of it was that if we didn't pay the men for two days they would load all our equipment on to the camels and take it back to Hadibo. Mike got out the long wooden case containing the 410 shotgun and I asked him not to open it but only to unbuckle the straps. Some of the men went away. Most of them were not interested in the problem: the camels all belonged either to the Sultan or to Ibrahim and the money wouldn't go to the drivers. Ali stood fidgeting, uncertain what to do, afraid of losing face once his bluff had been called. Then Neil and John returned from a bathe in the sea and selected suitable segments of tent poles. We were determined not to let our equipment go and the doubling of our strength ended the argument. The camel-men untethered their camels and left without being paid anything at all. It was another of those interesting situations. Only this time it was the Arabs who were at a disadvantage. We were leaving; most of our stores were already at the airstrip ready for the airlift; we were no longer dependent on Socotran transport and labour. The Arabs on the other hand were in danger of losing a day's pay (a not inconsiderable sum of £30) by continuing with their argument and being so proud as to refuse our quite fair offer of payment.

But it was essential to forewarn Peter and Richard of the position and bring back as much of the equipment remaining in Hadibo as possible in *huris*. Neil and John arranged with a sabre-toothed Mouri head-man to hire a canoe for the voyage to Hadibo and back. They arrived in Hadibo at 2 p.m. after three hours at sea, collected Peter's hamper of ancient pots, some paraffin, a lamp, a crate of skulls and Richard's *shamlahs*. Only the meteorological equipment, Richard's personal belongings, the large tent and the ice-boxes were left. There had been no message from the R.A.F., although we had sent our second Operational Immediate signal a day or so previously. Obviously something was wrong with the wireless system. And now trouble with the camel-men at the very last moment. . . .

John and Neil came back huddled in the bottom of the canoe, squeezed between the boxes. They arrived at sunset, returning through the scrub in the darkness guided by flares from my Very pistol at quarter-hour intervals. They came through the darkness singing "For Those in Peril on the Sea".

In Hadibo in the evening Thani bin Ali called on Peter. He had turned diplomat. Ibrahim had sent him because he was in our greatest confidence. Thani was very friendly and civil. He said that Ibrahim much regretted he could do no more for us until Mr. Botting paid the camel-men all their wages and the matter was settled. Peter said he didn't know anything about it but would see me tomorrow.

But to Peter's surprise, on the next day, before he had been able to see me, Ali bin Khaled arrived at breakfast-time and asked if we would like more camels. This was a complete change of front and so Peter ordered three camels and got four. He also brought a letter in Arabic from Ibrahim saying would he ask Mr. Botting to pay seven shillings (instead of fifteen shillings) for the return journey. The camels set off loaded with everything that could be spared and I met them at Qadhub.

I had set off at nine that morning in one of two canoes I was taking to Hadibo to transport all the equipment from Hadibo to the airstrip. A boy sat at the stern and his father at the bow, and all through the voyage through the green sea beneath the eroded yellow shore where the sea lapped gently into the whorls and caverns of the rock, in the cool of the morning, with a breeze blowing off the sea, they sang a song in time with the strokes of their paddles. "Ya-a-a-a, Abdull-a, ya-a-a, Abdull-a," they sang. They didn't seem to know any more words. They paddled strenuously without ever stopping while a few yards to port three relatives paddled in the other *huri* and held a conversation with my own boat-boys from time to time. The sea was calm and as the sun rose it glittered painfully and reflected the sun and burnt my sun-brown arms. We came after three-quarters of an hour to Qadhub. It looked a scruffy little place; the mud white-washed houses seemed to be decaying and the whitewash was stained dirty brown. A battered sort of mosque rose above the other buildings and the children ran down to the beach and stood between the canoes to watch us go by. The boatman pointed and said "*Gemal*", and there sure enough were camels, tethered in the shade of a great rock near the foot of the *aqaba*. We went in to the small cove to the east of the village and I got out of the boat and waded through the water to land.

Ali was there with four camels and their drivers. He took my arm and drew me to sit down. They were brewing coffee and wanted me to have some. I was very surprised to see him and glad to see the camels taking the equipment to the airstrip.

After a short time I left and paddled some of the way to Hadibo encouraged by all the five boat-boys. I landed at two, soaked to the skin from the waves that had sometimes splashed over into the boat.

Peter and Richard were in the house having lunch. The house looked bare and forlorn, a litter of paper and unwanted boxes, only a table still up and the refrigerator still making ice in the surgery. It was sad somehow to see the house now.

No message had come from the R.A.F. Radio communication with Mukalla was established three times a day—once at 8 a.m., again at 2.45 and lastly at 7 p.m. Nothing had come in the morning. I went round to the askaris' house at three and still nothing had come. I drafted the third Operational Immediate signal, drank tea with Omar Ali and the askaris and the pot-bellied merchant with the bad breath, and hoped to God some message would come in the evening. It was the very last message we could hope to receive, as I had decided to move with the ice-boxes to the airstrip the next day whether a message came or not.

In the evening Ibrahim paid us a social visit. We discussed business in Swahili; I said I did not wish to pay the seven shillings for the camels' return journey and Ibrahim said he did not mind, as it was up to me and I could pay them or not as I wished. Then the subject became more general. He talked about the prices *ghi* fetched in Aden. He told me that blankets were sold for fifteen shillings each in Aden and that Major Snell had bought 50 and a Royal Navy captain had bought a huge one for one hundred and fifty shillings. We talked about other visitors. He remembered Harold Ingrams and Sir Bernard Reilly who visited the island when he was a boy, and Major Spencer Cooke and Mr. Popov and others. He talked about the fluency of their Arabic. He was very friendly and I felt again that I liked him now.

We parted good friends after arranging for two canoes to take us to Mouri the next day.

Peter and Ali had sailed to the airstrip during the afternoon, taking everything except one sleeping-bag, one camp bed, a box of kitchen utensils and the vacuum boxes. Musa cooked us omelette and fish for dinner, and as we ate in the desolate courtyard amongst the whining, swinish mosquitoes Rubberlips came with a message. The message was brief but was all we wanted:

"Wednesday, 3 repeat 3 October."

We went to bed very relieved that all our planning for the last few days had been correct. We tossed a coin to decide who should sleep in the camp-bed and who in the sleeping-bag. I slept in the camp-bed and Richard slept in the sleeping-bag on the floor of the yard. I slept in my underclothes without any bedding. My underclothes were still wet with salt water and made my skin very sore, but there was nothing else to wear. At one in the morning I woke up feeling very cold and slept only sporadically, praying for the morning to come. I got up at 4.30 and Musa came soon afterwards and cooked breakfast for us of Porage and tinned sausages. We gave him a very large baksheesh for his excellent and willing service, said good-bye to Ibrahim and the merchants who had come this early to make sure that the goods they had bought were still there to take away. The orphan came in and cried again as he saw us preparing to leave. Good-bye, good-bye, we would never see them again.

The ice-boxes were loaded into one canoe with Richard and myself: Rubberlips and Mubarak into the other. We were paddled strongly by two Africans and took alternate puffs at Richard's pipe. There was nothing to do but relax during the three-hour journey to the airstrip. A school of flying fish jumped out of the water nearly into our boat. I saw Hadibo for the last time, white among the palms, and the mountains, and the *aqaba* and Qadhub.

We landed at Mouri at 10.30. I set off at once over the plain towards the airstrip. Richard organised a party to carry the ice-boxes and they arrived at the camp after half an hour. Omar Ali had already arrived to collect the camp-beds and mosquito nets he had bought from us, and he had already informed the others that the planes were coming, to their great relief. I had a quick cup of tea, a wash and shave and a change of clothes. I started to pay out Ali bin Khaled, counting out £30 in one shilling pieces, when we heard the drone of an aircraft. It came over from the north-west, and circled low over the airfield. Neil held out a red towel in a vain attempt to indicate the wind direction to the pilot, who was obviously very uncertain of the landing conditions, while Mike set fire to the scrub and Peter fired the Very pistol. I got frantic trying to pay out money to Ali and answering the merchants who clamoured round asking for items of equipment which I could not now find and paying the money back that they had given me, and trying to get myself ready and the boxes out on to the edge of the airstrip. It was chaos again for the umpteenth time. Screaming of Arab voices, trying to do many things at once, the shredding of nerves. Neil and Richard were suddenly surrounded by a horde of clamouring patients who had got wind of our departure and wanted a last final cure or tonic. The R.A.F. crew got out and added to the chaos.

A second plane arrived at midday. The last lot of porters, boys and men from Mouri and Qadhub, shifted our stuff to the aeroplane. An R.A.S.C. 2nd Lieutenant listed the loads and made sure each aircraft had a correct payload. I paid off the men for the last time as they sat in a circle round the almost empty money-box, a shilling for each boy and two shillings for each man. Richard and Neil got four more bedouin bloods to make the total a hundred, and packed the thermos boxes with ice the R.A.F. had specially brought over. We said good-bye to Mubarak, very disappointed because no fresh flour or cigarettes had arrived for the garrison. Ali bin Khaled stood under the wing looking very sad. I did not notice him till the door of the plane had been shut and the first engine was turning over. Then it was too late to say good-bye and Ali walked all by himself over to the camels, and as we taxied down to begin the take-off I saw him and his four camels slowly making their way over the plain towards Qadhub.

We took off at 1.30. We made a tight circle over the airfield and then flew low over the coast, at about 50 feet. We stared out of the windows at the hot, yellow, barren shore, lapped by the green sea, and at the occasional village of hovels and the lonely fishermen by their canoes staring up at us. We flew twice over Qalansiya as I filmed through the port-hole window, and then we flew north-west and saw the end of the island, a cliff of sheer rock obscured by drab clouds, vanish very slowly and unwillingly from sight. Then we were at 8,000 feet over the sea, feeling the coolness and the dryness in our nostrils, a strange, pleasant sensation.

We read letters from home and opened tins of cold stewing steak with a penknife. The civet cat in the biscuit box made the cabin smell.

APPENDIX

Short glossary of Arabic words

agal	cord of an Arab head-dress	mafi (mafish)	there is not
aqaba	a pass	magnun	mad, madman
barid	cold	meqaderih	corn (a Socotri word)
bass	enough; used in conversation in the sense of "Well, you see..."	muqaddem	head-man
		mushadda	headdress
		naam	yes
		na'ar	fire
		nana	a sweet
bermil (*plural* baramil)	oil drum	naqhoda	dhow captain
		Nasara	a Christian
biscot	biscuit	ndizi	banana (a Swahili word)
bombe	millet		
burma	pot	ngoma	dance (a Swahili word)
felus	money		
ferangi	Frank, a European	nugat	spots or stains
futah	loincloth, often reaching down to just above the ankles	qat	privet-like leaves of the tree *Catha Edulis*, chewed for its stimulating effect, recently banned in Aden Colony
haboob	wind		
hakak	flea		
harim	women, the women's quarters	rotl	measure of weight, approx. one pound
hina	here	sahib	term of respect applied to Europeans, literally meaning friend
humar	donkey		
huri	dug-out canoe		
ibra	needle, used for penicillin injection	salaam!	peace!
ismah	listen	sambuq	small dhow
jol	plateau	samn	*ghi*, a clarified butter
kafia	hat, used to refer to cloth of Arab head-dress	shaib	old, old man
		shamlah	blanket, rug
		shuf!	look!
kam	how much, how many	siqaya	water cistern for wayfarers
karib	near	tamaam	all right, O.K.
karrani	clerk, one who can read the Koran	tariq	path
		wasm	ownership marks, but used on Socotra to refer to branding in local folk medicine
kibrit	match		
khor	estuary		
kull	all		
la	no		
lakin	but	wen	where
leban	milk	ya!	O! (a vocative word of address)
leish	why		
luban	incense	zamaan	of long ago